NORTHWESTERN UNIVERSITY HUMANITIES SERIES
volume 18

SPEECH DEVELOPMENT

OF

A BILINGUAL CHILD

A LINGUIST'S RECORD

Volume III
GRAMMAR AND GENERAL PROBLEMS
in the First Two Years

BY

WERNER F. LEOPOLD

AMS PRESS
NEW YORK

Copyright © 1949, Northwestern University Press

Reprinted with permission from the edition of 1949, Evanston
First AMS EDITION published 1970
Manufactured in the United States of America

International Standard Book Number:
Complete Set: 0-404-50700-X
Set of Four: 0-404-50749-2
Number 18: 0-404-50718-2

Library of Congress Card Catalog Number: 76-129385

AMS PRESS, INC.
NEW YORK, N.Y. 10003

Table of Contents

Preface

Vol. 1 covers the vocabulary development in the first two years of my daughter Hildegard. Vol. 2 analyzes the sounds during the same period, both the fate of the standard sounds in the child's representation and the growth of a system of sounds in the child's language. Vol. 3 covers the remaining problems of grammar for the same formative stage: syntax and morphology.

While the child was making considerable strides in lexical and phonetic mastery of the models, the acquisition of the syntactic and morphological patterns remained in an incipient stage. Words were put together in an endeavor to express complex ideas as standard sentences do, but the child did not make much headway toward the subtle organization of standard sentences for this purpose. Particularly the formal signs for relationships of words, endings, articles, prepositions, auxiliary verbs, were as yet rudimentary. Most of the development along these lines came after the end of the second year.

In addition to these grammatical topics, this volume deals with problems of child language of a more general nature, some of which have commanded much attention in the literature of the field. Most of this chapter is devoted to a detailed discussion of the semantic development, about which no more than a hint has been given in vol. 1 (pp. 169–171, also 175–179). The often-treated topics of the development of concepts, original creation, child-etymology enter into this discussion. Such subjects as word-formation, opposition, antithesis appear incidentally in it. Most of the discussion is centered on an attempt to fit the child's semantic learning into the traditional classification of semantics: extension of meaning and restriction of meaning.

The last part of the volume (**635 ff.**) is devoted to problems of a very general nature: selectiveness of imitation, motivation, gestures, understanding and speaking, echolalia, memory, stages of learning, bilingualism. These aspects round out the picture of a small child's language learning, which the study as a whole tries to give.

The results recorded in this volume may be disappointing to some, because its topics unavoidably entail the consequence that often mere beginnings of developments are shown, much more so than in the first two volumes. This applies least to the sections on the learning of meaning; but the chapters on syntax and morphology are definitely torsos, although they should be interesting to those who find the almost intangible beginnings of a process as fascinating as its further development along well-established lines. The sections on bilingualism, too, are not very revealing, because the child was not bilingual in any full sense of the word by 2;0; she did not yet acquire two separate language instruments. I regret this shortcoming more than the others. I know that many readers are misled by the title of the work into expecting an emphasis on bilingualism, whereas the emphasis is really on the speech-development; I tried to forestall this misinterpretation by a clarifying remark in the preface of vol. 1 (p. VII). To mitigate the disappointment somewhat, I go beyond the two-year limit in the discussion of bilingualism and present some convictions which I have come to formulate for myself in the light of my experience.

The developments begun in the second year continued more energetically in the following years. Bilingualism in a more vital sense, the learning of two separate language-systems in alternation and eventually concurrently, also developed in later years, when Hildegard spent half a year in Germany, and continued to speak German to me after our return. All these developments can be followed in detail in the diary of the later linguistic history, which vol. 4 will present in chronological arrangement.

If anyone still doubts the value of the detailed study of children's language-learning, I can only point to the urgent calls for more exact records of individual cases, which are heard again and again in the literature. "Der schon oft beklagte Mangel an Beobachtungen der Sprachentwicklung" is reiterated by Fröschels (p. 61, cf. p. 94). Lewis (p. 168), after discussing the statistical method used by recent psychologists and educators, who take averages of the language development of many children, says: "But this method is certainly inadequate when we come to deal with the problem now before us: the relation of the forms of children's language to the process of their mastery of the conventional mother tongue. For this, once more, we need studies of individual children, recording their preconventional words, and the corresponding adult forms used within their hearing. Accounts of this kind, it need hardly be said, are almost entirely lacking;" thereupon Deville's record is highly praised, Stern's moderately so. Other references of the same type have been given in the preceding prefaces.

I am grateful to Professor R.-M. S. Heffner of the University of Wisconsin for reading the manuscript and recommending its publication to the editorial board of the Northwestern University Studies.

W. F. L.

Sister Bay, Wisconsin
25 July 1946

The publication of this volume has also been delayed by printing difficulties. In the meantime, Antoine Grégoire has unexpectedly published a continuation of his work, *L'apprentissage du langage:* II *La troisième année et les années suivantes*, Liège-Paris, 1947. This significant book (see my review in Language 24, 1948, pp. 323–326) covers in part the same ground as my present volume; but it was too late to use it for my study. I welcome the appearance of a parallel study from the pen of a well-known linguist. Fortunately, the coördination with my observations will not be difficult; Grégoire uses similar principles of classification.

W. F. L.

Evanston, Illinois
24 November 1948

Additional Linguistic Terms[1]

Back-formation (accepted translation of German "Rückbildung"), an
unetymological reduction of a seeming derivative to its supposed
base on the model of other couples of related words, like "pup"
from "puppy" (< French "poupée"), "edit" from "editor", "to
house-clean" from "house-cleaning". The phenomenon is related
to metanalysis, but applies to word-formation instead of sequences
of sounds.

Causative, a verb which expresses the causing of an action or condition,
like "to fell" = "cause to fall", "to sadden" = "make sad".

Doublets, two distinct words derived from the same etymon, like "phan-
tasy" and "fancy".

Hypothetical condition, condition contrary to fact, unreal condition.

Loan-translation, an expression borrowed from another language by
translation of its component parts into the native language:
"almighty" from Latin "omnipotens," "loan-word" from German
"Lehnwort", "back-formation" from German "Rückbildung",
"standpoint" from German "Standpunkt", "loan-translation"
from German "Lehnübersetzung", "superman" from German
"Übermensch"; "marriage of convenience" from French "mariage
de convenance", "It goes without saying" from French "Cela va
sans dire"; also called translation loan-word, semantic loan.
"Anglicisms" and "Germanisms" are loan-translations. My phrase
"modeled on . . . ", refers to loan-translations.

Metanalysis, Jespersen's term for faulty placement of the boundary-line
between successive words (cf. **467**). In this way, "a norange" (cf.
Spanish "naranja") became "an orange", "an ewt" > "a newt",
"an eke-name" > "a nickname", "a nauger" > "an auger", "a
nadder" (cf. German "Natter") > "an adder". In morphology,
metanalysis operates in cases like singular "pea" from singular
"peas" (< Latin "pisum") taken as a plural; "cherry" < Middle
English "cherris" < French "cerise". The phenomenon is related
to back-formation, which, however, does not operate on successive words. For this reason, the last-named examples might be
called cases of back-formation rather than metanalysis, contrary
to Jespersen.

Parataxis (paratactic) = coördination; the opposite of *hypotaxis* =
subordination.

Past tense is used, for the benefit of the lay reader, in the sense of simple
past tense, instead of the possibly more scientific term "preterite".

Primary element of a sentence (German "Satzteil"), one of the principal
units of syntax of which a sentence is composed, like subject, verb,

---

[1] Cf. vol. 1, pp. 5–11, and vol. 2, p. XII.

object. A *secondary* element is one which forms a part of a primary unit, like an adjective accompanying either a subject noun, an object noun, or a predicate noun. The terminology agrees with Jespersen's, but I do not follow him into the intricacies of his analysis in this aspect of syntax.

Sentence-adverb, an adverb which summarizes the content of a whole sentence, positively or negatively; "yes" and "no" and their synonyms.

Stem of a word, formally that part of a word which remains after it has been stripped of prefixes, suffixes, and endings, like "fog" in "befogged"; semantically the syllable or syllables bearing the basic meaning of the word apart from modifications called forth by the context. Technically there is a difference between "root" and "stem". This difference of comparative linguistics plays no part in this record.

Strong verbs, those verbs called "irregular" in elementary grammar which form tenses by a modification (ablaut, apophony) of the stem-vowel instead of by the addition of an ending, like "sing, sang, sung". *Weak verbs* are the "regular" verbs which leave the stem unchanged and add an ending, like "love, loved, loved".

Syndetic, connected by means of conjunctions; *asyndetic*, not so connected; in the latter case, logical coördination or subordination is left unexpressed.

Terminal unvoicing, not an accepted term. I use this term for German "Auslautsverhärtung," the devoicing of voiced consonants at the end of words. Cf. index, vol. 2, under *Final unvoicing* and *Unvoicing of final consonants*.

Umlaut = mutation, the partial assimilation of a vowel to the vowel of the following syllable, especially to "i," like German "Füsse: Fuss", English "feet: foot". In both languages, the plural ending used to contain an "i."

Syntax of the First Two Years

501. In studying Hildegard's linguistic development during the first two years, I have devoted a whole volume to the vocabulary and another to the sounds. In both areas there is ample material for observation and analysis.

In contrast, the treatment of syntax and morphology has a more limited scope. At the end of the second year, the child's speech was only beginning to step out of the pre-grammatical stage. From the point of view of adult syntax, most sentences were still incomplete. Grammatical endings and other morphological devices which serve to clarify syntactical relationships were in a rudimentary stage. In the first part of this volume, we shall follow Hildegard's first steps towards organized sentence-structure. Morphological features, as formal signs of a developing syntactical analysis, will be examined in the second part.

To understand the development of the child's early sentence, we must probe into the hidden processes of the child's mind, remaining conscious of the hypothetical nature of such inferences. Scholars who wish to restrict the domain of linguistics to the external form of language must refrain altogether from investigating children's earliest syntax, because there is very little form to deal with.

502. There is a great difference between the learning of vocabulary and sounds on the one hand and syntax on the other. The former are learned primarily by imitation of objective material heard again and again in substantially unvaried form; analogy and patterning, while by no means absent, play a subordinated part. Syntax, however, is nothing but pattern. Phrases and short sentences can be learned by imitation; but the application of syntactic patterns to ever-varying vocabulary material requires well-developed powers of abstraction.[1] It is not surprising that the learning of syntax comes last.[2]

503. For a long time after the beginning of speaking, the child's sentences consist of a single word. From a purely formal point of view, there is nothing of a syntactic nature to report during this extended stage. Functionally, however, a good deal will have to be said about the period.

The next stage is the expansion of utterances to two, then to three, and eventually to more words. To the end of the second year, the words of

---

[1] Delacroix (1934), p. 91: "Il y faut quelque puissance d'analyse." Bloch (1924) p. 43: "Ce n'est pas par de simples exercices d'imitation qu'il acquiert la possibilité de faire des groupes de mots, il faut que l'effort conscient soit presque continuel." The term "conscious" should, of course, be taken with a grain of salt.

[2] Fisher (p. 2) takes "control over the sentence" rather than over vocabulary as an indication of linguistic growth. At 6, "normal children have acquired all the ordinary speech patterns used by the adults about them." The vocabulary, of course, keeps growing after that stage. "There was a significant positive relationship between the complexity of sentence structure and the intelligence of the child" (p. 9).

such combinations are nearly always placed one after the other without such formal characterizations as endings and other morphological devices.

Eventually the latter also appear, first sporadically, then more and more systematically. A first move toward organized syntactical structure of the sentence is made before the end of the second year.

This rapid preview will guide us in the detailed examination of the sentence-development. The first stage to be analyzed is that of the one-word sentence.

504. The fact that Hildegard's earliest utterances were one-word sentences[3] is in harmony with the observations made on the speech-development of most children.

For a long period, one-word utterances serve the needs of a child satisfactorily.[4] In Hildegard's case, the pure one-word stage lasted from the appearance of the first spoken word, 0;8 or 0;9, to 1;4 or 1;5. Then two-word utterances appeared, although the first of these can well be considered combinations of two one-word sentences. The duration of the one-word stage was thus at least eight months for this child of slow-average speech development. The hesitation concerning the starting-point arises from the question whether the interjection listed as the first "word" 0;8 is recognized as a word or not. The end is set at the time when the first mechanically-imitated sentences appeared, which was at 1;5, with an imperfect forerunner, registered under *da* (*ist es*) in volume 1, at 1;4. Of course, mechanically-imitated sentences, even though they be complete from the point of view of standard syntax, are genetically not very different from imitations of one word. Independent combinations of two words did not begin before 1;6, and not until 1;8 were they clearly two-word sentences rather than two successive one-word sentences. Thus the one-word stage can well be said to extend over a whole year in Hildegard's case. Besides, one-word utterances were by no means discontinued. They remained frequent, decreasing markedly only in the last month of the second year.

505. Of course, one-word sentences are not unknown in the speech of adults. In colloquial speech, the only type which is of importance as a model for the child, they are quite common.[5] Speaker and hearer being in

---

[3] The term "rhemes", as taken over by Chamberlain (1901, p. 146) from Postgate, does not cover quite the same ground as "sentence-words" (pp. 141–143). The term is occasionally used by other writers, *e.g.* Bean and McCarthy. Most writers on the subject do not feel the need of a special technical term.

[4] Stern (p. 180) gives a list, from his own experience and from the literature, of the duration of the one-word stage. He finds that it lasts around half a year, with a range from 5 to 12 months. Kenyeres p. 200: six weeks to one year. K. Bühler (1926) p. 602 f.: months, sometimes a year. Decroly p. 129 f.: 4–12 months. There is much on one-word sentences in Romanes. Nice (p. 370): 4–9 months, average 6 months, for 16 English-speaking children; 4–12 months, average 6.6 months for 17 foreign children.

[5] Cf. Feyeux (p. 60), with examples.

thorough agreement about the situation referred to, one word often suffices to make the meaning clear.[6] The child makes a much more extensive use of this linguistic device because it fits the first period of linguistic development. In the phonemic analysis of sounds (vol. 2), we observed that Hildegard often started with a single series of vowels or consonants and progressed through a contrasting two-series stage to ever finer discriminations. The same observation applies to the growth of syntax. At first the understanding of a spoken sentence amounts to no more than understanding the word which represents the semantic peak of the utterance,[7] with the aid of intonation. In English and German, this is also the word bearing the strongest stress. Naturally, in his own early utterances, the child is satisfied with the reproduction of the one word on which his passive and active attention is concentrated. Later, when the child has the experience that the problems of a situation cannot always be understood and solved by means of a single word, both understanding and speaking must progress to a finer analysis.

506. Since the semantic peak and the phonetic stress do not put form-words (words used chiefly for the clarification of syntactic relationships) nor, in German and English, prefixes and endings in relief, it is not surprising that such elements are the last to receive attention.[8] During the period of one-word sentences, the words selected by the child are what would be called nouns, adjectives, adverbs, and interjections in the standard classification of parts of speech. Verbs appear also, but in very limited numbers. Actually, a break-down into parts of speech is futile as long as one word serves the purposes of communications usually cast in the form of complete sentences in standard speech (cf. vol. 1, pp. 166–168). Even when the utterances are extended to two and three words, such a classification is still too rigid, although it may be granted that the child is then beginning to learn the standard organization of a sentence. Not until verbs are combined in increasing numbers with other words, in our case in the last month of the second year, can we speak of real sentences in the child's language.

507. There can hardly be any doubt that the one-word sentence constitutes for the small child a complete expression of thought and feeling. The child is not aware of the fact that his sentence is incomplete in comparison with prevailing adult speech-habits. His attention in the understanding of spoken sentences is concentrated on the most significant word, which also bears the strongest stress. This word is at first reproduced alone, and since the child's environment is well equipped to understand the intention of such utterances with the help of the concrete

---

[6] Guillaume (p. 203) calls "sentence words" of this type "predicates of the situation".

[7] Cf. in this connection the observations on p. 27 f. of vol. 1 (with note 67) and Guillaume (p. 206).

[8] Guillaume (p. 204): Form-words are never used as sentence words.

situation which is at that stage always involved, this primitive mode of expression satisfies the needs of communication for an extended period.

The nature of these early communications is, however, not the same in all instances. Very often the child expresses a wish or request; at other times he asks a question. Sometimes he expresses lively interest, which he wishes to share. Again, he may make a statement reporting an observation he has made. The child has one formal syntactic device at his disposal from the beginning to distinguish between several types of utterances: intonation. This has been emphasized by Karl Bühler.[9] Gestures, a non-linguistic communication-device, help to make the meaning clear if the speaking situation does not give sufficient support for understanding (639–642).

508. It is not easy to make a clear distinction between the types of syntactical purposes just enumerated. There is no sharp cleavage between request and question. A question which would, in adult syntax, be cast in the form, "May I . . . ?" amounts to the same thing as a request like "I should like to . . . ". From there it is a small step to more peremptory requests of the types, "I want . . . ", "Give me . . . ", "Do . . . ". The more elaborate syntax of these standard formulations makes distinctions of this kind possible. But in the child's one-word sentences they merge imperceptibly one into the other. All these shades of meaning might be combined under the heading, emotional language. It might seem at first glance that emotional utterances can at least be kept separate from statements of fact and reports of experiences the child has made. Even this boundary-line, however, is not sharp. The lively interest with which the small child makes such utterances tinges them with strong emotionalism.[10] Besides, such a seemingly declarative operation as reproducing the name of an object can be complicated by the uncertainty which the child often feels with regard to the analysis of his experiences. It is therefore sometimes delivered with an interrogative intonation which asks for confirmation of the identification. In addition, all emotional utterances are attached to something factual, objective,[11] and no objective statement is ever made quite dispassionately. If there were no intention to influence the hearer, or at least an interest on the part of the speaker, present, the statement would not be made at all. This holds true even for adult speakers, and much more so for the small child.

The controversy between those who emphasize the emotional and volitional character of child-speech and those who insist on the intel-

---

[9] (1922) p. 82; cf. end of 489 in vol. 2. Hermann (1936, p. 547) exaggerates when he claims that the small child makes exact distinctions by means of intonation.

[10] O'Shea p. 55: "Regarding the matter psychologically, there is an interjectional element in most of the child's early words;" p. 56: "He can use 'horse' with interjectional function about as readily and effectively as 'Oh!' or 'Whew!' or 'Hurrah!' "

[11] Cf. Delacroix (1930) p. 295 f.

lectual aspects of it (515),[12] therefore loses its point, much as it has contributed to a better appreciation of the driving forces behind the speech of children, and therefore to a truer analysis of syntactic problems. All that can be said is that the preponderance of one or the other element varies. We shall try to steer as clear of the early mistake of comparing all utterances of children to the most intellectualized language-types of adults, as of the later exaggeration to deny the existence of any declarative statements. Delacroix[13] has a sensible view: the word has at first an ill-defined meaning and an ill-defined value; it refers to a nebulous complex, factually and emotionally; only gradually do its factual and emotional components become clearer, resulting in lexical and syntactic discriminations. This situation is again parallel to the gradual refinement in the child's mastery of sounds, which was found in the phonemic analysis of vol. 2.

509. Without losing sight of the fact that emotions, wishes, questions, and statements cannot be completely disentangled during the one-word stage, we shall look at a representative number of examples in which one or the other of these categories prevails. We shall generally have to take the situation into account and will often be compelled to emphasize fluctuations between categories. Since one-word utterances do not cease when the combination of several words has been learned, examples can also be taken from the later months.

Interjections (vol. 1, p. 171, item 9) are linguistic expressions of emotions in the language of adults. It is in this form more than in any other that the one-word sentence retains its footing in the fully developed speech, not only in the language of everyday conversation, but also in the elevated style of poetry.[14] The child's early speech is loaded with emotion. Its predominance decreases slowly, but it never disappears entirely.[15] It is no wonder then that interjections play a prominent part in the early utterances of children.

The very first item in Hildegard's speech which is listed as a "word" at 0;8 (vol. 1, p. 151) was a spontaneous interjection (p. 21). Not all of the first few words were interjections. Sometimes the emotional reaction attached itself to the factual material with which it was connected, and the form chosen to express it was a noun, adjective, or adverb taken over

---

[12] Cf. Stern pp. 181–185.

[13] (1930) p. 296.   Cf. Stern p. 123 f.

[14] The "expressions esthétiques", which Cohen (p. 112) mentions as a domain of the "complete" language by the side of the "explications intellectuelles", are of course linked with the emotional side of speaking. Piaget (p. 4) says that the driving forces of early speaking are "not only affective but also well-nigh magical". This statement is meaningless to me.

[15] O'Shea (p. 56) puts the decline of exclamatory or interjectional coloring as late as age 7 or 8 and says that it does not cease during youth. The restriction expressed in the last two words might well be omitted.

from the standard languages. Interjections, however, were prominent. Of the first eight words learned during 0;8–10, four were spontaneous babblings which had acquired a specific emotional meaning[16] and one was a spontaneous click which had been adapted to a function given to the same click in standard colloquial usage. All of these can be classified as interjections.

The spontaneous interjections disappeared quickly after the period of transition from babbling to speaking. New ones did not occur after 1;0, with the sole exceptions of kχ at 1;7 and 1;10 and bu:: at 1;11; the latter may not even be a pure interjection; it is probably based on standard words. Standard interjections, however, were taken over by Hildegard much more eagerly than words with factual content. One glance at the numerous words printed with an exclamation-mark in the German column on pp. 152 and 153 of vol. 1 shows how frequent these interjections were, especially at 1;1–2; several of the English words, printed without exclamation-marks, are likewise interjections. The percentage of new interjections remained high during the following months. Not until 1;10 did words with a clearer factual content gain a decisive ascendancy. Examples of standard interjections are *oh 1;0–7, *pooh 1;2–4 (intellectualized 1;4, 1;11, **515**), ei 1;4, hello 1;5, *huch 1;7, au 1;8, wehweh 1;8; also *sch 1;0–6, sh 1;6.[17]

Besides, the survey of new acquisitions does not yield an adequate impression of the strong position which interjections held during the first year of speaking. Although many of them were discontinued by the end of the second year (as indicated by asterisks), they often lasted for several months and during that time were used more frequently than other words. Just because interjections were early and frequent, they do not appear as new acquisitions in the later months.

Some of the items waver between interjections and other classes of words. *Kiek 1;1, 1;3 is a Low German imperative (**511**), but it cannot be doubted that its value for the child is closely parallel to that of pieks *1;1, 1;11, which can only be classified as an interjection. Imperatives in general are akin to interjections.

Again, *there 0;10 was not counted as an interjection in the preceding statement concerning the share of interjections in the first eight words. Yet there can be no doubt, on account of the way the child said it, that the interjectional admixture to the factual content of the adverb was as strong as in an interjection like pieks, which also had a factual content, namely the action of pricking. The same holds for the synonymous German da 1;0, which remained active and very frequent.

Another category not usually classified as an interjection is the sen-

---

[16] Preyer's claim (p. 93) that the growth of "inborn" interjections into words to express ideas "is not proved to exist", "has not been observed" is invalidated by this observation, unless "ideas" is to be taken in a purely intellectual sense.

[17] Cf. Gheorgov pp. 327 f., 421 f.

tence-adverb, particularly the negative. In saying *no*, the child expresses a strong emotional reaction together with a manifestation of his will. The two elements are welded together, but factual considerations do not enter at all in the beginning.[18] In fact, the stronger emotional value of the negative[19] explains the often-observed phenomena that it commonly precedes the affirmative in time of acquisition[20] and that it becomes fixed as a *no*-complex at times (Hildegard 1;8, Karla 1;9–10).[21] In the pre-speaking stage, the negative reaction is expressed by crying.[22] At E 1;3 this meant already "I do not want to" in Hildegard's case; the form of the utterance precludes all doubt as to its emotional character. This primitive reaction was not definitely replaced by the verbal negative until 1;6 (vol. 1, p. 112, also p. 110). From the beginning, the negative was sometimes used factually, as a statement (515); but the emotional and volitional implications prevailed until 1;11.

Even an "adjective" like *pretty* 0;10 was for a whole year no more than an emotive. It might well be said that it was used by itself as an interjection of delight. Not until 1;11 did it become a real adjective (vol. 1, p. 120). Significantly, it did not fall in line with regular sound-substitutions as long as it was an interjection (496).

The diary states on the occasion of a summary of Hildegard's small vocabulary at B 1;4 that an emotional admixture was nearly always present, but not always a wish.

510. Next to the one-word utterances which were primarily characterized by their emotional load, we discuss those in which a wish was expressed. Needless to say, there is no boundary-line between emotions and wishes. Wishes are intimately tied with emotions, but the methodological distinction is based upon the fact that wishes represent an active attitude, whereas the preceding category is essentially composed of passive reactions to the inner and outer world.

In the one-word stage there can be no clear distinction between emotion and wish. We find the same words used for both purposes, which are often mingled, at best with a preponderance of one or the other at different times. The situation and an intimate acquaintance with the

---

[18] Even later, parents will sometimes sorrowfully interpret a "no" as an untrue statement, whereas the child meant it only as an utterance of his personal reaction, or even as a compliant echo of negative rules laid down earlier. Cf. Delacroix (1930) p. 295 (he follows Stern).

[19] Jespersen p. 136; Delacroix (1930) p. 324 f.; Karl Bühler p. 235; Guillaume p. 16.

[20] Jespersen p. 136; Gheorgov p. 400 ff.; Decroly p. 196.

[21] Reynolds, in a specialized study of "negativism", fixes the peak at or below 2;0.

[22] Concerning similar pre-linguistic forms for giving assent to a command, see vol. 1, p. 93, note 170. An example for partial repetition of the command, mentioned by Decroly (p. 199) as a linguistic precursor of the affirmative adverb, is given in the text on the same page at 1;8. In Hildegard's and Karla's cases the practice was later than the acquisition of *ja*.

child are needed to decide the intention of the utterance. Aside from the pure interjections, in which the wish-element is often a subdued concomitant, we find the term of admiration, *pretty*, used at times from the beginning, E 0;10, with an added element of desire. The meaning of the adverbial interjection *da*, which was at first quite factual, became more diffuse at 1;1 and included the desire to have the object designated by it, at the least to 1;4. The same holds true for the later stages of the spontaneous interjection ˀə in its varying forms, from B 1;3. The interrogative intonation which accompanied it signified "May I have it?" rather than "What is it?" The same intonation was often attached to *da*. The interjection *m* 1;0 with reference to food carried not only the emotional reaction, "It tastes good", but also the announcement that she was hungry, which, of course, was not an objective communication, but contained the ardent wish to be fed. It would be futile to attempt a separation of appeals, requests, exhortations, and expressions of impatience from wishes or desires. It should be noted that negative wishes, unwillingness to do or suffer something, were at E 1;3 still expressed by crying and disgruntled squealing, when positive wishes had already a more articulate form. The remarks (**509**) about the later negative sentence-adverbs *no* and *nein* apply to wishes as well as to emotional exclamations.

In the summary of Hildegard's vocabulary at B 1;4, a classification is attempted in the diary with regard to absence or presence of a wish-element, as follows: with wish, three interjections (including interjectional adverbs and adjectives), no nouns, five activities; without wish, two interjections, ten nouns (persons, animals, objects), three activities. This rough classification indicates that interjections and activities (none in verb-form) had the greatest affinity to wishes, nouns the least.

Even at 1;8, when pure statements became frequent, wishes were still the most powerful stimulus for speaking. The conventional formula for expressing a wish, *bitte*, used alone 1;5–6, became exceedingly frequent because of the dominant importance of wishes. The fact recorded for 1;7 that she said *bitte* readily, whereas she disliked the equally conventional *danke*, is in line with this condition; *bitte* achieved results of importance to her, *danke* seemed to serve no useful purpose.

511. In the standard languages, the means to express wishes and related phenomena are statements with modal auxiliaries ("I want", "let us", "you shall, must"), polite questions ("Would you?" "Have you ... for me?" "May I?"), and imperatives. The modal auxiliaries were missing in Hildegard's baby-language. Imperatives existed only rudimentarily. The most fertile way of indicating wishes was an interrogative, rising intonation, supported by a questioning facial expression and, of course, the situation, although the preponderance of this method was not yet strong in the one-word stage.

Real imperatives did not occur before 1;4, because no verbs were in her vocabulary at that time. Yet the demonstrative *da* sometimes indicated the wish to have something as early as 1;0. The adverb *up*, which she used often to express such wishes as "Put me up on the davenport" (1;4, 1;6), "Take me out of bed" (1;6), "Raise the lid of the box" (1;4), "Put the periodical up on the mantel" (1;6), "Get up" (1;6), was functionally the same as an imperative. It expressed a wish and did not require interrogative intonation to make the intention clear.[23] All kinds of early utterances could contain a wish-element and be used like imperatives, no matter whether they were objectively based on nouns, adjectives, adverbs, or even interjections. The interjection *sh*, for instance, meaning "be quiet", behaves like an imperative even in the standard language, and was imitated by the child in the same way, with a gesture reinforcing its imperative character.

As far as real imperatives, based on standard verb-forms, are concerned, *up* 1;4 can be considered a forerunner. It is quite probable that the child was sometimes reproducing, to the best of her ability, such standard imperatives as "get up". The verb proper, standing in pretonic position before the more strongly stressed adverb, had to be dropped at this stage, by a normal phonetic rule (476). No observer without linguistic training would think of classifying *up* as anything but an adverb—a further sidelight on the more than dubious value of the classification by parts of speech of children's early words (cf. vol. 1, pp. 166–168), in which untrained observers often indulge. Verbs compounded with *up* were not reproduced in full until 1;10, and "get up" was not among them even by the end of the second year (vol. 1, p. 36).

One experience with the German word *hoch*, which was similar in meaning, clearly showed that for the child it was not an adverb. As reported in vol. 1, p. 91, I used the word 1;8 as an adverb of place while trying to give her directions, but she responded by a different action for which the word had become a habitual stimulus. It might be called an imperative in the function in which Hildegard understood it, because of the response in action which it received (she raised her arms). It was farther removed from a standard imperative, however, than *up*, because, when it was learned 1;11, it never resulted from phonetic omission of a preceding verb. "Heb (die Arme) hoch", which might be thought of as a parallel to "get up", had not been used. The more primitive form without a verb was in this case taken over from the presentation.

In different meanings, other adverbs appeared in functions similar to *up*. *Auf* 1;6 stood for "mach auf", *aus* 1;6–11 for "zieh aus", *away* 1;8 for "put, take it away", *an, on* 1;9 for "zieh an", "put on" 1;9, for "turn on" 1;10–11 (for "Licht an" 1;10), all as phonetic clippings of standard imperatives. In one combination the phonetic clipping can be

---

[23] Snyder's definition of imperative sentences (p. 412) as "any sentence . . . that calls for an action-response" is too wide for our purposes; it includes requests with interrogative intonation.

proved: **ma** 1;10 came from *come on*. Of course, the situation is closely parallel to the earlier synonym **mit* 1;8–10 from *komm mit*. The latter example is exactly like the other adverbs which I assume to be imperatives with phonetic clipping. It will be granted that the hypothesis has great probability. As late as 1;11, the noun *house* alone was said for "come into the house", the semantically and dynamically less prominent words being suppressed. When she addressed the imperative *away* to herself 1;8, preparing to put the cart away, its imperative and wish character faded out; it approached the character of a statement (515).

There are a few instances in which a standard German imperative of a simple verb was imitated mechanically even with an imperative ending, whereas later, when imperatives really became alive, they regularly lacked an ending. These examples are *backe* and **hacke* 1;11. In both of them the imperative character is faded in the standard language. They were actually no more than mechanical verbal accompaniments of two play-actions which were similar in character. The traditional nursery-game of clapping the hands together with the sing-song "Backe, backe Kuchen" had often been rehearsed by the time when she once spontaneously knocked two stones against each other. It is probable that the similarity of the action induced her to repeat readily the similar verbal symbol, *hacke*, presented by a friend who was watching her. The accidental character of the latter game prevented its verbal concomitant from becoming rooted in her vocabulary.

A real imperative of a simple verb, which Hildegard learned before 2;0, was the German *rollen* 1;8. It happened to be presented in infinitive form with imperative function. At first she attempted to imitate even the infinitive ending; but when the imitation of the word became less mechanical, the ending was dropped. This was in line with the simple morphological pattern of the stage, but it can also be attributed to the amalgamation with the English synonym *roll*, which, of course, has no ending in either the imperative or the infinitive. The imperative *trag* was used 1;11 in the sense of "carry me", without an ending and without expression of the object.

The Low German **kiek* 1;1 and 1;3 is, from the point of view of standard grammar, clearly an imperative, the earliest imperative she ever used. For the child, however, it was no more than a linguistic game-cue (509). It was replaced from *1;4, 1;8 by the English *peekaboo*, the imperative origin of which is disguised in the playful extension of the nursery standard. A verb with the real meaning "look" was completely missing until 2;1.

Most of the English imperatives which occurred are equally doubtful. *Rock, rock* 1;8, although it expressed a wish to be rocked in a certain rocking-chair, was hardly based on a real imperative, but on the verbal symbol with which her mother emphasized the rhythm of the rocking motion. *Open* 1;8 was really an imperative; but it cannot be proved that

the child felt the imperative function of the word. It inherited part of
the functions of the earlier *auf* and was later (1;10–11), in the two-word
stage, used like an adjective as often as like an imperative. *Dress* 1;10
was the clearest imperative of all. It meant "dress me", was so said at
1;11 and was based on this pattern of the presentation. Yet its function
was not essentially different from the older *on*, and it was also used as a
noun 1;10. We cannot assume that even the verb-character of the word
was clear in the child's mind, much less the imperative function. *Wait*
1;11 would seem to leave no room for doubt as to its imperative nature.
Yet it was a replacement of German **Augenblick*, which few observers
would classify as an imperative. *Blow* 1;11, when it meant "Blow up my
balloon", was an imperative; but the same word was used in other
situations, when it could not be interpreted as an imperative (512).

The negative sentence-adverbs fit in some way in every one of the
categories. In so far as they are equivalents of "Do not do that", they
can be called negative imperatives. This meaning hardly occurred for
*nein and *no*, which usually quoted interdictions of her parents. *Don't*
1;11, however, which Hildegard generally used by itself, as she heard
her mother often say it, was definitely a negative imperative.

Actually the situation is this. In the one-word stage, the child's
linguistic utterances were grammatically undifferentiated. The parts
of speech were not at all separated from each other. The child frequently
felt the need to express wishes, and seized on any linguistic means which
could be utilized to achieve the desired ends. Sometimes the words
chosen were based on the imperatives used by adults for the same purposes and came more or less close to them in the child's imitation. Just
as often words belonging to different grammatical categories were used
if they could be made to serve the same purposes. Words classified as
imperatives were such only from the point of view of standard syntax.
The child's linguistic analysis had not progressed to such distinctions.[24]

512. There were other wishes expressed by means which could even
less be called imperatives and which did not use interrogatory intonation to mark the utterance as a request. This category can be regarded
as an incomplete version of standard sentences with a modal auxiliary
of wish or will, the auxiliary being omitted. This interpretation, however, is again one of standard syntax. No consciousness of omission can
be assumed to have existed in the child's speaking practice. The distinction from the preceding category is arbitrary as far as the child's undifferentiated syntax is concerned.

Utterances which belong here differ from those treated under the

---

[24] Such obviously useful imperatives as "see", "look" were completely missing
during the first two years. Hildegard learned *look* at 2;1. Karla, with her sociable
nature, demanding participation of others in everything she did, used "look" to
the point of exasperation for many years after 2;0. She used *see* 1;10, not as an
imperative, however, but as a question.

heading of imperatives in not requesting another person to do something for her, but announcing an action which she was about to perform herself. For the child, however, there was presumably no conscious difference between imperatives and wishes which adults could not put in the form of commands. Announcements of her own actions might be regarded as imperatives addressed to herself or even as future tenses, but all interpretations of these kinds would operate with patterns which were as yet far beyond the child's crude syntax.

At 1;8, riding in her cart, she said *walk*, making it quite clear that she wanted to get out and proceed on foot. I have no doubt that she felt the utterance as being complete; for her, no auxiliary was omitted. *Wischen* 1;8 was probably used to accompany an action which she felt ought to be performed and which she performed at the same time herself, as in a two-word form 1;11 (520). *Away* 1;8 was not only used as a clipped imperative, but also as an announcement that she was going to put something away. *Ride*, which she said in reduplicated form 1;8 with her hands on her cart, in the house, signified "I want to ride" or "I want to go outside for a ride". It was the successor of *sch*, which had been used 1;0–6 for riding motions, and was only slightly more articulate than it. It would be idle to try to decide whether it was a verb or a noun. In fact, it is not even certain that it was at this stage a word distinct from the homonymous and rather synonymous *outside* 1;9. As early as 1;3, and very often later, she said *by-by*, which meant the same thing, "I want to go outside, for a ride, for a walk", a wish which she entertained and uttered constantly. *Blow* 1;11 meant "blow up my balloon", imperative (511), but soon also "blow the whistle", "blow the nose", etc. At least in the last function, she did the blowing herself, so that the verb was not an imperative; but, to be sure, we cannot be certain that her definition of it was as accurate as ours; it may have meant "wipe my nose" as well as "I want to blow my nose".

When she was asked 1;8 whether she wanted to go to bed now, she answered *Bett*. This primitive form of assent amounts to "Yes, I want to go to bed now". It comes close to the standard affirmative sentence-adverb, which involves no modal auxiliary.

513. Questions, marked by a rising intonation or high pitch, fall into two distinct categories. Those that by their purpose might be paraphrased by "May I . . . ?" "Will you . . . ?" are questions containing a request. They are similar to the utterances discussed in the preceding sections. The other type, questions amounting to "What is it?", are questions concerning facts. They are related to statements devoid of a wish-element.[25]

---

[25] Snyder (pp. 412–416) uses a classification of questions in four categories, which is adopted or adapted by other authors. Two of these categories are logically subdivisions of requests. Although they apply to older children, nearly all the categories are already found in the one-word stage.

The questioning intonation was learned early. The first "word" to which it was attached was the interjection *ʔə? in its varying phonetic forms, the first meaningful "word" which she learned (0;8). In the beginning it was a demonstrative used to call attention to something. From B 1;3, however, it had interrogative intonation and meant "May I have that?" The more conventional German word *da* (B 1;0) passed over from demonstrative into request function in a parallel manner at E 1;3. At 1;6 *auf* and *aus* were said with the intonation of a question to express the wishes to open ("aufmachen") a box for her or to take off ("ausziehen") articles of clothing. During the same month, she said the noun *light* with strikingly rising intonation to express the desire to be allowed to operate the light switch.

The latter device, to say a verb or noun with interrogative intonation, became the favorite way of asking for permission in the last half-year, when the growth of the vocabulary made this more specific form of request possible. By this time, several words were usually uttered coherently. As an intermediate, but overlapping stage between the primitive interjections and adverbs and the more specific words, she used from 1;6 the German *ja*, not as an affirmative, but as a request for permission, as is possible in the standard language. This use of *ja?* became very common at 1;8. In fact, at that time *ja* served only this purpose, *all right* being used as the affirmative answer to the request. A little later 1;8, *hm? was learned, and was used for a short time as a request for permission or approbation. Only then did *ja* become an affirmative, often used as an answer to the question *hm?*

At 1;8, during a certain routine performance in the bathroom, she would point to different places on the rim of the bath-tub where we usually sat watching her, saying in succession: *Mama? Papa?* This meant: "Will you sit in your customary places?"

The pattern of interrogative intonation for requests continued into the stage of several words (521, 529). At 1;11 the diary states that questions were still used "very frequently" as a means to express requests.

514. The interrogative intonation was also used to obtain information. The emotional element was not lacking in such questions. They were asked with lively interest, with the purpose of having her curiosity satisfied or her knowledge and experience extended. She wished to grow into the adult way of looking at the world and into the adult way of expressing this way in words. This subconscious intellectual wish is, however, so different from conscious wishes for the fulfillment of practical needs or wants that it is better to exclude it from the definition of wishes for our purposes.[26]

Factual questions date from about 1;5. In view of the limitations of

---

[26] Curme (1931, §2) says with regard to the standard language that the question does not only call for a statement, but is at the same time emotive since it contains an expression of will.

her vocabulary at this early stage, it is natural that the same words of vague content which were earlier used for emotional reactions and wishes were also utilized for asking questions for information. The primitive interjection *ʔə? and the interjectional adverb *da* were both used at 1;3 in a way which should be considered a forerunner of such questions. Pointing at one picture after another on the wall, she uttered either the one or the other in a high-pitched voice. These interjections were not yet questions. They merely expressed her lively interest in pictures. It was, however, only a small step from this usage to asking for the name of an object.[27] At 1;5 the similar interjectional adverb *there, spoken with rising intonation, was definitely interpreted as meaning "What is that?" to which it could, however, not be traced phonetically. *There ceased to be used after 1;5. It is conceivable that the German synonym *da*, which displaced it, had the same function at times. It might even phonetically be based on "that" or "das". No such usage was, however, recorded.[28] The interjection ʔə? probably served this function in its later stage, 1;5-6, since it is listed (vol. 1, p. 72) as one of the successors of *there. The later *this* 1;8 is never recorded as a question for the name of an object.

After all is said, the fact emerges that Hildegard, in spite of Stern's generalized claim,[28] did not make much use of questions for the names of objects. *There* is really the only word for which this function is definitely established, and only exceptionally. The observation holds not only for the one-word stage, but for the following stages as well. It is characteristic of Hildegard's mental processes. Undoubtedly she asked for the name of an object occasionally later; as a rule, however, she did not solicit information, but waited patiently until it came to her of itself.

Names with interrogative intonation represent a different type of questions. At 1;6 she uttered the names of persons in their absence in this manner. *Mama?* clearly meant "Where is Mama?" and amounted to a complete sentence, a question for factual information, with a subdued emotional component since she missed the person, but not usually with longing or unhappiness.

The word *this* was used once, late (1;11), as a one-word question of a different kind, as a question for confirmation, to check whether she had understood a direction correctly. She had been told to bring a small rug from the living-room. Doing so, she asked: *This?* It was not even a question for checking on the linguistic understanding, but for ascertain-

---

[27] Preyer (p. 232) corrects Darwin's term "interrogatory sound", attached to a wish for food in this case, into "a very strongly marked tone of longing", "which should mean the same thing". There is a difference, but there is also a close relationship between the two intonations.

[28] Stern (p. 192) says that observers easily fail to recognize the questioning character of early primitive words. Although I do not exclude the possibility of such an oversight, I have too much confidence in my observations to suggest it more than tentatively.

ing whether the rug which she brought was the one intended. The diary marks this question specifically (but erroneously, **522**) as the first question for confirmation. This type is also a factual question, but not one for vocabulary information. Similarly, at 1;8 I once varied the familiar question, "Wie gross bist du?" to test her comprehension, asking: "Wie gross ist Papa?" She asked back *Papa?* and unhesitatingly raised my hand to show that she understood.[29]

The first interrogative, non-permanent, was used for a few days 1;10: *why*, in the sense of "Why am I not allowed to do that?" Its intellectual meaning was not clear to her. For that reason it was dropped soon. It was more or less an emotive to express her disappointment.[30]

In looking back over the questions of the one-word stage the reader will notice that they indicated mostly requests. Questions for linguistic or factual information were rare.

515. Questions about facts lead over into statements concerning facts, or declarative sentences.[31]

Much attention was once devoted to the problem whether the child's early language has more statements of a comparatively dispassionate, intellectual nature or more utterances which serve the will and the emotions. After an early phase of over-emphasis on logic in the examination of child-language, under the influence of the older grammar of standard languages, which was itself under the sway of logical analysis, a violent reaction set in, which laid much stress on the emotional and volitional character of child speech. Meumann was the outstanding representative of this younger school. This controversy can by now be considered settled. Will and emotion do indeed dominate children's early speech, particularly in the beginning. As recent linguistic scholars have emphasized, these elements continue to play an important part in the speech of adults, especially in the colloquial use of language. Even in the most intellectualized types of language, say in science and philosophy, they are not entirely absent because the will to convince motivates even such utterances, spoken or written. Quite early the child also makes statements which do not aim at the fulfillment of any practical desires. They still contain the emotional element of lively interest, which the child wishes to share with the environment; otherwise there would be no

---

[29] The incident shows, too, that she did not understand "Wie gross" intellectually. It was for her merely a cue for a certain action.

[30] Or, as Lewis (1938, p. 163) states it for the boy K. as late as 2;9: "why" serves at first only to ask for further explanation. "No doubt there is some rudimentary notion of causal connection present". Omission of a negative on which the meaning of the sentence hinges did not otherwise occur in Hildegard's language (but cf. **694**). Bloch (1924, p. 28 f.) reports it from 2;2 to 3;6. Karla used *why* mechanically, without clear meaning, at M 1;11. She may have learned it from Hildegard.

[31] Snyder (p. 412) defines the declarative sentence as "any sentence . . . whose value does not depend primarily upon a response."

point in making the statements. But this admixture is almost as faint as in declarative sentences of adults and can be disregarded.[32]

The first "word", *ˀə, must again be examined in this connection. Being originally a spontaneous interjection, it was laden with emotion. From the very beginning (0;8), however, it contained also a demonstrative element, which was later reinforced by the gesture of pointing. As early as B 0;9, Hildegard used it not only to address persons (a vocative function in the service of the will), but to call attention to objects beyond her reach (demonstrative, imperative statements, full of emotion, but not strongly volitional; paraphrase: "Look at that!") and to the fact that she had dropped toys out of reach ("I have lost my toy", statement of fact, to be sure with the undertone of "I should like to have it back"). At B 1;0 she used the interjection in a special phonetic form and with a special gesture to call attention to music; paraphrase: "Listen! Music! How pretty!" The high-pitched ˀə which accompanied pointing to pictures (mentioned in **514** as a forerunner of questions) was more clearly a demonstrative. The diary characterizes it specifically as devoid of wish. The interjectional form, partly justified by the imperative component of calling attention to the object, was largely due to the extreme limitation of vocabulary and syntax, which precluded a more specific statement of the type "This is a . . . ".

I grant that none of these utterances is clearly a statement, although I think they are forerunners, because they show the progressive diminution of wish and even of emotion. *There 0;10–B 1;0, based on a standard demonstrative, was more clearly a statement. It did not lack a strong emotional component, to be sure; all early utterances betrayed the lively interest which prompted them. No wish component is, however, ever recorded for this word. At M 0;10 she used it as an answer to a question about a picture, pointing to it. It amounted to "there it is". The emotional concomitants of joy and astonishment which the answer contained according to the record do not diminish the declarative character of the statement. A variant with the vowel ı: may even have contained germs of *this*. Its successor, *da* 1;0, was often used for wishes, quite frequently with interrogative intonation. At other times, however, it was clearly declarative. In the vocabulary summary of 1;4, "there it is" was listed as one of its two established meanings, with falling intonation. During the same month it began to pass over into the complete declarative statement *Da ist es*.

Pretty 0;10 was an interjection rather than an adjective and therefore less clearly a vehicle of statements. The logician might think that such

---

[32] An excellent treatment of the intertwining of affect, "conation", and objective reference in the child's early language and of the growth of objective reference can be found in Lewis, chapter IX (summary: p. 162 f.). Cf. Macdougall p. 574. The fact that words are used early with very slight emotional value is emphasized by Bloch (1923) p. 670. Cf. Jespersen p. 134.

a word was clearly an evaluating statement or even a judgment, and early observers did. With better psychological insight, however, we cannot fail to see that the word, as one of the very few earliest words, carried an overload of implications and was pressed into the service of expressing a great number of contents for which more specific terms were still lacking. The record states expressly (vol. 1, p. 24) that the object referred to was not necessarily pretty at all, and the assumption that the child's judgment differed from ours would miss the point. *Pretty* was a vague term of admiration, of interest, and of wish. Still, although it did not express a judgment except in the haziest way, it was often used like a demonstrative, with the same pointing gesture as *there*, and moves on that account into the outskirts of the category of statements.

Ticktack, ticktock 0;11, one of the first permanent words, was never used with wish. It was always an objective statement expressing the fact that she recognized an object as falling within the classification covered by the term.[33] The vagueness of the definition in her mind helped her to apply the term correctly to a variety of kinds and shapes of watches and clocks (1;0). It also misled her later (1;0–9) to apply it to a considerable number of very varied objects for which its use is not sanctioned by adult practice. But no matter whether it was used rightly or wrongly, all these one-word sentences were statements, in which interest and enthusiasm were emotional by-products and not the mainstay of the utterance.

Once 1;6 she wanted to play with the toy of a visiting baby, but desisted with the statement *baby*, "It belongs to the baby". This utterance, thwarting her wish, was as free from the wish component as could be desired.

These nouns may serve as examples for early statements without wish and with subdued emotion. It will be recalled (510) that this condition held true for 10 nouns designating persons, animals, objects at 1;4, more than for words derived from other parts of speech. Probably we should state this less categorically for four names of persons included in this summary (Papa, Mama, Dada or Carolyn, and Marion), which were no doubt also used for appeals, in addition to answering questions like "Who is this?" and stating spontaneously the fact of recognition. On the other hand, even interjections could be used for statements in the absence of better vocabulary items. When, for instance, she said *pooh* in a primitive version 1;4, she meant to communicate the fact that she had had a physiological accident in bed or that she imagined her doll to have met with the same mishap. The interjection used by her mother on previous occurrences to record an emotional reaction was utilized

---

[33] Lewis (1937, p. 41) defines "declarative speech" as "the child's use of a word merely to draw the attention of others to some object." The definition seems rather too narrow, but it applies to the case under consideration. Lewis's first case 1;6 concerns the same word with reference to the picture of a watch.

in a non-standard, but perfectly efficient way to communicate a fact.[34] At 1;11 the interjection became Hildegard's synonym for "dirty" and thus the carrier of purely factual statements. At 1;10 already, it was the exact antonym of *dry*, with which she announced triumphantly the progress of physiological training upon awakening in the morning. *Wet* was not used for this purpose.

At the stage of expanding vocabulary, numerous nouns were said for the purpose of rehearsing the names of objects. For instance, at 1;8 I made her say the names for the parts of the face and she added *nose* on her own impulse. Such statements of linguistic facts are a special branch of factual statements. No useful purpose would be served by multiplying examples.

The methodical distinction between wishes and factual statements which we are trying to make in this analysis has value for digging up the roots of the speaking process, but it cannot be assumed to have existed in the child's mind. In instance after instance she used the same vocabulary item for both purposes. The dearth of vocabulary explains this economy, but there is no indication that the child felt at all embarrassed by the duplicity of functions given to the words. The interjectional adverb *up* was usually an expression of wishes of varying nature. But as early as 1;4, the month in which the word was learned, she also used it for stating a fact. Having been told in German to get up, she did so and said *up*, giving the word not only a slightly different meaning (static position instead of upward motion), but also a different function, the statement of an act already performed. If it should be claimed that the utterance, at this early stage, might have been rather a delayed echo of the cue translated into English, there is no doubt that by 1;8 statements without wish were made with this word. Shortly after her mother had risen, Hildegard once pounded the empty bed and said *up*. From then on, she often used it factually, both for stating that something was up in a high place or was moving up. By this time the utterances usually had two or three words, but one-word statements still occurred. In answer to the question, "Where are you?" she said *up*, meaning "upstairs", 1;11; cf. also *away* 1;8 (511). After pushing a drawer in, she exclaimed *zu!* 1;11, which meant "It is shut". Also at 1;11 she said *home* in the sense of "She went home"; this was part of a three-word utterance, but amounted to a separate sentence.

The adjectives *hot* 1;4 and *heiss* 1;5 were used to make statements concerning radiators and other hot (or cold) objects, with a serious expression of caution. The fact, learned from experience and instruction, outweighed the emotional overtones.[35] At 1;8 she used the adjective *nass*

---

[34] A parallel intellectualization of the emotional term is illustrated by Karla's language. She developed the fixed expression "to make pooh" as a synonym of Hildegard's more standard *A-a*.

[35] Preyer (p. 144) records the same word at 1;10 as "the first spoken judgment", eight and a half months after the imitative acquisition of the word. There was no such lag in Hildegard's case.

as a pure statement of the fact that something was wet. Even when she
discovered that my overcoat was wet and stated the fact excitedly with
this word, it was a declarative statement, in spite of the emotional overtones. All statements made with the English synonym, *wet*, which was
older (1;7) and won out over the German competitor, were of a similar
nature. Although more commonly used in utterances of at least two
words (*all wet*), simple *wet* also occurred. Even earlier, from 1;5, *all*,
standing for "all gone", and the German synonym *alle* 1;7 made statements of fact not always accompanied by regret.

The diary observes at 1;8 that pure statements of fact had unmistakably become frequent recently. This month should be considered the
time when intellectualized speech made marked inroads into the earlier
predominantly emotional and volitional utterances. Of course, by this
time most utterances consisted of more than one word.

Words based on standard verbs were often used to make statements, in
addition to other functions. Since such words were entirely absent until
1;4 and did not become numerous until 1;11, examples belong to the
latest stage, when few utterances had one-word form. At 1;10 she sometimes used *break* practically in the same function as *kaputt* and *broke(n)*.
The latter was an adjective rather than a verb form. At any rate all
three words were used for statements of fact, not even with the emotional
component of regret which would have been desirable when she was to
blame for the breakage. At 1;11 she stated dispassionately the fact that
a baby was crying by saying *cries*, in the stem form without the ending,
which was characteristic of the stage. In spite of the monosyllabic form
of the utterance, it approached the character of a complete sentence, the
addition of the subject being, for this particular activity, almost as
superfluous as for meteorological events like "it rains", "it thunders"; in
both situations Spanish, for instance, dispenses with the subject. A
month before, she had reported "The baby cried" in the same phonetic
form, *cry*, with falling intonation, relating a past experience.

These examples do not make a better showing than verb forms used
as imperatives or as vehicles of wishes, but this is largely due to the fact
that we are confining ourselves here to one-word utterances, which had
become rare by the time when most verbs were learned.

The picture of the various types of one-word sentences is rounded out
by mentioning the affirmative and negative sentence adverbs, which have
one-word form commonly in standard speech. They were often used to
express willingness or unwillingness (**509**), or to ask permission (**513**) or
to give it, usually to herself. In the latter function they come close to
declarative statements. Later they often were pure statements of facts,
although sometimes fictitious facts, specifically *ja* from 1;6 and especially
from 1;8 (hardly **yes* 1;4), *no* from 1;6, *m-m* (colloquial negative) from
1;6, **nein* 1;8–9; *all right* from 1;8 served exclusively to give consent.

In looking back over the statements, we find that declarative sentences
existed, along with wishful and primarily emotional utterances, from

the first months of speaking and became rapidly more and more numerous, especially from 1;8.

516. Proceeding to two-word utterances, we shall find the situation a little more complicated. The same categories of utterances will appear again, but the improvement in the length of the utterance does not amount uniformly to an improvement of the syntax. If for instance a statement like *wet* is extended to *all wet*, the syntactic situation remains the same. If two one-word utterances are said in succession, a way is paved for the development of more complete sentences. If finally the two words are, say, a verb (or what can act like a verb) and an object, a real start is made toward a conventional complete sentence. While adhering to the convenient classification by the mechanical length of the utterances, we need to keep in mind these differences in syntactic character.[36]

517. Most standard interjections consist of one word. Therefore we cannot expect to find additions to the stock of real interjections in the two-word stage.

The interjectional adverb *da* began to be extended into the complete sentence **Da ist es* 1;4–5. Hildegard's forms **da:i** 1;4 and **da:ɪ** 1;5 may be called one word or, because they are based on two words of the model, two words. Even when the complete sentence was imitated mechanically 1;5, it was hardly more than an exclamation.

The regretful interjection *oh* was replaced in part of its functions by the compassionate phrases **armer Wauwau!*, *armer Mann!* 1;7–10. These exclamations display an important progress in linguistic analysis. The English synonym *poor* took the place of the German adjective 1;10–11: *poor Mama, poor Papa*. The exclamation, *naughty rock-a-baby* 1;11, with which she scolded the rocking chair after she had fallen over with it, was also composed of a real adjective and a noun, although the noun was developed from the first line of the ditty, "Rock-a-by, baby", which contains a playfully extended imperative and a noun in the vocative. *Pretty dress* and *pretty coat* 1;11 (the latter a child-etymology for "petticoat") are similar exclamations replacing unspecific interjections.

Otherwise the two-word stage brought, in the domain of interjections, the practice of combining a name of a person or animal with the interjection in one intonation group. The vocative, itself related to interjections in character, served to make the exclamation more specific: *nein-nein, Mama* 1;7 **(519)**, *hello, Papa* 1;7, *hello, man* 1;10, *hello, Katz*

---

[36] There is a good psychological explanation of the syntax of one- and two-word sentences in O'Shea, Chapter III. Delacroix (1934, p. 88) emphasizes that the appearance of sentences is not an event psychologically, because one-word utterances had already served the purposes of sentences. Linguistically it is a milestone nevertheless. Bloch (1924, pp. 19–22) analyzes the first two-word sentences of his three children linguistically in categories very similar to mine. These pages are among the most important in the literature of infant-linguistics.

1;10. The comma which is conventionally inserted in writing these combinations is not in agreement with the manner in which Hildegard said these phrases. *Here, Papa* 1;9, said while handing things to me, is similar. It was a complete utterance. The stress distribution of the adult model was faithfully reproduced.

A transition from interjection to statement appeared in several utterances containing the word *Wehweh* 1;8. The plaintive tone in which she usually said it made the word retain its emotional value. But the fact that it was coupled with another word which localized the pain, transformed the utterance into a statement of fact (523), in which the interjection served as a subject and the other word as a predicate. "Wehweh" is often used as a noun in standard nursery German.

The combination *pretty please*, which occurred once 1;9 when she looked longingly at sweets which were out of reach on the mantel, can hardly be called an interjection. Its first word was an emotive expressing her pleasure (509), to which the wish to have the sweets was added. It was not an adverb reinforcing *please* (vol. 1, p. 56).

518. This phrase leads over into wishes expressed by two words. If we leave aside again for the present the wishes which can be equated with imperatives (519), those in which a modal auxiliary seems to be omitted (520), and those which had interrogative intonation (521), a few two-word combinations remain which expressed wishes in varying syntactic forms.

At 1;9, when she had just learned *please*, she rarely said the word by itself, but combined it with the familiar German synonym *bitte*. This double expression of a wish reinforced the appeal in the same manner as by saying *bitte* twice, but did not change its syntactic character, which remained the same as in the one-word stage. *Big by-by*, used at the same time, looks as if it represented a great step forward syntactically. The observer who looks only at the form of the utterance and its relationship to the standard language would say that it consists of an adjective and a noun. Actually its value for the child was quite different. It has been shown (vol. 1, p. 54 f.) that *big* was more commonly an emotive. It was therefore suitable as a means of intensifying *by-by*, which expressed the ardent wish to go out for a ride in her buggy. The only progress over the one-word stage lies in the fact that *big* had the overtone of specifying the wish to go for a ride in the street instead of being merely pushed out on the balcony; this added an intellectual element to the emotional request. *Big* was also combined with *A-a* 1;8. If it had really been an adjective it could have been quite useful to distinguish one physiological function from another, but Hildegard made no such distinction at that stage. It merely served to underline the wish character of the utterance, just like the simultaneous expression *bitte A-a*. This parallelism shows that the adjective character of *big* was still very hazy, although the child used it only before words which could be construed as nouns. Both

versions contained a word to indicate the wish and a word to specify its
domain. In this respect they represent a step forward from the one-word
stage, in which either the wish or the specification had to be inferred from
the situation. *No A-a* 1;11 is similar in those situations in which the
phrase was used as a negative wish. One word expressed the wish by
means of a negative, the other specified it. *Down bitte, bitte up* 1;7, with
the wish word subordinated in stress (and, as late as 2;1, *no bite* meaning
"don't spank me") should be interpreted in the same way, but can be
regarded as imperative in function (519).[37]

Conditions are different in wishes like *This bottle* 1;8, *Hase Bett* 1;8
and *My auf* 1;11. The first example expressed the object of her wish in
two words. The other two represent a decided progress in syntactical
analysis. They can be interpreted as elliptic forms of "The bunny should
also go to bed" and "I want to get up". It is not possible to separate
them clearly from other examples which will be examined in the category
of sentences omitting a modal auxiliary (520). I am convinced that the
pattern of wish-expressions by means of a modal auxiliary was still
below the threshold of active linguistic experience. The wish was implied, not expressed, and in this regard the versions were less mature
than those treated above. Syntactically, however, they were much better,
because they specified the subject to which the wish referred and the
action to be performed. The actions were indicated in a primitive, but
quite understandable manner by words which cannot be called verbs,
but which should be called predicates. These two-word sentences were
grammatically complete in a sense, since they did not require either the
subject or the predicate to be supplied by the situation.

519. The expression of wishes by two-word imperatives cannot be expected to show the same kind of progress, because the standard languages
commonly dispense with the expression of the subject to whom the command is addressed.

Two-word imperatives are recorded from 1;7 and 1;8 on, but the combinations differ greatly in character. Some of them consist of two words
merely because they are compound verbs. During the one-word stage, the
adverb was reproduced alone because it was more strongly stressed.
Now the verb proper preceding it also received its share of attention
and the combination was said in full: *go away* 1;10, *walk in* 1;10 (echo
of "walk right in"), *push in* 1;10, *pick up* 1;10; *throw away* 1;11, *cover
up* 1;11. In two or three of these expressions, the standard language
requires an object, especially in the last one, which meant "cover me up".
The child dispensed with it, because she concentrated her attention
on the two words with the strongest stress.[38] The object was implied by

---

[37] Sully (p. 174) gives an example "No Babba look", which he interprets as
"Babba will not look". I wonder whether it had not better be understood as a
primitive negative imperative. For negatives at the beginning of a series of words,
cf. K. Bühler p. 235.

[38] Bloch (1924, p. 27) likewise reports omission of the object at 1;11.

the situation and was dynamically subordinated in presentations of similar structure. The imperative *lie down* 1;11 sometimes passed over into an announcement of her intention, "I am going to lie down".

With simple imperatives the two-word span allowed the addition of the name of the person addressed; in the one-word stage either one or the other had been said alone.[39] *Come on* 1;10, which was contracted into one word by the child, was a real imperative. It was always followed by a name (*Papa*, *Miau*) in the vocative, with or without a pause. It took the place of *mit* 1;8, which must be interpreted as the child's equivalent of the imperative "komm mit", shortened by omission of the pretonic syllable. This word was at first used with interrogative intonation (521), but at 1;9 and 1;10, before it was replaced by the English synonym, it had the exclamatory tone of the imperative. It was likewise accompanied by a vocative (*Mama*), which preceded it at the imperative stage, with a pause. At 1;8 she said *Mama up*, "Mama, get up", every morning.

Another group of two-word imperatives represents a much more significant advance in syntax, namely those in which a direct object was added to the verb. The first example occurred at 1;8: *open door*. It was quoted from the finger-game, "This is the church", and the mechanical imitation explains the early date of its use. The construction was premature, but it was used with full understanding, and not always as a quotation. Hildegard applied it at once to situations in real life. The next example is *watch Mama* at 1;9, but the diary entry is not full enough to show whether it was an imperative. It is more probable that it meant "I want to watch Mama" (520). The best example is *dress me* 1;11. The object had the main stress, the verb a strong secondary stress. The distribution of stress reveals the effort which was needed to put the two elements of the new construction together. Thus the last month of the second year should be regarded as the time when this construction was really learned. During the preceding month she had expressed the same idea more simply by *bitte dress*, utilizing the two-word span to add the wish-word *bitte*, but omitting the object. Even at 1;11 the incomplete three-word phrase *pretty dress on?* (529) was used more frequently than the new imperative with an object. Examples like *nose blow* and *coat button*, with their failures in word-order, reveal that, at M 1;11, she was still experimenting with the new pattern for expressing "commands" together with the object to which they applied.

There is another category of two-word combinations which were syntactically less advanced. *Bitte dolly* 1;8, *bitte drink* 1;10 consisted of a vague wish-word and an object, but did not express the verbal idea "give me", which was clearly implied. Only from the point of view of standard speech does this construction belong under the classification of impera-

---

[39] Vocatives were not included in the discussion of one-word imperatives (511), but their relationship to imperatives cannot be doubted. When the child calls "Mama!", he means "Mama, come here". Some imperative idea is always implied in the vocatives of adults, at the least an appeal for attention.

tives. Otherwise it is closely related to the wishes without an imperative (518). The examples *down bitte* and *bitte up* 1;7 can be repeated here because they amount to standard "Take me down, Lift me up, please", but I do not claim that the child had in mind any more than the two words which she actually said. *Bitte dress* 1;10 is slightly different because an imperative was used, accompanied by the wish-word, but not yet by the object "me", which was judged to be implied. *Buch away* 1;8 and *water on* 1;11 were much better. To be sure, the imperatives ("put", "turn") were missing, but the more important part of the predicate and the object were expressed. The expression was similar to *Hase Bett* 1;8 (518). The child's grammatical analysis was not sufficiently advanced to distinguish between the two expressions with confidence. For the adult, the former contained a grammatical object, the latter a subject; but the child probably felt no such difference. In fact the utterance *Buch away* was broken up into a sort of question and answer by the intonation. It marked a transition from two correlated one-word sentences to a two-word sentence.

The final category of two-word imperatives is that of negative imperatives. The negative required one word, which left the other free for indicating the content of the wish. *No bite*, as late as 2;1, was a primitive form (518). *Don't sh* 2;1 was a more standard expression, the interjection *sh* assuming the function of the verb "sleep". This pattern began to be used 1;11: *Don't spiel* (527). The addition of a specifying word was a considerable step forward from the one-word negative *don't* 1;11 (511), for which the situation had to supply the interpretation. In situations where the negative sentence-adverb *nein-nein* still sufficed without specification, there was now room for the addition of the vocative *Mama*, 1;7. The combination was uttered as a single intonation-phrase. I count the reduplicated *nein* as one word.

520. Wishes expressed in a form which is felt by adults to lack a modal auxiliary gained in expressiveness during the two-word stage. Again, the progress was not significant in the instances in which the verb consisted of two words instead of one, like (*I want to, I will*) *pick up, knock down, wisch ab, go Bett, go by-by*, all 1;11. The improvement was phonetic, the dynamically subordinated verbs being reproduced along with the more strongly stressed complements. In fact, in the last example she actually said *by-by, go by-by*: first the old form without a verb, then the new one with the verb.

Syntactic improvement appears in examples in which both the verb and the object are expressed. *Bau, Haus* 1;9, meaning "I want to build a house", was said with level stress and a pause between the words (actually in a four-word utterance, which was composed of two separate sentences, however). The stress indicates that we are here facing two one-word sentences, on their way toward becoming one two-word sen-

tence.[40] In *Watch Mama* 1;9 (**519**), *Ring bell, Spiel Haus, Spiel piano*
1;11, all announcing her intention, "I want to . . . ," "I will . . . ," the
combination of verb and object into one stress-group was achieved.[41]

In some instances she expressed not the object, but the subject of the
desired action. The verb was suppressed during the two-word stage, the
predicate being expressed by a different part of speech with the function
of a verb. A striking early example is *I! by-by* 1;8, which amounted to
"I want to go by-by,"[42] but was at best a forerunner of this sentence-
pattern. *I*, learned and used in a mechanical manner, had more emotional
than grammatical value (vol. 1, p. 33). *My auf* 1;11 (**518**), "I want to get
up", shows the construction in better development, *my* being her subject personal pronoun at the time. *Hase Bett* 1;8 (**518**) is similar if we
accept the interpretation "The rabbit should also go to bed." "Should"
is also the implied modal auxiliary in *This outside* said with level stress
1;9; but I would not dare to separate this interpretation from "I want
this to go outside" (cf. **563**).

521. In the domain of questions used to express wishes and requests
for permission, the syntactic progress over the one-word stage (**513 f.**)
was slight until the last two months. Acceding to the summons to go to
bed, she expressed her consent and then added *Mama? Papa?* 1;8, showing the way out of the room with her arm. She meant: "Will both of you
please accompany me?" This form of request differed hardly at all from
the one-name request of the same type used at the same time. Each
name still had its own interrogative intonation so that the utterance was
essentially a double one-word sentence rather than a single two-word
question.

In other examples the two words were not parallel. In the same situation, preparing to go to bed, she expressed the same wish repeatedly
1;8 by saying *Mama? mit?* or *Mit? Papa?* The name was logically subordinated to the question proper, "Will you come along?," but had not
yet been depressed into vocative function by the sign of intonation. It
retained the interrogative tone which it needed when it was the sole
carrier of the request. Formally these questions were still sets of two one-
word questions.

---

[40] What Preyer (p. 151) reports as the first two-word sentence of his son, as
late as 1;11: "Heim, Milch", is definitely a set of two one-word sentences, two
wishes ("I want to go home; I want to drink milk") or a wish and a specification.

[41] Bloch (1924, p. 25) found the verb "play", in its literal meaning and in "play
the piano", missing even during the third year. Karla used it, in English form, as
early as Hildegard.

[42] "Want" is not classified as a modal auxiliary, but "will" is. The function of
the two verbs is similar. In German, "wollen", the equivalent of "want" and
"will", is called a modal auxiliary. In sentences like (*I want*) *this bottle* 1;8, I
consider the verb a full verb, in German as well as in English; but when another
verb follows, I treat "want" as a modal auxiliary. The conventional classification
is formal, not functional.

The combination of two words into a single question, however, was also achieved at 1;8. *By-by auto?* and *By-by choo-choo?* were requests with added specification.

Radio on? and, with avoidance of the difficult noun, *This on?* 1;10 meant "May I have the radio on?" *Water auf?* 1;11 was a request to have the faucet opened. In these last examples, the expression of the objects represented syntactic progress.

522. A smaller number of two-word questions contained no wish element. They served the purpose of obtaining factual information.[43] At 1;6 she asked: *Marion? Dodo?* (the latter name even, irregularly, with the rising intonation of the question on each syllable separately), meaning "Where are they?,"[44] and, in slightly less primitive form, *Mama? by-by?* in the sense of "Where is Mama? Did she go out?" Because each word had its own interrogative intonation, the utterances amount to two successive, related one-word questions. That is the way in which a two-word question originates. The next step is to combine the two words of the second example into one unit of intonation, turning the first item from a separate question into the subject or object of the question expressed by the second item. This represents a considerable syntactic progress. She took this step at 1;9 with the question *Schuhe aus?* This happened to be not a question for factual information, but for confirmation of a fact about which she must have entertained a slight doubt. The difference between the two types of question is small, but real. The utterance was an answer to an adult's question, "What is the maid doing?" Since the fact that the latter was taking Hildegard's shoes off was indisputable, the interrogative intonation which the child gave, rather exceptionally, to the statement of the fact must have meant something like "Is that what you are referring to?"[45]

By 1;8 she had understood that the adults' questions often called for statements of facts. It is recorded that she answered them habitually by *yes* or *no*, even when she did not understand them, and that she did not bother about the agreement between her answers and the facts. This means that she understood the linguistic function of this type of questions. The fact that she had not yet learned to assume a responsibility for the validity of her answer is not within the province of language.

---

[43] Cassirer p. 35: "Dans la question s'exprime pour la première fois une curiosité dirigée non vers la possession d'un objet, mais vers l'acquisition d'une connaissance."

[44] A few days later she would answer the question herself (531).

[45] Lewis (1938, p. 157) discusses questions for information (boy K. at 2;5): "He is making a tentative statement of his knowledge, and demanding corroboration of it." I have no example of exactly the same situation, in which the term "knowledge" would be applicable. This is due to the exceptional caution characteristic of Hildegard's speech. Interrogative intonation for corroboration was regular with Karla in later years (for instance now, at age 8) whenever I said something to her in German and she gave the English equivalent of the crucial word in a questioning tone to check on her understanding; cf. **987.**

Let the reader be reminded, as a parallel, that a lie may be linguistically correct, and a truth linguistically offensive, although ethically the situation is the reverse. We are here concerned only with the language.

523. Two-word statements were in part as primitive as statements during the one-word stage, namely when the utterance was a predicate to a subject implied in the situation. The predicate was sometimes a compound verb like *push in* and *wisch ab* 1;11, which hovered in the twilight zone between an imperative addressed to herself and a statement of what she was doing. (*The cat*) *go(es) away* 1;10 was clearly a statement, without imperative character; the personal ending was not expressed. Very commonly a predicate adjective was accompanied by a reinforcing adverb, most frequently by *all*: *all sticky* 1;7, *all wet* 1;8 and 1;10, *all nass, all gone, all dry* 1;10, *all through* 1;11. *Right da*, half translated from "right there", 1;11 is comparable.

A noun accompanied by an adjective as the predicate of a situation is similar in character. *Mein Ball, my stocking* 1;7, in part still with level stress, were statements amounting to "This is my . . ."; but it should be remembered that the colloquial language itself often dispenses with subject and verb in such asseverations of ownership, particularly in the teasing game in which Hildegard learned the construction. The discussion in vol. 1 (p. 99 f.) shows (with many examples) how *my* developed from a vague emotive into a dispassionate possessive from 1;8. In the one-word stage 1;6 she had simply said *mine* in the same phonetic form as an emotional statement of ownership or of taking possession of an object. *Big Bau* 1;9 is a combination of adjective and noun only for an observer who transfers adult patterns indiscriminately to child-language. Actually Hildegard used the verb *bauen*, without an ending, in a vague manner lacking grammatical analysis and added to it the emotive *big*, which was hardly a descriptive adjective. *No A-a* 1;11, when it meant "I have finished going to the toilet", was a statement of fact, but not an adjective with a noun, although it seems to be that from the point of view of adult syntax. *No book* occurred at 1;11, with "no" as an adjective, perhaps accidentally. For the negative sentence adverb, the one-word version *no* sufficed. Sometimes, however, the child said *no, not* at 1;11, reinforcing the adverb with the newly learned "not".

In all preceding instances the two words of the utterance form, more or less, a unit. They belong together syntactically. The same holds true of combinations consisting of a genitive (or possessive) of a noun and another noun. The genitive had no formal sign until E 1;10, and then only in *Mama's* and *Papa's*. She learned to say *June's dolly, Bates's dolly* at 1;8 when her claim, *my dolly*, was taken at its face value and disputed. The idea of possession was developed in this way and secondarily filled into the adjective *my*, which had merely been an emotive previously. Hildegard used genitives also when no genuine ownership was meant. *Florence's Liebling* 1;11 is an example.

In *Joey's kimona* 1;10 and *Florence's dolly* 1;11 the things belonged to her; the person named was the donor; the name was added for purposes of identification. Two-word phrases like *Auto noise* 1;10, *choo-choo train, A-a paper, egg ball* (the latter with level stress) 1;11, belong together even more intimately. No great progress over the one-word stage was involved. They are essentially compound nouns of the same character as *street-car* or *toothbrush*, which happened to be treated as single words. No sharp boundary line exists between these types of compounds. *Baby Hildegard* 1;11, a phrase with which she identified her picture, is different, but comparable.

There were, however, many two-word statements which represent syntactic progress, because the two words belonged to different parts of the adult sentences on which they were modeled. They vary in character. A few were complete sentences[46] consisting of subject and verb. *Mama? sh, Dada? by-by* 1;6 show the transition from two one-word sentences to one two-word sentence. A question about the person, her activity or her whereabouts, received an immediate answer in the intonation of a statement: "What is Mama doing? She is sleeping"; "Where is Carolyn? She has gone out." The next step was to omit the interrogatory tone: 1;8 *Dada wäscht!*, an excited communication with level stress still betraying the origin in two one-word statements: "Carolyn is doing something interesting! She is washing!" During 1;8 the clear combination of a subject and a verb in a single dispassionate statement was achieved: *man sh*, meaning "the woman (in a picture) is sleeping", *Frau m*, "the woman (in a picture) is eating". The two verbs involved happen to have primitive form, but they had definitely lost the emotional value of interjections in these objective statements of fact. A real verb was involved in *Fritzchen steht* 1;11. *I do* 1;11 as an answer to questions like "Who likes candy?" was a complete sentence, but it was learned by mechanical imitation and meant for the child no more than simple *I*. In fact it might be called a particle expressing desire.

These utterances were syntactically perfect because the standard language needs in such instances only two words to express the idea completely. Where the standard required at least three words because the predicate was not a simple verb, the child was forced to omit one of them while the sentence span was limited to two words. In statements with subject and predicate the auxiliary verb, usually a mere copula, was omitted. It is unstressed in the standard and functionally much

---

[46] "Complete" means in this chapter syntactically complete, or containing subject, verb, object when needed. It does not mean that all minor words of the standard sentence were also present. Boyd (p. 187) states that, at age 2, every sentence is childish; prepositions, conjunctions, articles, and auxiliary verbs are only 3.4% of all the words used (25% at age 3 and age 8). Bloch (1924, p. 28) says that even when the pattern of complete (even complex) sentences has been evolved, those words are omitted "que l'idée principale estompe momantanément" (age 2;6).

less important than the complement which carries the real meaning of the predication. Neither phonetically nor semantically does it engage the attention of the child. At 1;8 this construction was still in a preparatory stage. *Mama? bad(en)!* did not yet conform to the pattern "Mama will baden". It amounted rather to two correlated sentences: "What is Mama doing? She is getting ready to bathe". By the tests of intonation, facial expression, and situation, the child was not uttering a wish, but a statement of fact. When she switched the light off and said *Light aus* at the same time, it is doubtful whether it meant "the light is out (off)" or even "I am switching the light off". Probably she was using an imperative-equivalent, executing the command at the same time.

From 1;9, however, statements of the type "this is . . ." became frequent: 1;9 *this mine; this oil-spoon;* 1;10 *this church* (reproducing the line, "This is the church", in a nursery rhyme); 1;11 *this zu* ("this, the door, is shut"; high pitch on the first word, low pitch on the second, an effective device to set off the subject from the predicate); *this nass* (with level stress); *this in; here church* (substituting "here" for presented "this"); *this paper-ball; this (is for the) nails.* The emergency subject *this* was useful because it circumvented the exigencies of a limited vocabulary, particularly in statements which did more than give the name of a thing.[47]

Often at 1;11, sometimes earlier, more specific subjects appeared in factual statements: 1;9 *bath alle* ("the bathing is over"); 1;10 *by-by dunkel* (undoubtedly not analyzed as "the outdoors is dark", but expressed with a pattern in which *by-by* acts like a subject); 1;11 *door open; door zu; hottey da* ("the horsey is there"); *cry-baby da; choo-choo da; meow da; meow out* ("the cat is outside"); *Mary Alice Bett* ("is in bed"); *Mary Alice (must) eat. Auto alley* 1;11 reflected the adult statement, "Autos are only in the alley (not in the yard)".

As all these examples show, the word which took the place of the predicate had varied character from the beginning. It could be a noun (**547 f.**), a possessive pronoun (**548**), an adjective (**549**), an adverb (**550**), or an infinitive (**545, 575**).

Another category of two-word statements consisted of verb and object. The omitted subject was supplied by the situation: (the cat) *drinks milk* 1;10, (she) *picks flowers* 1;11, (I) *bite Papa* 1;11, (the cat, who had just been mentioned) *bites me* 1;11.

The lack of a third word was a serious syntactic deficiency when the verb was omitted because the child had the desire to express both subject and object. The complete predicate had to be inferred from the situation. Although this could be done, the statement gave the impression of being syntactically more imperfect than the preceding utterances, because this omission is not customary even in the colloquial

---

[47] Cf. Goodenough p. 343.

form of standard speech. *My Wehweh* 1;10 was not what it seemed to be, a noun preceded by a possessive adjective. *My* had at that time regularly the function of the subject personal pronoun. "I have an ache" was the idea. We cannot be sure of the noun character of *Wehweh*, which retained the interjectional element of a plaint. The object was unmistakable in *Papa apple* 1;8 and *meow oatmeal* 1;11. In both utterances the verb "eats" had to be supplied (cf. **580**). For the former example the diary stresses the fact that the subject was not said with the interrogative intonation which was still common during 1;8. It was clearly a two-word statement, and the child confirmed the correctness of my interpretation by reacting to it with a laugh of satisfaction.

This leaves a group of statements in which both subject and verb were missing, but an adverb was added to an object: (I am putting the) *meow in* (the rocker) 1;11. In the other examples, the word which can be called an object was *Wehweh*. It may, on account of its interjectional nature, be considered a complete predication. It was used, however, for specific communications: *Wehweh—da! knee Wehweh, da Wehweh, Wehweh eye* 1;8. The syntactic vagueness of *Wehweh* makes the interpretation uncertain. Instead of "(I have a) Wehweh (in my) eye", we might also paraphrase "(A) Wehweh (is in my) eye", as was done in **517**. The adverbial nature of "(in my) eye, knee" is also a syntactic interpretation which runs ahead of the child's linguistic development. It might be best to abstain entirely from pressing these utterances into any adult syntactic pattern, their form being too primitive. It cannot be doubted, however, that they were two-word communications largely declarative in purpose.

The statement *Ring, Mama* 1;11 was also primitive in form. It consisted of two one-word sentences with the idea, "This is my ring; Mama gave it to me". This pattern was to develop into Hildegard's version of phrases like "a ring from Mama", which supplanted such less logical expressions as *Florence's dolly* for "a dolly from Florence". *Hoch Hand* 1;11, "I am raising Papa by the hand" assuredly was not thought out in any grammatical form; the utterance was unorganized.

The absence of a wish element is clearest in the utterances which referred to past events. Some such instances occurred even in the one-word stage (**515**). No formal sign of the past tense was developed during the two-word stage. The example *Ring, Mama* is a statement which included a reference to a past event in primitive form. At 1;8 Hildegard pounded on the bed which her mother had just left in the morning and stated *Mama up* in the same words which she otherwise used every morning as an imperative. She altered the function of the words without a change in form; but we cannot assume that a past tense, "Mama got up," was implied. A statement of the result in the present tense, "Mama is up", is a more convincing interpretation. At 1;9 she stated *Dada ironing*, "Carolyn was (did) ironing"; but again the tense was not beyond doubt; in the situation in which it was said it may also have been a generalized statement, "Carolyn does the ironing (in this household)". There were clearer instances at 1;11: *Mama Kuss*, "I gave Mama a kiss"; *by-by street-car* after she had come home from a ride in the street-car; *Papa patsch*, "Papa spanked me". *Wake up*, frequently said 1;11 for "I woke up", is less clear; it may stand for "I am awake". *Go away* 1;10, a statement also consisting merely of a two-word verb, is equally doubtful: "The cat went away" or "is walking off".

524. We are at the end of the discussion of two-word sentences. Some of them were syntactically as simple as the one-word utterances, but many others represented a step forward in the direction toward organized sentences. Instead of one word giving a meager clue for the intent of the utterance while all other circumstances had to be inferred from the situation, the child was now able to single out two different parts of speech for specification,[48] thus adding greatly to the clarity of the meaning which she intended to convey. The aid of the situation was still needed in most instances, and the only formal signs separating the two words syntactically from each other were intonation and stress, which were sometimes used effectively for the purpose. The words selected from the standard pattern of the sentence were two which were important for its organization. We might therefore speak of a progress from a one-item syntax to a two-item syntax, in parallelism with the advance from a single series to a double series which we found in the learning of sounds.

There is room for doubt whether the transfer of this pattern from phonetics to syntax does justice to actual conditions in the child's language. We must not forget that in languages with dynamic stress like English and German, the syntactically important parts of speech usually have the strongest sentence-stress. We would expect the child's attention to be concentrated on the words which were put in relief by the stress, just as we found in the learning of words that she paid most attention to the syllables with main (and secondary) stress. From this point of view, the progress might appear as being of phonetic rather than syntactic character.

There is one important difference, however. In the utterance of sentences the child no longer imitated always a fixed sequence of sounds, but put varying words together independently. That is why it was important to segregate utterances like "I do", which were indeed imitated as a whole without variation, from others which were composed in a more original manner and not mechanically learned as a unit. Thus it

---

[48] Stern (p. 199), speaking of the improved understanding of the child, expresses the progress by means of a metaphor. From the flood of sounds rushing in on the child in adult sentences, two wave peaks are now recognized by the child where formerly only one was seen. Trettien (p. 132), speaking of the first two-word sentences, says: "These are the mountain peaks of language which make their appearance in the mist."

can be said that the child had learned to recognize stress as a device used in the organization of syntactic patterns. This is proved by the fact that, along with sentences like *open (the) door*, in which she reproduced the two stressed words of the presentation, Hildegard said *Dress me* with a stronger stress on the object than on the imperative, contrary to the normal presentation. In cases like this, she used stress clearly as a device to underline a syntactic pattern containing two different parts of speech.

The degree of originality in the handling of sentence patterns varied. In *open door* she repeated a combination which she had heard often in exactly the same form. In *door open* and *door zu* she expressed two different meanings with one pattern, but both utterances had been heard from adults in the form which she reconstructed from memory. *Dress me* was an original sentence, because nobody had taught her to say so and she had never heard the identical utterance from an adult. The example proves conclusively that she had learned the syntactical pattern. The exaggerated stress was due to the effort still required to apply the pattern.

It would be satisfying to find a sequence in the learning of the parts of the sentence as we found it in the learning of sounds. It is not easy to discover such a sequence. Even in the one-word stage the utterances represented different elements of the standard sentence. In the two-word stage a verb, or a part of the predicate without the verb, was usually present. Sentences containing a subject and an object but no verb in any form occurred to the end of the second year, however (523). Subject (*Hase Bett* 518, *Dada wäscht, man sh, Frau m* 523) and object (*open door* 519) both appeared during the same month, 1;8. The analysis is complicated by the fact that the standard varies. Imperatives usually lack a subject in the standard languages, and not every sentence requires an object. The pattern subject — verb can be called earlier since it was fully alive and independently handled at 1;8, whereas the pattern verb— object remained imitative with regard to the words used in it until 1;9 (520) and was not common until 1;11.[49]

At 1;10 several utterances had three words including an object, and at 1;11 the complete pattern subject — verb — object was mastered.

The situation seems to be this. During the one-word stage a single, syntactically undifferentiated word was used to give a clue to the intended meaning. Syntactic differentiation began in two-word sentences, and the first pattern learned was the combination of a subject with a predicate, at 1;8. The pattern verb — object became active at 1;9, common at 1;11. The way was paved for complete three-word sentences consisting of subject, verb, and object.

---

[49] Stern (p. 199) finds a variety of grammatical patterns represented from the beginning in sentences consisting of more than one word. He thinks that the combination verb — object is particularly common.

With this survey we have encroached on the domain of three-word sentences, which need to be examined now. Adhering to the mechanical principle of counting the number of words in a sentence, we shall again find some that do not represent a significant syntactic progress. Others, however, will disclose the growth which became possible with the widening span of attention.

525. As early as 1;5 two complete three-word sentences were in Hildegard's linguistic repertory, *Da ist es* and *I see you*. Both were exclamations used in definite situations and differed from one-word interjections only in the accidental fact that they were based on simple three-word combinations in the prototype. The child cannot be assumed to have been aware of this difference, although the inclusion of both unstressed syllables in the imitation of each of these items is remarkable for this early stage. Both phonetically and syntactically the items were examples of that premature correctness, achieved by mechanical imitation, which distorts the picture of organic growth, as we have observed previously. Neither of them survived beyond the month 1;5. Original three-word sentences did not begin until three months later, and then in a more primitive form.

Interjections and exclamations did not often consist of more than two words (*oh my gosh* and *you naughty meows!* 2;1 lie beyond the two-year limit). I find only one example, *Wehweh — da — au!* 1;8. The three words were strung up with level stress, which makes the utterance a series of three one-word sentences rather than one three-word sentence. Besides, although it is true that *au* is certainly an interjection, that *Wehweh* has largely the same character, and that *da* could be used as an interjection (**509**), Hildegard happened to make this utterance to communicate the fact that she had teething pains. She supplemented the linguistically primitive formulation with the efficient gesture of putting her finger in her mouth with the adverb. The intonation was not even that of lament, but that of a quiet statement. The example is a striking illustration of the fact that, at the stage of insufficient vocabulary and syntax, the stock originally serving emotional purposes can be pressed into the function of dispassionate statements, where this utterance really belongs (**531**).

526. By the time that utterances had reached three words, the category of wishes expressed by means other than a question, an imperative, or a sentence lacking a modal auxiliary became depleted. With the progressing organization of sentences nearly all of the wishes fall into one or the other of these latter classifications. *Ride Papa's neck* 1;10 expressed her wish in a primitive form, which was perhaps not an incomplete version of "I want to ride on Papa's neck" (**528**); but it would be so analyzed in terms of standard syntax, and we never claimed that this represented also the child's analysis. *Dolly ride buggy* 1;11, "I want the dolly to ride in the buggy", is parallel. *Put hat on* 1;11, recorded in the diary merely for its phonetic form, with no indication of the circumstances, could be anything from "I want to put a hat on" over "I want the hat to be put on" to the imperative "Put the hat on". These utterances were much more specific than those in the one-word (510) and two-word (518) stages and represented progress also because they contained verbs; but they were not yet mature formulations of wishes, and the very fact that verbs were present makes them fit better in another category (528).

527. The three-word imperatives of 1;10 are mostly doubtful because the circumstances are not recorded. *Dicke(n) Bauch wasch(en)* (actually four words, because the adjective was said twice) may not have been an infinitive (pronounced without an ending) used as an imperative, as is possible in German, but an incomplete version of "I want to . . .", "I am going to . . .", or even a statement in the present tense with arbitrary word-order. *Wash baby's dress* is like the first example except that it is clearly English. *My shoe brush* may have meant "brush my shoe", with imperfect word-order. *This oil weg* meant clearly "Put this oil away."

The more numerous examples of 1;11 vary in their syntactic character. Few of them lacked a verb, like the last example of 1;10. *All balls da*, late in the month, meant "Put all the balls there" (into the net-bag, in which they were kept). The utterance showed little syntactic improvement. It had three words merely because the object noun was extended by the addition of a numerical adjective. *This on beads*, also after the middle of the month, was even more primitive. It meant "Put this on, the beads (around my neck)". The object was expressed twice, once vaguely, then more specifically, but without a pause in the utterance. In both utterances and in the last example of 1;10, the fact that the object required two words led to the sacrificing of the verb, which was already present in many two-word imperatives. *Come on, Papa, auf!* contained two imperatives, one with and one without a verb; but *come on* (one word in the child's language) and the vocative were merely signals for attention; the specific imperative ("get up") lacked the verb.

All other examples contained a verb. When an intransitive verb consisted of two words, room was left for the addition of a vocative: *Papa lie down* (frequently said) (cf. *Mama wake up* 1;10). Since the addition of a vocative is merely a device to beam the imperative in the right direction, the vocative being linked by intonation with the imperative but not really entering into its syntactic structure, it is more significant that Hildegard filled the space left by the compound transitive verb sometimes with an object: *Put hat on* (but cf. 526).

With a simple verb there was room for a two-word object; two examples of 1;10, if they were really imperatives, illustrate this scheme, clearly *Wash baby's dress*, less so *Dicken Bauch waschen*, because *dicken Bauch* had become one word for the child; even so, the fact that *dicken* was said twice in this instance brings the utterance in line with this group.

The best form of three-word imperatives is the most common scheme in which a vocative, a simple verb, and an object were combined: *Papa hol Maus; Papa, push me* (on the tricycle); *Papa feed my*, "Papa, feed me", all at 1;11 (*Mama bite Hildegard* 2;0). These sentences were said fluently and without apparent effort. They occurred later in the month than *coat button* and *nose blow*, in which the word-order was still inadequate; but some of them were earlier than *Dress me*, which had a strained stress distribution (519, 524). Our findings confirm that the combination of an object with a verb in the imperative was not made before 1;10, did not become frequent until 1;11, and showed evidence of unfamiliarity occasionally even then.

A negative imperative, which consumes one word for the negative adverb, happened to occur with a verb which needed no object, so that there remained room for the addition of a vocative: *Don't spiel, Miau* 1;11, "Don't play, meow".

528. Wishes which would be expressed with the aid of a modal auxiliary in standard syntax continued to lack the modal invariably in the three-word stage. One of them had no verb at all and was therefore syntactically primitive: (*Let us go*) *way down* (*to the*) *beach* 1;11. It expressed nothing but an adverbial phrase, which consumed all three words, with omission of the standard preposition.

The other examples contain a verb, which would be an infinitive in the full standard version. Adverbial phrases without prepositions were added to it: (*I want to*) *ride* (*on*) *Papa's neck* 1;10; (*I want to*) *go* (*into*) *Mama's Bett* 1;11; (*I want to*) *lie* (*in*) *Papa's Bett* 1;11.

Dolly ride buggy 1;11 expressed a wish. *Dolly* was not a vocative, and *ride* was not an imperative. The paraphrase "I want the dolly to ride in the buggy", might seem to assume too advanced a syntactic pattern. This utterance could be classified as an unorganized wish (526). Still, (*I want to, am going to*) *ask Papa* (*to put this*) *on* 1;11, in which the presence of a verb before the object makes the same kind of paraphrase more compelling, makes it credible that the child was beginning to evolve this construction (563).

There were other examples in which the absence of a modal auxiliary was felt more definitely, because a subject was expressed before the "infinitive". These, however, were not wishes and will be found among the three-word statements (531). Our method of dealing with the omission of modals as a sub-category of wishes is beginning to break down, because the child's statements included a greater variety of shades of meaning. This methodological embarrassment is a source of satisfaction, because it reflects the growth of the child's language beyond arbitrary classifications suitable for the first steps.

529. Wishes said with interrogative intonation, although they contain the ideas, "May I . . .?" or "Will you . . .?" were from the beginning of this study methodically separated from those in which a modal auxiliary could be said to be omitted, because the interrogatory intonation was considered the more significant feature. A three-word utterance of this kind, which, however, was not one three-word question, occurred at 1;8: *Walk? Schnee? ja?* She meant "May I go for a walk in the snow?" and reinforced the eagerness of the request for permission with the question, "ja?", which often served this purpose. The utterance was cast in the form of three separate questions, each with its own interrogatory intonation. This device is the forerunner of utterances combining several words into a unit. Occasionally level stress lingered on into 1;11, but not in wish-questions, which had by 1;11 a unified intonation. *Pretty dress on?* can be paraphrased by "May I put a ...?" It expressed the object in two words, but lacked the verb part of the predicate. *Papa on me?*, two days later, meant, "Papa, will you put this on for me?" It lacked the verb and the object, but contained a vocative instead. Imperfect as this question is, it pointed forward to the development of prepositions out of the adverbial part of compound verbs, which got under way soon after the end of the second year (see the diary). This step was not assumed to be completed yet, in view of other utterances at the same time; but this utterance comes close to it; "on me" would make as good sense as "on for me", since she was talking about an article of clothing, which I was to help her put on. Both these utterances were late in 1;11. There were others at 1;11 which contained a verb: (*May I*) *da slide down?*, the local adverb *da* pointing to the banister of the stairs; (*Shall, May*) *I spiel Nackedei?* "May I go without clothes?" The last question is the only one of this type in which a subject was expressed. (Concerning *I*, cf. 559).

530. There are again few examples for factual questions. The last examples in the preceding section lead over to them. If, instead of "May", we paraphrase these questions with "Shall I", "Do you want me to", the question for permission is changed to an inquiry about an adult's wish, a request to a challenge. At this late stage it is not improbable that such a variation in the underlying sentiment was taking place. Utterances were becoming more finely shaded in their intention, although the formal signs were not yet developed to express these shades of meaning. *My room, Taschentuch?* 1;11, however primitive in form, meant, "Shall I go, Do you want me to go, to my room to get a handkerchief?" *Papa mehr bathe?* 1;11 implied "Do you want to bathe more, longer?" and was definitely not a wish of her own, but an inquiry about my wish. (*Dodo make A-A?* 2;1, "Dodo, are you making A-a?", a clear question about a fact, without suppression of a modal auxiliary, lay beyond the two-year limit.)

The first interrogative adverb, the only interrogative really learned, occurred also in three-word questions 1;11: *Where* (*is*) *my ball?* and, with a vocative: *Dasch, where* (*is*) *Hildegard?*

I have no examples of questions for linguistic information. Three-word questions like "What is this?" could have served this purpose; but the copula was still below the threshold of attention, so that two words would have sufficed. Such questions, however, were not even asked in two words (522). "What" did not occur (until 2;1), and it was characteristic of Hildegard that she did not often ask such questions. She waited instead until the information came to her unsolicited (cf. 514).

531. Statements of fact increased greatly in number on the three-word level. Hildegard's language was becoming more intellectualized. The emotional and volitional elements receded.[50]

Again we find that the syntactic character of the utterances varied; but along with some incomplete sentences, in which the situation still had to help the understanding, we encounter many more which were complete with subject, verb and object, and others which lacked only the copula, which even some standard languages, like ancient Greek and modern Russian, omit (579).

A forerunner was the three-word utterance *Marion? Dodo? Away!* 1;6, which was still cast in the pattern of three one-word sentences, namely two questions (521) and one answer. The pattern was improved 1;8: *Marion Joey away*; the three words were separated by pauses and had level stress; but this corresponds to the stress in the standard version, "Marion and Joey are away". The question-and-answer pattern was still used at 1;8: *Shoe? Mama's shoe* and *By-by auto? No!* In the latter, a question asking for permission was followed by her own negative answer; this amounted to the negative statement, "I cannot go out for a ride".[51] The three-word utterance *Wehweh — da — au* 1;8 was also a syntactically immature sentence. On account of the emotional character of the words used, it has been discussed in 525, but was found to be really a statement in the primitive form of three one-word sentences with inadequate vocabulary.[52]

A few sentences were still syntactically incomplete in the last month. *Mama new hat* 1;11 meant, with the aid of the situation, "This is Mama's new hat". In the recapitulation of a story in the form of answers to questions, she stated its most interesting point with *All piece broke* 1;11

---

[50] In the light of the preceding discussions it is obviously impossible to assign a definite time to the change from emotional and volitional speech to intellectual speech. The transition is gradual. Hetzer and Reindorf set the time at 1;6 for children in cultured families, and at 1;9 for children in uncultured families.

[51] This preparatory pattern for negative statements, often observed in children's language, was used by Karla M 1;11: *(May) Karla (get) all dirty? Oh no!* Cf. K. Bühler p. 235, O'Shea p. 117, Sully p. 174.

[52] Gabelentz (p. 346) reports a similar utterance of three one-word sentences: "Au! Wauwau! Happ! (= gebissen)" and comments: "Hier ist in rohester Weise die Synthese des Gedankens in einer dreigliedrigen Rede zum Ausdruck gebracht; ein Kind, das so spricht, redet schon in menschlicher, das heisst gegliederter Sprache. Die Synthese aber besteht in einer blossen Aneinanderreihung, sie ist ohne bindenden Mörtel wie eine cyklopische Mauer: die Sprache ist i s o l i - r e n d." The transition from three one-word sentences to one three-word sentence in the standard language is treated by Curme (1931) §2a, last paragraph.

for "all broken to pieces". The question had furnished the subject, and the copula was dispensible. The remainder was still primitive in its arbitrary rearrangement of words. *All sticky candy* 1;11, an utterance in which the adjective was phonetically imperfect and its interpretation not certain, meant "My hands are all sticky from candy". Presumably she showed her hands, which provided the subject. The copula and the preposition were regularly omitted. *Bottle pieks, Wehweh* 1;11 was an ingenious, though clumsy ,way of giving a description of a medicine dropper, "This is a bottle (an object made of glass) which pricks and hurts (is pointed)".

The number of statements which merely lacked the copula (523) was rather large in the last two months. Since such sentences cannot contain an object, either the subject or the predicate consisted of two words. Two-word subject: 1;10 *This book mine;* 1;11 *This door open; All babies Bett*[53] (translated from German presentation; part of a seven-word utterance; preposition "in" omitted); *Da my ball* (in answer to her own question, *Where my ball?*); *Mary Alice's Wehweh alle.*[54] The latter amounted to a negative statement, "Mary Alice has no pain any longer"; it was accompanied by head-shaking. Two-word predicate: 1;10 *This my spoon; Papa all wet; This my rock-baby;* 1;11 *Wash all dry; Meow up Baum;* negative: *Miau not da* (in a five-word utterance); *No, not da* (without subject; *no, not* formed a unit for double expression of the negative; in *No, Florence's Liebling,* however, we have two sentences said to deny and correct the implications of a question).

This is mine 1;11 was sometimes said with a dissyllabic form which might represent "this is". In view of the consistent omission of the copula in all other examples, some of which were based on the same combination "this is . . .", it is better to interpret the second syllable of dɪtə as containing a vowel of transition.[55]

Some of the syntactically complete statements had no object because none was needed. In that case the predicate consisted of a compound verb: 1;10 *my go away; Mama wake up;* 1;10 and 1;11 *my wake up; my walk down.*

All other examples contained subject, verb, and object. None was earlier than 1;11. Some of the earliest had level stress, which betrayed the effort needed for the new pattern: *Mama calls, meow* (the pause shows that the familiar pattern was restricted to subject and verb and that the object was added without as yet entering into a syntactic unit);

---

[53] In some of these examples, "to be" is more than a copula. Hildegard omitted the full verb as well (579).

[54] Karla used the same construction with level stress E 1;10: *Grandpa, auto, gone,* "Grandpa's auto is gone."

[55] Ament (p. 172) registers the first complete sentence for the 626th day (E 1;8): "da is lulu"; it has the copula expressed. Two of Stern's children, alone among those surveyed by him (pp. 200–202), had a copula in the first sentences of more than one word, at 1;5 and 1;2 respectively.

Duck, bite, me.[56] This stage of transition, however, was ephemeral. Almost at once, such statements were made fluently: *Papa spielt Ball; Meow makes A-a* (the verb "make" was marked as an innovation; it was still rare); *Mama washes (my) hands; I spiel this; Mama reads book* (secondary stress on verb, main stresses on subject and object); *Meow bites Wauwau; Papa reads book.* The ending of the third person singular was never expressed; the verbs had basic stem forms. (At 2;0 the diary notes that the supply of verbs increased strikingly. They were needed for, and used in, statements of this type.)

Omission of a modal auxiliary in sentences which do not express wishes results in statements which are syntactically less complete; but they represent a progress in the expression of finer shades of meaning. *Mama sh mehr, Mama mehr sh* 1;11 was not a wish, nor a simple statement of fact, but a reproduction of her mother's decision: "Mama wants to sleep more, longer". *Mary Alice eat, home* 1;11 consisted of two primitive sentences, but expressed the advanced idea, "Mary Alice must (has to) eat, she went home". *No, (I must put) shoes, on* 1;11 was an utterance with which she recalled an adult injunction, checking her impulse to run out of the house without shoes. It had level stress. This primitive way of stringing up words made the interpretation hazardous; but I have no doubt about the intended meaning.

532. I have omitted from the preceding section all statements which referred to the past. We no longer need this separation to make sure that the utterances represented factual statements; but it is still useful for organizing the wealth of examples.[57] Besides, it is interesting to see how the number of statements concerned with past events increased. As a rule there was still no formal sign of the past tense. For this purpose, as for the third person singular present, the verb had the unchanged basic form. The morphological development lagged behind the learning of syntactical patterns. (For the possibility that the ending of the weak past tense was lost for phonetic reasons, cf. **142** and **148**. This explanation does not apply to strong verbs, which were also used in their present or infinitive form. The hypothesis, interesting as it is, is therefore not convincing.)

At 1;9 Hildegard said *Marion? Dodo? Da!* She was in her bed and pointed to the day-bed in her room. She meant to convey the idea that her cousins had slept there. That was a week before. The form of the utterance was primitive. It consisted of two questions and one answer.

---

[56] Karla also used level stress at 1;11: *Mammy, coming, soon.* The use of an adverb of time to indicate future has no parallel in Hildegard's language.

[57] Stalnaker (p. 231), examining nine children 2;4 to 4 years old, finds that "the declarative sentence takes the lead at all ages"; the next most frequent type is the "request or command", only exceptionally the interrogative sentence. But her classification is open to objections; for instance, "I want a stick", is listed as declarative (p. 233), which is too mechanical a classification. Boyd's much more careful and detailed observations made on his daughter from age 2 to age 8 show different results (p. 183).

The three words were not yet combined into one sentence. It is interesting, however, for the comparatively long span of memory involved. Most statements, even much later, referred to events which had just happened.

Strangely enough, the only other example which involved as much as a day of time elapsed between the event and the statement, was also early, 1;10: *Papa this on*, namely "Papa turned the shower on yesterday". I had turned on the shower while she was in the bath-tub to tease her. The shock was vividly remembered. The statement lacked the verb proper.

All examples of 1;11 referred to the immediate past. All had a verb except the rather late *Mary Alice (went) home, (to) eat*. With intransitive verbs no object was required and the predicate could consist of two words: *Taschentuch fall down; My fall down; My wake up* (if it meant "I woke up"; more plausibly it amounted to "I am awake", **531**). Sometimes no object was expressed, but an adverb was added instead, being felt as more essential: *Mama da bite*, "Mama spanked me here", cheerfully indicating with a clap of her hand where the punishment had been administered; *Miau kratz da*, "The cat scratched me here".

The remaining instances had an object: *Mama call, meow* (statement following the event immediately, so that it might be called a present tense, **531**). *Mama buy balloon* (when Hildegard came home with the balloon from a shopping trip); *Papa make Bau*, "Papa has built something (with blocks)"; *Mama call Mary Alice; Mary Alice ride, me* (in the second half of the month; object still not an organic part of the statement); *Mama kiss my*, "Mama kissed me".

Of these examples, *Papa make Bau* is especially interesting, because it is an expression hardly possible in standard colloquial speech. It shows all the more impressively that the pattern subject — verb — object asserted itself in spite of the limitations of vocabulary. The verb *bau(en)* was used as a noun, because a noun was needed in the pattern.

One verb actually occurred in the form of the past tense, first, early 1;11, only in the fixed utterance *Mama forgot toothbrush*, meaning "Mama forgot to brush my teeth", later in an original statement with the same pattern: *Papa forgot this*. Hildegard did not use a present-tense form of the same verb. Awareness of formal distinctions between tenses cannot be inferred from this isolated past-tense form (**586**).

533. Three words was the normal length of sentences during the last month of the second year, although sentences of one and two words continued to occur. Longer sentences were less common,[58] and utterances of more words frequently consisted of two or three grammatical sentences placed side by side. Subordination was not yet learned except in rudimentary beginnings. Since many sentences in the three-word stage were already grammatically complete, no syntactic progress can be expected

---

[58] Decroly (p. 132) sets the beginning of sentences containing more than three words at 1;3½–11.

to be disclosed by the examination of longer sentences. It will, however, be carried out, because the length of sentences and utterances has some interest in itself.[59]

Continuing with the same classification, we find no more examples of interjections and exclamations nor of wish questions. Interjections cannot be expected to run to lengths of more than three words. Exclamations might, but did not, probably because three words was still the normal length of sentences; in all categories the number of examples decreases beyond this span. The explanation for the absence of wishes cast in the form of questions may be the same. It should lead over into the adult type of polite requests with "May I". A pause in the use of this type of request would, however, not be surprising. In spite of all social training, the utterance of wishes in the more emphatic form "I want" comes more naturally to children.

534. Wishes so primitive in form that they do not fall easily into one of the other categories were naturally rare among the utterances of four words; there are no certain examples even in the three-word stage (**526**). As early as 1;9, earlier than most three-word sentences, Hildegard produced the four-word sentence *this, big, baby, bottle*, after her mother had told her that she had drunk from this bottle when she was a little baby. It was a wish. She wanted it after her interest in it had been aroused. The wish, however, was vague. We might call the utterance an emotional statement. Since the bottle could hardly impress her by its size, the word *big* was still the old emotive with vague intellectual content. The level stress was also a primitive feature.[60]

535. Imperatives of four words belong to 1;11. At 1;9 she said *Mama, mit! Bau, Haus!* and *Mama, mit! Oino, Wauwau*. These were utterances of four words, but each consisted of two grammatically separate sentences, a two-word imperative followed by a rough explanation of the wish and of the circumstances which produced it. In the first example, the addition might be another imperative, "Build a house" or an announcement of her own intention, "I want to build a house with blocks". The blocks were not yet at hand, so that the crude formulation included the wish to get them. In the second example, the addition was a clumsy statement of an exciting fact: "The uncle brought me a bow-wow", actually an Easter cake in the shape of a lamb.

Most of the four-word imperatives of 1;11 had this length because of an added vocative. *Papa dear, wake up* contained a stereotype two-word vocative and an imperative complete in two words. *Papa this hang up*

---

[59] A specialized study on "length of sentences" is that of Nice. Boyd (p. 187) confirms Nice's results. Smith (1935, p. 210) claims: "Sentence length is indicative of size of vocabulary". Her study gives statistics of the length of sentences in the conversations of 220 children aged 18–72 months.

[60] Jespersen (p. 135) records a four-word statement with "a pause between the successive words" for 1;10.

had a one-word vocative not separated from the two-word imperative by pause or stress, and in addition an object in a non-standard position. *Papa, this da down* ("put this chair down from the terrace") lacked the verb, but made the intention quite clear by the two adverbs, at least one of which indicated the direction of the desired motion. *This, on, my neck* ("hang this little bell around my neck"), though imperfect in form, is nevertheless more interesting. In the level stress the utterance carried the egg-shells of an earlier construction: "(Put) this on, (namely around) my neck". But the four words really belonged to one sentence. They were linked more intimately than can be claimed for an imperative and a vocative. The adverb *on* was on its way toward becoming a preposition.[61]

(At 2;1 the pronoun *you* was added to imperatives in many examples: *you do this; you wash me; you feed my; you button my shoe*, the pronoun even said in reduplication, with a stress on the second *you*. I interpret this practice, which is not so common in the standard language, as an indication that Hildegard was learning the pattern of a complete statement and extended the habit of including a subject to imperatives.)[62]

536. Four-word utterances expressing the child's intention give clearly the impression of lacking the auxiliary "I want to" or "I am going to". *Spiel Haus, knock down* 1;11 consists of two coordinated two-word sentences. *Ask Mama this aus* 1;11 ("I am going to ask Mama to take this article of clothing off") and *Watch bake cake Mama* 1;11 ("I want to watch Mama bake a cake", with undeveloped word-order) point forward to a subordination of one idea to the other (**563**). *This dolly up Bett* 1;11 may be interpreted as a simple four-word wish. The paraphrase chosen at the time of observation was: "I want to take this dolly upstairs to bed" (cf. **563**). The utterance lacked the main verb in addition to the auxiliary, but was more unified than the preceding examples.

537. *Papa all through eat?* 1;11 is a clear factual question lacking the copula. It meant: "Papa, are you all through eating?" It is interesting because it shows that the ending "-ing" had not yet been learned (**578**).

538. Four-word statements often consisted of two sentences. Examples begin as early as 1;8. *Knee Wehweh, da Wehweh* 1;8, every word with the same amount of stress, made a plaintive statement in two words and added to it a parallel statement accompanied by pointing, to make sure that she would be understood. *This big Buch, da!* 1;9 did not mean "This big book is there", but "This is a big book, there it is". The second sentence again underlined the reference of the first. *Wauwau! Meow bite Wauwau* 1;11 identified a bark which she heard and added a fanciful statement about the reason for barking.

---

[61] Karla M 1;11: *Glenna (was) on (a) bus*, also with level stress on the three words; E 1;11: 'In ˌhau, "Let us go in, into the house."

[62] I have considered and rejected the hypothesis that this construction represents standard "Will you . . .?" with omission of the modal auxiliary. The interrogative intonation, which had long been characteristic of this way of expressing wishes, was never present.

Of more interest are several four-word statements consisting of two correlated two-word sentences. She examined two brushes 1;8, pointed to them in succession, and said *This (is a) brush (and) this (is a) brush.* The intonation was rising on the first sentence, falling on the second. Although the intonation was the same as in utterances like *Shoe? Mama's shoe* (531), which she made at the same time, it clearly did not indicate question and answer about one object, but served as a device to link two correlated statements about two objects. The same is true for *This (is) Dodo's (and) this (is) Dodo's* 1;8, said with reference to a pair of overshoes. (*This is) Dada's hat (and) this (is) mine* 1;10 is a little more advanced. There is not merely correlation, but contrast, and the formulation of the two sentences is not exactly parallel.

At 1;10 and 1;11 there were several unified four-word statements. *My buggy (is) way down* (in the basement) 1;10 lacked chiefly the colorless verb. *This (is) my rock-baby* 1;10 ("my rocking chair," 531) lacked nothing but the copula. In *Papa (has) my comb da* 1;11 the absence of the verb was more keenly felt; "have", whether as an auxiliary or as a full verb, was completely missing from the vocabulary (580). *Mama fix bed my* 1;11 ("for me") was complete with subject, verb, and object, but still imperfect in the personal reference.

539. Four-word statements referring to past events do not add anything to the syntactical development. *Ja, Mama da bite* 1;11 consisted of two separate sentences. *Ja*, being an answer to a question, was complete by itself; the second sentence, which gave supplementary information on the same topic, has been treated as a three-word statement (532). Two other examples 1;11 were syntactically primitive because they lacked verbs and used the four-word range instead to extend other parts of the sentence. *Rita's house big A-a* suppressed subject and predicate and consumed two words each for the object and an indication of place. *Meow all wet me*, late in the month, had curiously undeveloped form for this stage. It used the stereotype phrase *all wet* for the description of a condition, but inserted it into the pattern of a complete sentence with subject and object, so that it came to take the place of a verb stating an action performed before the time of the utterance (the cat had licked her). "Wet" can be a verb in English, "all wet" cannot. It is unlikely that Hildegard meant to use the verb "wet". "The cat got me all wet" would be a formulation more in accord with child-language, but the word-order makes this interpretation unconvincing, too. The utterance shows a well developed syntactic pattern, the application of which miscarried because no satisfactory simple transitive verb for the intended purpose ("licked") was available. It was an emergency solution, good enough to convey the intended meaning clearly (cf. 549).

540. A span of four words really marks the upper limit of the length of sentences during the first two years. There were instances of coherent utterances consisting of five to seven words rather early; but they were grammatically composed of more than one sentence. *Bitte dress, my wake*

up 1;10 was a two-word imperative, with an added statement of three words to explain the wish. *Stockings! Mama hangs up stockings* 1;11 was a four-word statement extended to five by emphatic anticipation of the object. It combines a primitive mode of utterance, which called attention to the things which excited the child's interest by means of a single word, with an explicit statement of the facts in a complete sentence. Such a formulation is, of course, quite possible in the lively colloquial speech of adults ("Snow! It snowed last night"). The primitive form of the first part does not mean linguistic immaturity. *Miau da, Miau not da* 1;11 was composed of two statements linked by contrast. The additional word (**538**) was necessary to accommodate the negative; the copula was missing as before. The negative was stressed in the second statement; the adverb of place was stressed and overlong in the first part, unstressed and not so long in the second. The contrast between positive and negative statements was consciously practiced in the last half month (**627**).[63]

In less mature form this process was much older. (*Should I put on*) *this hat? Ja. This hat? No* 1;8 did the same thing in the form of four sentences divided into questions and answers. Monologs of this type, with the answers "Yes" and "No", were common at 1;8. (*This is*) *no Mama's stocking, here* (*is*) *Mama's stocking* 1;9 was also a six-word utterance of the same type, in reversed order. It preceded the acquisition of the word "not", which would be more fitting, by two months. *Where my ball? Da my ball* 1;11 shows question and answer of parallel structure.

Mary Alice Bett ("is in bed"), *all babies Bett, night Bett* 1;11 was a seven-word recitation partly inspired by my remark, "Alle Kinder sind jetzt im Bett". It consisted of three separate parallel statements, the meaning of the last one being rather obscure.

(Single sentences of six and more words began just after the two-year limit. *I put my hat my room* 2;1 was a unified six-word statement rather perfect in form, lacking nothing but a preposition. *Look, Papa, my automobile on my wheel* 2;1, seven words, was less complete and less unified; but the imperative and the vocative were more closely linked with the following statement than was the case in most of the earlier examples. The mother's baby book states for 2;0 that Hildegard "repeated and originated" sentences up to eight words long; but no example is given. On account of my absence from home during 2;0 I have no record of such sentences. I suspect that they were eight-word utterances rather than eight-word sentences.)[64]

---

[63] Snyder (p. 419) states that antithetic statements of this kind are typical of age 2;6, with reference to the studies of psychologists. She gives the example: "Not dat boat hot; dat boat hot"; also in reverse order. Cf. Delacroix (1930) p. 324 f.; Stern p. 206 f. (with examples from the literature, 1;9–2;9); Bloch (1924) p. 39 (age 2;6).

[64] I have a record of a sample of Karla's speech at E 2;3, an account of an imagined happening, which was composed of sentences three to seven words in length: *Vati, I took your pencil the other day. You can't have it. I threw it away—*

541. The preceding classification of examples by the length of utterances and sentences is too mechanical to give by itself a clear picture of syntactic growth. The stages overlap chronologically, and a rapid glance back over the findings is needed to improve the perspective.

We have seen (**504**) that the pure one-word stage lasted nearly a year, from 0;8 to 1;7. The combination of two words into one unified sentence began at 1;7 in the category of exclamations (**517**), in which we cannot speak of a grammatically organized sentence.[65] A start toward syntactic analysis was made in other categories of two-word sentences (**518–523**), the time of the earliest examples varying in the subdivisions between 1;8 (**518, 521, 523**) and 1;10 (**523**). The pattern subject — verb began at 1;8, the pattern verb — object at 1;9 (**524**).

There was no long interval between the learning of sentences with two words and sentences with more than two words, as there was between the beginning of the one-word and of the two-word stages.[66] Three-word stentences (disregarding three-word utterances consisting of more than one sentence) began at 1;10, but so did four-word sentences, for which there is even one example at 1;9 (**534**), antedating the three-word examples. Some of the three-word sentences were grammatically complete at 1;10 (**531**), but the pattern subject — verb — object was not achieved until 1;11 (**531 f.**). Many three- and four-word sentences were incomplete. No example had more than four words in a single sentence (**533–540**)[67]

---

in the garage. It's broken. I can't fix it. Vati can't fix it either, each item in many repetitions in varying order.

[65] Stern (pp. 200–202), in a survey of sentences of more than one word in the literature, finds that they begin between 1;1 and 2;0, most commonly at 1;6 and 1;7. Bergmann (p. 243) found no sentence before 2;0, mostly two words in the third year. Cornioley (p. 43) observed two-word sentences from 1;4–5. Charlotte Bühler (p. 160) reports Hetzer and Reindorf's findings that 28 children of cultured families began to use sentences of two and three words between 1;1 and 1;4 and all used them between 1;9 and 1;11, whereas 28 children from uncultured families did not begin until 1;9–11 and some were delayed until 2;0–6. Nice (p. 370) found the first two-word sentence at 1;1–2;3, average M 1;5, in the speech of 20 English-speaking children; at 1;1–11, average 1;6, in that of 20 foreign children. Bloch (1924, p. 19) records the first two-word sentences for his three children at the ages 1;10, 1;6, and E 1;11 respectively. K. Bühler (p. 233) sets the time for the beginning of original two-word sentences at the middle of the second year. He realizes that two one-word sentences represent a stage of transition, as does Stern (p. 199); cf. also K. Bühler's remarks 1922, p. 82. Trettien says that the first sentences appear in general between 18 and 20 months; he gives as examples "car stops" and "Papa's nose".

[66] Bloch (1924, p. 20) says that "on ne peut pas parler d'un stade de langage de l'enfant qui serait caractérisé par le groupement de deux mots . . . très rapidement, on peut presque dire immédiatement, . . . davantage." Actually, however, he had recorded (p. 19 f.) for his three children a gap of two weeks, one month, and seven months (!) respectively.

[67] K. Bühler (1926, p. 603) designates, in a generalizing survey, the end of the second year as the stage of sentences composed of two or three words, with fluid syntax. In his book (p. 234) he states that sentences of more than two words

(until 2;1, when six words were used in an utterance which was clearly a unified sentence, **540**).[68] If we disregard the single occurrence of a four-word sentence at 1;9, we may state that there was a lag of two to three months between the earliest two-word sentence and the earliest sentence of more than two words.[69] There was no gap at all between three and four words, and one of three months between three or four and more words.

542. A backward glance at the development of the parts of speech will also be useful.

During the long stage of one-word sentences, no parts of speech can be assumed to exist in the child's syntax, as has often been emphasized in the course of this investigation. No matter on what part of adult speech the child's words were based, they were used for the purpose of uttering a wish or a predication concerning the situation at hand. For the child the words were grammatically undifferentiated. We can speak of a single series of syntactic units. To call the situation the subject, and the uttered word the predicate, is psychologically correct, but linguistically it is not justifiable to speak of two parts of speech when one of them is not expressed at all, nor felt as missing.

Syntactic analysis begins with those two-word utterances in which the two words do not belong closely together (as they do in utterances like *all wet*, **516**), but represent in some way separate units of thought (like *Hase Bett*, **518**). A transition is made by two correlated one-word utterances, in which two predications are not on the same level (like *Mama? mit?* **521**, or *Dada? by-by*, **523**).

At this stage the single series is beginning to split into two series of syntactic units. The child has begun to understand that adult sentences are organized and contain several separate units of thought-expression which are in some way contrasted with each other and yet linked together by some kind of coherence. It is necessary to emphasize that the grasp of syntactic organization must be dim at first, growing gradually in clarity. Yet, from this moment on, the child's utterances begin to resemble organized standard utterances, and we may speak of subjects, objects, verbs etc., if we keep in mind that the sharp separation of these parts of speech is at first still ahead of the child's linguistic development and ap-

---

begin soon after 2;0. Nice (p. 370 f.) observed that one of her daughters, who spoke the first sentence at 1;8, used, at the age of "two years", during one day seven three-word sentences, 352 two-word sentences, and 683 one-word sentences, the average being 1.35 words. "Single sentences in this period may be fairly long, but a representative series will give an average of more than one and less than three words."

[68] Schlag (p. 224) found an average length of 4.62 words for children six years old, and of 7 words for children eight years old, with a variation from one to seventeen words. Boyd (p. 187) finds that the average number of words increases, from age 2 to age 8, from 3.3 to 8.5. The average length of conversational sentences in the works of novelists is 10–11.1 words.

[69] Nice (p. 371) found that the stage of two words lasted three, seven, and "at least 13" months respectively with her daughters and estimates the average as perhaps four to seven months.

plies to the utterances a logical analysis which is only dimly realized in the young speaker's linguistic behavior. The child gropes for the imitation of standard syntactic patterns without fully realizing at once what is happening.

543. Words which may be called the subject of an utterance were used for the first time at 1;5 in the sentences *Da ist es* and *I see you* (525). These sentences, however, were learned by mechanical imitation. Their grammatical organization was not appreciated by the child. They were syntactically premature. Therefore they were soon dropped from the vocabulary and did not become productive.

These mechanically imitated sentences did not even pave the way for the learning of syntactic patterns; for at 1;6, Hildegard began to approach them in a quite different manner. She expressed what the adult would consider the subject and the predicate of one sentence separately in two or three sentences, giving the "subject" the form of a question. There are several examples at 1;6 of statements of the type *Mama? sh*, "Mama is sleeping", *Dada? by-by* (523), *Marion? Dodo? away!* (531). There is at least one example of a question built in the same manner: *Mama? by-by?* "Did Mama go by-by?" (522).

This stage lasted several months. At 1;8, *Mama? Bad(en)* (523) interpreted as "Mama is going to take a bath", followed the same pattern. *I! by-by* (520) is different because it did not use a question but an exclamation for the subject, but is otherwise comparable. One example was found as late as 1;9 (531).

In the meantime, however, the pattern of question and answer had become so well grooved that the two elements were joined together as one breath-group. The disjointed intonation was given up. The subject had no longer the form of a question. Thus the utterance gave the effect of one two-word sentence and was approaching the standard syntactic pattern. Since all of children's speaking efforts are constantly striving toward a more and more faithful imitation of standard practices, I have no doubt that the standard pattern was indeed the ideal at which the child aimed and which it reached gradually as her powers of analysis and synthesis grew.

The diary records no examples for 1;7. During that month she spoke many two-word phrases, but they were not sentences which could be said to contain subjects. It seems as if the child needed a breathing spell for the impending effort of building sentences. From 1;8 there are many examples, some still loosely organized like the examples with *Wehweh* (523), or *Hase Bett* (518), others quite clearly consisting of subject and predicate like *Dada wäscht* (523) or also subject and object like *Papa apple* (523).[70] At 1;9 a flood of statements with the pattern *This (is)* . . . began (523).

---

[70] Boyd (p. 188) says that the subject was omitted by his daughter at age 2, rarely at age 3. Guillaume (p. 22) found subjects expressed from 1;8.

Words which can be called subjects were at first only names of persons, exclusively so at 1;6, often at 1;8. Designations of persons by common nouns (*man, Frau,* **523**) started at 1;8. The impersonal demonstrative pronoun *this,* useful because it obviated the necessity of specifying the thing meant and served to overcome the limitations of the vocabulary, became common from 1;9. Specific subjects designating things belonged to 1;11, with one forerunner at 1;9 (*bath alle,* **523**). Personal pronouns were not used until 1;11. (The example *I! by-by* 1;8 contained *I* not as a pronoun, but as a mechanical wish-word, **520**.) The only pronoun was *I* and its synonym *my.* Her own name was not used as a substitute (*Where (is) Hildegard?* 1;11 in a hiding game was a quotation of my formula. The pronoun of the second person appeared at 2;1, **535**).

From 1;10 the subject could consist of two words. Forerunners were the utterances of three related one-word utterances of 1;6–9 (**531**), in which the persons about whom she wished to make a statement were named with interrogative intonation, in one example 1;8 even without this intonation. In the last two months the subject was once a designation of persons accompanied by an indefinite numeral adjective (*all babies* 1;11, **531**), in all other cases things accompanied by the possessive adjective of the first person (*my buggy* 1;10, **538**, *my ball* 1;11, **531**), by a name in possessive function (*Mary Alice Wehweh* 1;11, **531**), or by the demonstrative adjective *this* (*this book* 1;10, **531**, *this door* 1;11, **531**, *this dolly* 1;11, **536**).[71] Specific subjects designating things in this form were one month earlier than in one-word form, if we disregard the one example of 1;9 (*bath alle*). Probably we should not disregard it, but say that the use of impersonal subjects began slowly at 1;9, considering as accidental the fact that such subjects in one-word form did not become common until 1;11.

544. The first object expressed together with a verb appeared in the same mechanically imitated sentence *I see you* 1;5 (**525, 543**). The pattern was not recognized by the child. The ephemeral use of the sentence did not lead to the learning of the construction.

I disregard, as I did for subjects, the one-word sentences, to which syntactic classifications cannot be applied. Two-word sentences begin to come closer to the standard organization of sentences, but a good deal of more or less arbitrary interpretation is still needed to reconcile them with standard patterns, and this holds as well for some sentences of more than two words, a few of which continued to lack a verb to the end of the second year. Many of the sentences interpreted as imperatives (**519, 527, 535**) and as requests in question form (**521, 529**) seem to the adult to contain an object; but when no verb was expressed we have no assur-

---

[71] *All balls da* does not belong here, but under two-word objects (**544**). The paraphrase "All balls are there" (vol. 1, p. 30) is erroneous. The diary interprets the meaning, on the basis of the situation, as "Put all balls there" (**527**).

ance that the child was casting the utterance in the pattern assumed. In a few instances, in which the missing verb would be "have", the inference is nearly inescapable that the pattern subject — verb — object was reproduced incompletely: *Papa (has an) apple* 1;8 (**523**), *My (= I have) Wehweh* 1;10 (**523**), *Papa (has) my comb da* 1;11 (**538**), *Meow (has) oatmeal* 1;11 (**523**). In the latter example, the omitted verb was reconstructed as "eats", but "has" is also possible, and in any case the construction is the same.

We are on firmer ground when the verb is expressed by the child, and she did this frequently from the two-word stage on. The first example was *Open (the) door* 1;8 (**519**).[72] It was quoted from a rhyme, but used with full comprehension in situations in real life. There were a few examples at 1;9 in which the pattern became productive: *Watch Mama* (**519**), *Bau, Haus* (**520**). In the latter, the level stress revealed that the pattern was still unfamiliar. At 1;10 the construction was not yet frequent: *Drinks milk* (**523**), *Dicken Bauch waschen* and *Wash baby's dress* (**527**). At 1;11, however, there is a wealth of examples (assembled in sections **519, 520, 523, 527, 529, 531, 532, 535, 536, 538, 540**). In a few instances, level stress or garbled word-order indicated that the construction was not yet perfectly familiar. With a noun object, free word-order was used in *nose blow* and *coat button* (**519**);[73] level stress and pause separating verb and object occurred in *Mama calls, meow* (**531**).[74] The other instances of lack of fluency involve the object pronoun *me: Duck, bite, me* (**531**), *Mary Alice ride, me* (**532**). *Dress me* was said fluently, but with unorthodox stresses, which also betray the effort still needed for the application of the pattern (**519**). At the same time, there were, however, many other utterances in which no effort was visible, even involving *me: Bites me* (**523**), *Papa, push me, Papa feed my* (**527**), *Mama kiss my* (**532**).

The survey confirms the conclusion reached earlier (**519, 524**) that the pattern subject — verb was learned sooner (1;8) than the pattern verb — object (1;9–11). Even after the addition of an object was achieved, the older pattern, which was adequate for intransitive verbs, asserted its primacy in examples like *Mama calls, meow* and *Mary Alice ride, me*, in which the pause between verb and object gave the latter the effect of an afterthought. The exaggerated stress on the object in *Dress me* 1;11 marked the newness of the progress from the earlier formulation *Bitte dress* 1;10 (**519**), in which no subject was needed and the object was suppressed. The complete pattern subject — verb — object resulted from a combination of these two constructions. It was not possible before the three-word stage and was characteristic of 1;11. It was by no means present in all three-word utterances, in fact, it was not needed in all situa-

[72] Bloch (1924, p. 27) found objects omitted at 1;11. Guillaume (p. 21) found them added at 1;8.
[73] Cf. also *Papa this hang up* 1;11 (**535**).
[74] Karla 1;11 said 'mami fĭk, 'dæt *Mammy fixes (fixed) that.*

tions (imperatives, intransitive verbs), and incomplete two-word utterances continued to occur at 1;11 (**519**). The extension of the two-unit syntactic stage to the three-unit stage was a gradual, halting process.

All objects expressed were direct objects with the exception of *Mama Kuss* 1;11 (**523**), in which both a direct and an indirect object were expressed from the point of view of standard syntax. The primitive form of the utterance makes it hazardous to assume that the child had reached this stage of sentence-organization. It is safer to assume that she made the communication in an amorphous manner, by placing the two items of greatest importance side by side without using a developed pattern.

The kinds of nouns used as objects differ from those used as subjects by the fact that they were rarely names or designations of persons. *Watch Mama* 1;9 (**519**), *Bite Papa* 1;11 (**523**), *Ask Papa on* 1;11 (**528**), *Mama call Mary Alice* 1;11 (**532**), *Ask Mama this aus* 1;11 (**536**) are the only examples. At 1;8 they were all nouns denoting things: *door, dolly, Buch* (**519**), *apple* (**523**), *hat* (**540**). At 1;9 *Mama* (**519**) shared the field with *Haus* (**520**) and *Schuhe* (**522**). At 1;10 they were again all things: *drink* (**519**), *radio* (**521**), *milk, Wehweh* (**523**), *dicken Bauch, baby's dress, this oil* (**527**); *Wehweh* and *drink* were a little more abstract than the others, which were all quite concrete. At 1;11 there were too many examples to be repeated here. With the exceptions just mentioned, all of them denoted things, generally of a concrete nature. *I spiel Nackedei* (**529**), *Papa make Bau* (**532**), and *Rita's house big A-a* (**539**) were more abstract, but the abstract character of the last two examples is questionable; the noun-form of *Bau* was probably coined just to make the utterance more concrete, and *big A-a* may still have been an amorphous predicate rather than the object of an omitted verb. One object was a designation of an animal: *Meow bites Wauwau* (**531**).

The object consisted sometimes of two words from 1;10 as did subjects (**543**), with a forerunner at 1;8: *This hat? ja; this hat? no* (**540**). The word accompanying the object was the indefinite numeral *all* (*all balls* 1;11, **527**), the possessive adjective of the first person (*my comb* 1;11, **538**), a noun in possessive function without formal characteristics (*baby dress* 1;10, **527**), an adjective of emotional rather than descriptive character (*pretty dress* 1;11, **529**, *big A-a* 1;11, **539**), a stereotype epithet hardly analyzed as an adjective (*dicken Bauch* 1;10, **527**), or the demonstrative adjective *this* (*this oil* 1;10, **527,** *this dolly* 1;11, **536**). As in the case of subjects, no article was ever used with the noun. *This on beads* 1;11 (**527**), loosely constructed, rather contained the pronoun *this*, with a specifying noun in apposition. *This, big, baby, bottle* 1;9 (**534**), the only example of an object consisting of more than two words and a very early one, is dubious. Although it designated the object of a wish, it may have been a statement of the type "This is . . ." with a strong wish-component. Then it would not contain an object, but a predicate complement consisting of an emotional adjective and a compound noun of a type which she often used (*oil-spoon, A-a paper*). The utterance was premature and therefore produced haltingly.

Pronominal objects were, as in the case of subjects, the demonstrative *this*, from 1;10, used less frequently as an object than as a subject, and the pronoun of the first person, *me* and its synonym *my* 1;11 (never her name). The addition of *me* involved apparently greater difficulties than that of other objects. A contributory explanation for the halting utterance of *me* is the fact that the word was new at 1;11; but we might as well say that it was not acquired earlier because its function did not become clear to the child until that time. Omission with transitive verbs (*trag*, "carry me") continued to occur during the last month.

545. The predicate took varying forms from the beginning. It could be a simple verb or a compound verb, the latter at first with omission of the verb proper, later complete. More commonly it consisted of a noun, a possessive, an adjective, or an adverb or adverbial phrase, always with omission of the copula required by standard syntax.

Simple verbs appeared early among the words of one-word sentences (**511, 512, 515**); but the earliest ones, like *kiek* *1;1, *1;3 and *peekaboo* *1;4, 1;8 have lost their verbal character even in adult usage, and later ones, like *rollen, rock* 1;8 and *backe, *hacke* 1;11 were likewise no more than action-cues, the verbal origin of which was immaterial to the child. Others, however, even in one-word sentences, denoted actions more definitely: 1;8 *open, walk, *wischen, ride*, 1;10 *dress, cry*, 1;11 *trag(en), wait, blow*. As long as utterances consisted of only one word, we cannot be sure that they were verbs for the child, particularly since most of them were English and were not necessarily verbs in the standard language. The examples of the last two months belong to a stage in which Hildegard used organized sentences along with survivals of one-word utterances. At this stage it is probable that verbs were recognized as such and really used as verbs.

In sentences of two or more words, verbs are more clearly restricted to a function similar to that of standard syntax. The earliest examples, interestingly enough, contain interjections pressed into the new syntactic pattern subject — verb: *Mama? sh* 1;6, *man sh, Frau m* 1;8 (**523**). Immediately, standard verbs were also used in the same pattern, confirming its emergence: *Dada wäscht, Mama? bad(en)* 1;8 (**523**); the latter example, more primitive in structure, is less convincing than the former, because the etymon could also be the noun *Bad*, which had identical form in the phonetically and morphologically undeveloped speech of the child. The pattern verb — object appeared during the same month 1;8 in *open door* (**519**), imitative in the choice of words and containing a verb which was used at the same time as an adjective. It was not until 1;11 that simple verbs became numerous in sentences. Examples are: *dress, blow, button* (**519**), *steht, do* (in restricted function), *hol, push, feed, spielen* (**527**), *call, bite, make, read, eat* (**531**), *fall, buy, ride, kiss, forgot* (**532**), *ask,* *bake* (**536**), *fix* (**538**). Most of these verbs were not used before 1;11. The few that were did not have verbal character indubitably before 1;11.

546. Compound verbs, which show more clearly that they are verbs, were earlier than simple verbs, both in rudimentary and in complete form. They consist of a verb proper and an adverbial element which is linked more or less intimately with the verb. It is generally more strongly stressed than the verb, which commonly stands immediately before it. Therefore the verb proper is bound to be omitted at first for semantic and phonetic reasons.

Thus we get adverbs in a function very similar to verbs in the one-word stage. In the two-word utterance these adverbs are combined with other words, which seem to act as subjects, objects, or other parts of speech, the adverb taking the place of what would be the verb in a conventional sentence. Because the adverb forming a part of a compound verb and the adverb modifying the sentence as a whole (**550**) cannot always be separated, at all stages there is room for doubt concerning the exact character of the adverbial element.

Adverbs used alone in this manner were 1;4 *up* (**511, 515**), 1;6 *aus*, *auf* (**511**), 1;8 *mit* (**511, 521**), *away* (**511, 512**); 1;9 German *an*, English *on* (**511**), 1;10 *by-by* (**511, 512**). The latter is one of the dubious cases. If "go by-by" is compared to "go out", *by-by* may be interpreted as a part of a compound verb; but it is equally possible to paraphrase it by "go for a walk", and then *by-by* would rather be an adverb modifying the sentence (**551**). The clearest case is *mit*, which was used in the function of "komm mit". Its place was taken 1;10 by *come on*, the first syllable being clipped off for phonetic reasons (**476**), but leaving a remnant in the child's form, which makes it exceedingly probable that the verb part of "komm mit" was also omitted phonetically, without leaving a trace.

From 1;7 or 1;8 such adverbs were combined with another word, still without the verb proper. In *down bitte* 1;7 (**519**) we cannot be sure that a verb was suppressed ("put me down"). The desired direction might be expressed by a signaling adverb without any verbal idea. *Buch away* (**519**), *Mama up* (**519**), and *Light aus* (**523**), all at 1;8, might be similar. But *Mama (got) up* (**523**), also at 1;8, referring as it did to an action already completed, shows verbal character more definitely. *Mama, mit!* 1;9 (**535**) was based on the presentation "komm mit"; the adverb filled the place of a compound verb; in German grammar it is usually called the separated prefix of a verb; for *Schuhe aus?* 1;9 see **551**. During the last two months, when adult syntactic patterns had been learned, there is less doubt about the character of utterances in which this primitive construction continued to be used: 1;10 *Radio on? This on?* (**521**), *This oil weg* (**527**), *Papa this on* (**532**); 1;11 *Water on* (**519**), *Water auf?* (**521**), *Meow in, By-by street-car* (**523**), *This on beads, Come on Papa, auf* (**527**), *Ask Papa on* (**528**), *Pretty dress on? Papa on me?* (**529**), *No, shoes, on* (**531**), *This da down, This, on, my neck* (**535**), *Ask Mama this aus* (**536**).

In the examples *Papa on me?* and *This, on, my neck*, the word *on* was on its way out of the adverbial classification; it was preparing to become a preposition, repeating the process which had taken place in the standard language (551).

During the last two months, the intensification of the child's attention for finer details made the addition of the verb proper possible. The first example was *Pick up dolly* 1;9.[75] At 1;10 we find *come on* (511, 527), *go away*, (519, 523, 531), *walk in* (519), *push in* (519, 523), *pick up* (519, 520), *wake up* (523, 527, 531), *walk down* (531) said in full, in varying functions. At 1;11 *throw away* (519), *cover up* (519), *lie down* (519, 527), *knock down* (520, 536), *wisch ab* (520, 523), *put on* (526), *slide down* (529), *fall down* (532), *häng up* (535) were added to the list of maturer expressions.

547. Full verbs were, however, not the most common form of predicates, particularly in the months preceding 1;11. Much more typical were predications by means of a noun, possessive, adjective, or adverb, with omission, from the point of view of standard syntax, of the copula "to be".

During the one-word stage, the many words based on standard nouns can be taken as predicate nouns in all instances in which the utterance amounted to "This is (a person)", "This is (a thing)", for instance *Ticktack!* 0;11 (515). This interpretation, however, is hazardous. At the pure one-word stage, statement and wish were still too much intertwined. When the wish-element predominated, the standard paraphrase would be "I want a . . . ", "I want this . . .", and the noun would act as an object. Actually no syntactic analysis was yet attempted at this time. In the later months, when syntactic patterns had been acquired by the child and statements and wishes separated, such an interpretation has more validity.[76]

Two-word sentences which consisted of a noun with an attribute do not differ syntactically from one-word sentences, except for the fact that they bring out the noun-character of a word more clearly: 1;7 *mein Ball, my stocking,* 1;8 *June's dolly, Bates's dolly, my dolly,* 1;10 *Joey's kimona,* 1;11 *Florence's dolly* (523). *Florence's Liebling* 1;11 (523, 531) was unquestionably a predicate noun; it was an answer to the question, "Bist du Papas Liebling?", followed the syntactic pattern of this question, and would have to be paraphrased by "I am . . ." instead of the usual copula "is".

---

[75] The example does not appear in the foregoing survey of syntax because the diary fails to record the circumstances. The utterance might have been an imperative or an announcement of the child's intention. It was misunderstood at first, which testifies to the fact that the construction was new.

[76] Naming-exercises, like the enumeration of parts of the head 1;8 (515), hardly belong here. Adults say nouns in isolation in such situations. Psychologically they are predicate nouns ("This is the nose", etc.), but not linguistically.

The pattern was clearer when the subject was expressed: 1;8 *This (is a) brush (and) this (is a) brush* (**538**); 1;9 *This (is an) oil-spoon* (**523**), *This big Buch, da!* (**538**); 1;10 *This church* (**523**; imitation of the presented line, "This is the church"), *This my spoon, Papa all wet, This my rock-baby* (**531**), *Dada's hat, this mine* (**538**; second sentence confirming the pattern incompletely expressed in the first sentence); 1;11 *Here church* (original variation of the presented line), *This paper-ball* (**523**), *Wash all dry* (**531**). Sentences without an expressed subject continued to occur, but in the later months the syntactic intention can no longer be mistaken: 1;9 *No Mama's stocking, here Mama's stocking* (**540**); 1;11 *Ring, Mama* (**523**); *Mama's new hat; Shoe? Mama's shoe; Bottle pieks, Wehweh* (**531, 538**).

548. Often the predicate complement expressed possession, from the moment that the idea of personal ownership developed. It was expressed by means of a noun, usually without formal possessive characteristics, or of a pronoun, the latter only in the first person. The first example was as early as 1;6, when she checked her impulse to take a visiting baby's toy, saying *baby* (**515**). Linguistically this early instance was amorphous. It expressed the idea of personal property without a formal possessive. *Mine*, said alone 1;6 with the emphatic gesture of clutching the claimed object, looks like a clear possessive; but it was actually a game cue, which might just as well be paraphrased as "I got it first". *This mine* 1;9 (**523, 531**), *This book mine* 1;10, however, contain the same possessive pronoun in more intellectualized function. *Dada's hat, this mine* 1;10 (**538**) contrasts a statement in the form of a predicate noun accompanied by an attributive possessive with another statement expressing the subject and a predicate possessive pronoun. *This Dodo, this Dodo* 1;8, (**538**) similar in thought pattern, but different in its formal expression, uses a predicate possessive without formal sign. The formal signs were practically always missing. The pronoun *mine* had the same phonetic form as the adjective *my*. The nouns showed no trace of the possessive ending "'s", except for the two names *Mama's* and *Papa's*, in which it was added E 1;10. The diary does not indicate, however, whether these possessives were used as attributes or as predicates. Attributive possessives, of course, do not belong in this section, but the preceding one. They appear also as a part of subjects (**543**) and objects (**544**).

549. Predicate adjectives would be very early if we included one-word utterances mechanically, merely because they were based on standard adjectives.[77] As early as 0;10, *pretty* would then be called a predicate adjective. We have, however, claimed that the word was predominantly

---

[77] O'Shea (p. 70) agrees that "nice" is at first a sentence-word; "but a term like *virtuous* is never employed until the sentence-word period is outgrown, and the word discharges adjectival function alone". This striking discovery demonstrates the obvious.

the carrier of emotional reactions with only the vaguest intellectual content, and found that it remained phonetically isolated, on account ˎ f its interjectional character, for the long period in which it was not yet a real adjective. Rather early, some one-word sentences could be claimed to have more factual content: 1;4 *hot*, 1;5 *heiss, all*, 1;7 *alle* (the two latter in the sense of "gone, absent"), *wet*, 1;8 *nass* **(515)**.[78] Even then, their adjective character was not beyond doubt. It became clearer when the adverb *all* was added to them: *all sticky* 1;7, *all wet* 1;8, *all nass, gone, dry* 1;10, *all through* 1;11 **(523)**. Later one-word sentences (1;10–11, **515**) can more confidently be assumed to consist of predicate adjectives.

This was clearly the case when the subject was expressed, but Hildegard rarely did this before 1;11, and the number of examples is surprisingly small: *This zu, Door open, Door zu, This nass* **(523)**, *This door open, Mary Alice Wehweh alle* **(531)**, all at 1;11. *By-by dunkel* 1;10 contained a predicate adjective, but hardly a subject **(523)**. *Meow all wet me* 1;11 **(539)** used a two-word predicate adjective in a clumsy construction, in which it seemed to take the place of a verb. This gives the impression that the syntactic analysis was still hazy; but it may be unfair to draw such a conclusion from a single failure. The personal reference may have been loosely added as an afterthought to avoid the misunderstanding that the cat was all wet. The earliest example of the construction subject—predicate–adjective is *Bath alle* 1;9 **(523)**.[79]

Late sentences of several words containing predicate adjectives without a subject were *All sticky candy* 1;11, where the subject "my hands" was superfluous because she displayed them, and *All piece broke* 1;11, which certainly contained a predicate adjective (synonymous with *kaputt*), in spite of the loose word-order, because it was a quotation from a story **(531)**.

550. Adverbs and words which stand for standard prepositional phrases with adverbial function are not called predicate complements. Hildegard, however, used them often in much the same way, particularly in utterances of two words. The most frequent category is made up of adverbs of place. The omitted verb could be a form of "to be", usually "is" and "are". It is not simply a copula, since it has the meaning of "be located, situated"; but its semantic value is not much greater than that of a copula.[80] It is not surprising that the child paid no at-

---

[78] Stern (p. 256 f.) says that adjectives are first tactile, thermic, and kinesthetic, later optic (brightness, colors); cf. Decroly p. 192. The adjective "hot" is often early or the first; cf. Gheorgov p. 379.

[79] Curme calls "over" an adverb used as an adjective (1935, §8a) and "through" a predicate adjective (1931, index). English *all*, German *alle* and *zu* are in the same category; cf. Curme (1922) §222, 2B.

[80] To see how diffused the boundary line between the two functions of "to be" really is, cf. note 82. Erdmann (p. 42) shows that the meaning of the copula itself varies greatly.

tention to it. The verb "be" (like "have") was not expressive enough to be incorporated in the vocabulary and syntax of the first two years (579 f.).

The demonstrative adverbs of place *there* 0;10 and *da* 1;0 were used in a variety of ways in the first months of speaking; often they were hardly more than interjections, but in some instances the intention of stating a fact outweighed the emotional components (515). *Up*, at 1;4, more convincingly at 1;8 (515), seemed to have the function of an adverb of place as in the standard language. As long as these words were said in isolation, however, it is not safe to call them adverbs. Because the vocabulary was extremely limited at that stage, these words had to serve in all kinds of functions including that of verbs.[81]

Some of the later one-word utterances indicated place more definitely. *Bett* 1;8 meant "Yes, I want to go to bed" (512), but, repeating as it did a word of the question directed to her, it had more or less the function of an affirmative sentence adverb (and sentence adverbs, not being part of a sentence, but sentences by themselves, receive only marginal consideration in this syntactic survey). *Home* 1;11 (515, 531), meaning "she went home", at a time when more complete sentences were within the child's range, was rather definitely an adverb of place implying the direction of motion. *House* 1;11 (511), conveying the imperative idea "come into the house", can at this late stage be regarded as elliptic.

Two-word sentences did not make the adverbial idea much clearer than early one-word utterances when the added word was merely the conventional wish word *bitte*: 1;7 *down bitte, bitte up* (518 f.), or when the adverb was modified by another adverb: 1;11 *right da* (523). There are many other sentences of two or more words, however, in which the subject was expressed and a question asked or a declaration made about its position. The word or words indicating the latter are then static adverbs of place, the semantically unimportant verb "to be" being suppressed. The first examples at 1;6, *Mama? by-by?* (522) and *Dada? by-by* (523), are inconclusive because they were not yet real two-word sentences and because the nursery-word *by-by* is syntactically vague; "went by-by" is a better paraphrase than "is by-by". Actually no verb was missing; *by-by* was a syntactically amorphous signal rather than a part of speech. *Marion? Dodo? Away!*, also at 1;6 (531), comes much closer to a sentence containing a static adverb: "they are far away". *Marion Joey away* 1;8 (531) expressed the same idea in improved form. *I! by-by* 1;8 (520) was primitive again with regard to both words. *Wehweh* with an added localization: *da, knee, eye* 1;8 (523,

---

[81] It should be remembered that this is the case even with adverbs in the standard languages: "Forward!" "Onward!" "Down!"; "Vorwärts!" "Auf!" "Zurück!" "Herein!" O'Shea's claim (p. 69) that "up" and "down" were not strictly adverbs until the "third year, and I should prefer to make it a year later", seems unduly conservative.

538) was more definite as far as the adverbial part of the statements
was concerned; I consider the nouns designating parts of her body as
incomplete versions of prepositional phrases with adverbial value,
parallel to the adverb *da*, but of course not consciously elliptic. The
examples of 1;9 are again primitive in form: *Marion? Dodo? Da!* (532)
and *This big Buch, da!* (538). *Here Mama's stocking*, also at 1;9 (540)
had better form, but the adverbial value of *here* is a little doubtful.
The statement was contrasted with *No Mama's stocking*, which is best
paraphrased as "This is not Mama's stocking", and Hildegard used
Here church at 1;11 as an original variant of the presented line "This is
the church" (523), giving the word *here* the value of a local demonstrative pronoun rather than of a local adverb. This slight ambivalence in
the function of "here" exists in standard speech, of course, and may be
negligible.

In the last two months, adverbs of place became better established in
constructions of this type: 1;10 *My buggy (is) way down* (538); 1;11
This (is) in (523)[82], *Hottey da, Cry-baby da, Choo-choo da, Meow da,
Meow out, Mary Alice Bett, Autos alley* (523), *Where my ball? Where
Hildegard?* (530), *All babies Bett, Da my ball, Meow up Baum* ("is" or
"went"?) (also *No, not da*, without subject) (531), *Miau da, Miau not
da* (531, 540).

551. Adverbs of place in a dynamic function indicating a motion in a
certain direction like *up, down* or with a goal expressed (like *home*,
simple adverb, or *(zu) Bett*, standard prepositional phrase), were also
frequent. With them the suppressed verb was not a form of "to be",
but a verb of motion, and for that reason it can often not be decided
whether the adverb is independent or part of a compound verb (546).
One-word adverbs of this type are included among the examples at the
beginning of **550**; in fact, most of them were dynamic.[83] *By-by* 1;3
(512), when said alone, belongs here, too; but the adverbial character
of this primitive word is doubtful. For a long time it was probably no
more than a signal indicating a wish amorphously. Later it became more
intellectualized, until, at 1;11, she said once *by-by, go by-by* in succession. This utterance marked the transition from signaling to syntactic

---

[82] Curme (1935) calls "in", "out", "up", when used in this way, adverbs used
as adjectives (§8a), but includes one example of "in" in the same type of construction under adverbs (§15, 2a). I consider them adverbs pure and simple. I
would call "in" an adjective in the colloquial expression "He is all in", meaning
"He is exhausted"; but that is a different matter, which does not enter into consideration here. The line of demarcation is very fine. "He is out" can be paraphrased by "He is out of the game", making "out" an adverb, or "He is disquali-
fied", making it an adjective. In "He is down and out", the adverbs may be said
to act as adjectives.

[83] Ament (p. 170 f.) cites Lindner's opinion (p. 69) that children prefer dynamic
adverbs of place to static ones, apparently with disapproval (his wording is not
clear).

use of the word. Whether it should be called a specifying adverb or a part of a compound verb (546), remains in doubt.

In sentences of more than one word the "adverb" entered into a relationship with another word which restricted the completeness or the vaguenes of its reference; but its syntactic function continued to be ill-defined. *Hase Bett* 1;8 (518, 520) conveyed the idea that she wanted her bunny to go to bed; but whether the unstressed preposition "to", "zu" was omitted for phonetic reasons or the goal of the desired motion was just named without any syntactic organization, is impossible to decide. The syntactic immaturity of *I! by-by* 1;8 (520) has been emphasized before. *This outside* 1;9 (520) was clear in its meaning, but not in its syntactic pattern. *Schuhe aus?* 1;9 (522) is clearer, but the adverb, which did not have the concrete meaning of "out" but the figurative meaning of "off", must be based on the separable prefix of "ausziehen", probably remembered from its use in the imperative, "Zieh deine Schuhe aus!" (546). Even at 1;11 the functional value of the adverb was not always clear. *My auf* (518, 520) meant "I want to get up"; the subject was clear, but not so the function of the adverb. *All balls da* (527) conveyed the idea "put them there"; the directional form "dahin" was not learned, which is probably due to syntactic immaturity, but might also be attributed to the absence of such a formal distinction in English, which furnished her speech-patterns at the end of the year. *Down* in *Way down beach* (528) expressed the general direction in which she wished to go, *beach* the specific goal, but in primitive syntactic form, all three words of the normal span being taken up by adverbial expressions, which left no room for subject or verb. *My room, Taschentuch?* (530) is incomplete in its first sentence. It meant "Shall I go to my room?" *Mary Alice home, eat* (532) clearly meant "went home"; the verb was omitted, but the subject was expressed. In *This da down* (535), the last adverb gave the direction in which a chair was to be moved; *da* probably meant again "dahin", giving the same direction in a less specific way. In *This, on, my neck* (535), the adverb *on* also gave the general direction ("put it on"), rather certainly as a part of a compound verb, and *my neck* specified the goal of the requested motion more accurately. (The conversion of *on* into a preposition, prepared by such combinations as this, was completed at 2;1: *My automobile on my wheel,* 540.) *This dolly up Bett* (536), said more fluently, did the same thing, probably in a more standard construction, since Hildegard must have heard the phrase "up to bed" frequently.

552. The function of these adverbs and adverbial phrases, both static and dynamic, was much clearer when the verb was expressed. Disregarding those cases in which the adverb belonged so intimately with the verb that it can be regarded as part of a compound verb (546), we find an early example at 1;8: *Walk? Schnee? ja?* (529). Of course, the utterance still had the form of three one-word sentences; but in their connec-

tion the noun corresponded to standard "in the snow"; at any rate it specified the place in which Hildegard wanted to do her walking. At 1;10, *Ride Papa's neck* (526, 528), in a single sentence, was equally clear; the noun was not the object of the verb; "ride" was used intransitively. The same is true of *Dolly ride buggy* (526, 528). *Go Mama's Bett* and *Lie Papa's Bett* (528) are of the same type. *Da slide down?* (529) contained *down* as part of a compound verb and the independent adverb of place, *da*. *Mama da bite* and *Miau kratz da* (532) are other illustrations of the use of *da* as an independent adverb; it was the most frequent one in Hildegard's vocabulary. *Go Bett* and *Go by-by* (520) show the same use of adverbs, but not in original treatment, since both are based on fixed standard phrases. The preposition was omitted from all adverbial phrases (556).

553. There are a few examples of adverbs of place used in contexts without a verb, in which no form of "to be" could be supplied. *By-by dunkel* 1;10 (523) was a queer expression, the nearest standard paraphrase of which would be "It is dark outside", making *by-by* a static adverb of place not linked to an expressed subject by means of "is". It is not probable, however, that Hildegard was using this pattern. She meant to state a fact, "dark", and make clear to what the statement referred, namely not to any part of the house in which she was; she pointed at the window to make the intention unmistakable. The effect was that *by-by* appeared psychologically as the subject about which an utterance was made, and *dunkel* as the predicate. It is possible that she was actually applying the pattern subject—predicate, which she was just learning to use, in an unorthodox way. The utterance was, however, only dimly organized syntactically. We cannot go so far as to say that *by-by* had turned into a noun. It did, in this utterance, lose its usual wishful function and its dynamic character ("I want to go for a walk"), just as the emotional component of fear usually present in *dunkel* was reduced. It is the objective, factual character of the sentence which suggests that it may have been cast in a familiar pattern of statement. In *Papa my comb da* 1;11 (538) the suppressed verb was "has"; *da* was a static adverb of place. In *Rita's house big A-a* 1;11 (539), both subject and verb were suppressed; "I made" was the idea; *big A-a* was the object, *(in) Rita's house* an adverbial phrase, which again specified the place statically.

554. Indications of place account for the vast majority of adverbs and adverbial phrases.[84] There are, however, a few examples of adverbs with different functions.

By-by auto? and *By-by choo-choo?* 1;8 (521) contained nouns specifying the wish *by-by* in an instrumental way. In the standard language

[84] Adverbs of place are generally observed to be earliest; cf. Ament p. 170, Decroly p. 196, Gheorgov pp. 298 ff. and 399 ff., Stern p. 261.

they would be prefixed by the preposition "by (means of)". *Hoch Hand* 1;11 (523) was primitive in the use of the signal-clue *hoch* instead of subject, verb, and object; but the instrumental function of "(by the) hand", an original addition, was perfectly clear and explicit enough.

The interrogative *why?*, used for a few days 1;10 as a one-word sentence (514), was an adverb of cause, the meaning of which was not yet quite standard. The category was given up for the time being (until 2;1). Cause was also expressed in the none-too-clear statement (*My hands are) all sticky (from) candy* 1;11 (531).

An adverbial phrase of purpose appeared rudimentarily in *This (is for the) nails* 1;11 (523), with reference to a nail-file. *Mama fix bed my* 1;11 (538), in which *my* meant "for me", is not the same construction, but comparable with regard to its standard form.

Mama sh mehr 1;11 (531), in two versions with different word-order, contained an adverb of degree used in the function of an adverb of time ("Mama wants to sleep more, longer"). *Papa mehr bathe?* (530) was similar. The very common word *mehr* 1;5 (like the ephemeral synonym **more* 1;6) was usually used as an adjective. In one-word sentences it had sometimes adverbial function, when it amounted to "Do it more". It is a striking fact that real adverbs of time were missing. *Now* 1;8 was only used occasionally in the phrase *Now this* and indicated succession (relative time) rather than definite (absolute) time.[85]

Simple adverbs of manner were completely missing.

Sentence-adverbs like "yes" and "no" and their synonyms do not belong here. They are semantically complete sentences by themselves. Negative adverbs, which reverse the meaning of a sentence and are inserted in it, do belong in this category. This practice started at 1;9 with *No Mama's stocking* (540), in which the sentence-adverb *no* was used in the function of *not*, as proved by the fact that the utterance was contrasted with an accompanying positive statement. The pattern developed out of monologs at 1;8 in which the contrast was cast in the form of questions and answers, with correlated affirmative and negative answers in the shape of sentence-adverbs. *Not* was learned 1;11. The first example was *No, not da*, in which *not* was used correctly. Subsequently,

---

[85] Karla used çum, soon, frequently in the first half of 1;11, quite correctly: *Mammy, coming, soon*. In this example, the adverb served to indicate the future. O'Shea (p. 158 f.) states that children have great difficulty in the correct use of adverbs of time, without referring to age. Decroly (p. 196) also finds more confusion with regard to adverbs of time than with regard to adverbs of place. Stern (pp. 261, 263) says that adverbs of time are found only very exceptionally before the end of the second year and do not develop vigorously until the third year. Preyer (p. 173) distinguishes "succession in time", which his child understood at 2;4, from other indications of time, which he did not know how to handle; cf. p. 178, bottom (2;6). Neugebauer (1915, pp. 299–301) emphasizes that time distinctions were equally difficult with regard to adverbs and verbs; cf. Court about "yesterday, today, to-morrow" at age 2;9.

however, *no, not* was used as a unit by itself, representing a reinforced sentence-adverb. At the end of the month, finally, *Miau da, Miau not da* (**540**) showed full comprehension of the function of *not*. *Don't* 1;11, sometimes alone as a sentence-adverb replacing *no-no*, sometimes joined with a following verb (*Don't spiel*), was another negative, the etymology of which must have been obscure to the child (**624**).

For all classes of adverbs it is to be noted that the classification is purely functional. No formal sign of the adverbial function was developed, neither the ending "-ly" nor prepositions to indicate and distinguish adverbial functions.

555. We have finished the examination of the growth of syntactic patterns in simple sentences, having passed in review the primary elements of the sentence. Conjunctions did not enter into the survey because Hildegard did not learn any of them during the first two years.[86] Interjections stand by themselves syntactically. They do not enter into the texture of sentences and have no place in the discussion of organized sentences. Exclamations like *Poor Mama!* (**517**) show a limited amount of organization, but their structure is the same as that of many two-word subjects and objects. Vocatives are linked a little more intimately with the remainder of an utterance, but do not form an organic part of it.

556. There remain to be examined the secondary syntactic elements, those which do not form a unit of the sentence by themselves, but enter into a combination of several words which form such a unit.

Prepositions are such secondary units. They never stand alone in German, and only in subordinate clauses and questions in colloquial English. Not much need be said about them, because Hildegard did not learn prepositions in the first two years. The preposition *of* does appear in the Vocabulary at 1;11; but it was only used occasionally and uncertainly, and only in relatively fixed combinations like *piece of toast* and *drink of water*. The preposition *on* was on the threshold of being developed out of the adverb *on* (*this, on, my neck* **535**, *Papa on me* **529**), but the development was not completed (until 2;1). *Auf, aus, mit,* and *in* were always adverbs (also at 2;1, *in* became a preposition.) *Through* and *zu* were only adjectives, or adverbs used as predicative adjectives. No other prepositions existed in any function. In fluent utterances at the end of the year, prepositions were omitted without pause and therefore without consciousness of omission.[87] Their pretonic position and their slight semantic weight explain the omission. Syntactically they are quite important for adverbial phrases, but their im-

---

[86] Gheorgov, who studied the language of his sons to 3;7 and 2;8 respectively (p. 389 f.), found coördinating as well as subordinating conjunctions to be late (pp. 319 ff., 415 ff.) For a conspectus of conjunctions culled from the literature, cf. Decroly pp. 211–221.

[87] Karla 1;11: **he gɛt ʔaɪ**, *the hair gets in my eyes*. Her first preposition came on the last day of the second year: *Vira makes (made) lemonade for you*.

portance for the organized sentence in this function was only beginning to be grasped by the child at the end of the year (550–553).[88]

557. Adverbs were used not only as primary elements of the sentence, but also as secondary elements reinforcing other elements, namely adjectives and adverbs. The number of adverbs used in such a way is small; *right, way, too,* and *all* make up the complete list. *Right* occurred only in the fixed combination *right da* 1;11, which fell short of being an imitation of the standard fixed combination "right there" merely by the fact that the primary adverb in it, which had been dropped from her vocabulary in English, was replaced by the familiar German synonym. This fact proves that the child was able to analyze the phrase correctly. The German language does not use a fixed adverb to reinforce "da". The English idiom made an impression by its usefulness and was unhesitatingly reproduced in hybrid form. *Way* was combined monolingually with *up* and *down* from 1;7 and 1;10, in faithful imitation of a common colloquial idiom. In *way up high* 1;11, the whole phrase *way up* may be considered a reinforcement of *high.* The fact that the function of *way* was understood can be gathered from its use with two different words (with *down* three months later than with *up*) and from the retention of the glottal stop preceding *up*, contrary to the presentation. Hildegard's use of the adverb of degree *too* illustrates neatly how such unstressed pretonic words gradually stepped into the range of observation. Before 1;10 it was always omitted before "big" and "much" when the meaning of the utterance clearly implied it (examples 1;8–9 in vol. 1). At 1;10 she learned to add it before "much", "hot", "big" and other adjectives.

All was by far the most common adverb used as a secondary syntactic element. It was also the earliest to be learned: 1;7 *all sticky;* 1;8 *all wet;* 1;10 *all nass, all dry, all gone;* 1;11 *all through, all broken to pieces. All*

---

[88] Stern (p. 279) states that prepositions are one of the latest parts of speech, and that the first examples occur almost never before the end of the second year, sometimes as late as 2;6 or later. Most observers agree: Sully p. 182 (third year); Bloch (1924) pp. 32–34 (absent third year, while relationships already implied; but "avec" from 2;6 for his three children; cf. earlier occurrences of prepositions noted by Decroly p. 208 f.); Preyer p. 168 (from 2;3, first imitatively, then independently); Bergmann p. 241 ff. (girl 2;11, boy 4; pet preposition "in", which serves for all prepositions); Guillaume p. 216 (missing at first, although spatial relations are understood and expressed early; then misuse, exchange; finally clumsy handling at age 2–3); Decroly pp. 207–209; Ament p. 171 (first preposition, "zu", at 2;11). Some observers (like Ament) do not distinguish between prepositions and adverbs or separated verbal prefixes. Smith (1933, p. 188) found that "at two years, 42 per cent of the infinitive signs and 18 per cent of other prepositions were omitted" by 220 children; but the observation is not worth much, because "at two years" means in this study 1;6–2;5. Gheorgov (pp. 312 ff. and 411 ff.) observed prepositions to appear rarely at the end of the second year. A few observers, however, record them earlier: O'Shea (1;7); Bohn p. 585 (none before 1;6; then seven in one month); Kenyeres p. 202 (early, 1;5–8; in Hungarian, prepositions are really suffixes; the type of the standard language makes a difference, of course); cf. Tögel (1;10) and Pavlovitch (1;9) (Decroly p. 207 f.)

right 1;8 belongs here from the point of view of standard syntax; but it was imitated as a fixed unit.

The only adverbial element used in this function which was based on a standard prepositional phrase was *to pieces* in the last example of 1;11. It lost the preposition, of course. Although the expression was a direct quotation from a story, the word-order was garbled. The child's version was *all piece broke*. This might mean that the adverbial element was placed analogically in the same position as simple adverbs in this function. At any rate it reveals that the construction was still unfamiliar.

No in *no mehr* 1;9, Hildegard's form for English "no more", might be called an adverb of degree modifying *mehr*. Its semantic value is the same as that of "not" (554), but its attraction to the following word makes it here a secondary adverb.

558. Adjectives were also used in secondary function, as attributive adjectives. The first example is *mehr* at 1;6, one month earlier than the first secondary adverb. She had said *mehr* (and ephemerally *more*) since 1;5 in one-word form. It was rather natural that she soon extended the meaning from "more to eat" to "another ball" and other usages which often did not have the sanction of the standard languages. Then it became often necessary to specify to what the wish applied, and this was done by adding a noun of specification: 1;6 *mehr A-a, mehr Ball;* 1;8 *mehr light, mehr Baby;* 1;9 *mehr milk*. It is not certain that the word formed a close enough unit with the following one to be called an attributive adjective. Perhaps it remained an adverb of quantity, even in the extended meaning "another", which standard grammar would certainly call an adjective.

The next example, *arme* 1;7 in combinations like *Armer Wauwau!* (*Der*) *arme Mann!*, was used rather definitely as an attributive adjective. They were emotional exclamations, in which the adjective consisted of a single vowel just like the interjection *oh* 1;0–7. Still, it was never used alone; the exclamations had the same structure as the standard models, and the variability of the noun in them shows that the structure was understood. The adjective, however, hardly deserves the designation of a descriptive adjective. These were not learned, in attributive function, until much later.

The other examples of 1;7 concern the possessive adjective *my, mein*. The word had been learned one month earlier as a one-word utterance, as a game signal rather than a possessive pronoun (559). The idea of possession, however, developed rapidly, and a noun indicating a thing was added to it: *mein Ball, my stocking*. At first, level stress sometimes betrayed the emotional origin of the possessive, but rather quickly it became a real adjective, used unemotionally and paralleled by nouns in possessive functions (*June's dolly* 1;8).[89]

---

[89] At 1;8 one of Egger's children (p. 46 f.) did not even understand the shifting reference of "my"; at 1;9 he did. Egger found possessives used correctly in gen-

The next month brought the demonstrative adjective *this*, which was at once used frequently, earlier and more frequently than the corresponding demonstrative pronoun. The other adjective used several times at 1;8 was *big*. I have shown (518) that its meaning was emotional rather than intellectual; it was not clearly a descriptive adjective (although I thought it was the first one at the time and so designated it in the diary). It was always used as an adjective preceding a noun, however. There were several more instances of *big*, with equally vague meaning, at 1;9. Otherwise this month brought no progress.

At 1;10, in addition to more examples of *my* and *this*, there was *poor*, which took the place of the German synonym *arme*, still only in compassionate exclamations, and *dicken* in the stereotype phrase *dicken Bauch*. The meaning and descriptive character of *dicken* was so vague that it can be called non-existent; but its syntactic function of an attributive adjective began to become clear to the child; she doubled it in one instance.

It was not until 1;11 that descriptive adjectives in attributive position became really alive, much later than stressed predicative adjectives (549): *nice cake, new hat, pretty dress, pretty coat* (with child-etymological application of the new pattern to the misunderstood "petticoat"); also *Papa dear, Mama dear* in close imitation of a less common standard pattern, for the time being only with these two names. *Naughty* occurred only in a scolding exclamation, but was a fully understood adjective, which was also used in predicative function. The adjective function of *no* in *no book, no A-a* was less clear; it was not yet well separated from the adverb *no*. The limiting adjectives *this* and *my* and the emotive *big*, only slightly more intellectualized, continued to be used. The indefinite numeral *all* was added to the list: *all babies, all balls*.[90]

The first element of compound nouns resembles the attributive adjective in its function. A sharp boundary line cannot be drawn. Hildegard used many of them, imitatively and independently. Examples are: 1;9 *baby-bottle, oil-spoon;* 1;10 *Auto noise;* 1;11 *A-a paper, egg-ball, Ei ball, choo-choo train.*

Articles were not used at all during the first two years. Their slight semantic and syntactic value[91] and their subordination in stress did not yet allow them to engage the child's attention. Even when quoting from a nursery rhyme, Hildegard omitted the articles in *This (is the) church* and *Open (the) door* 1;10–11. The few instances of the indefinite article

---

eral about 2;0, at the same time as personal pronouns. Ament (p. 168) records "mein" for E 1;8.

[90] Treitel (p. 345) assigns adjectives to the third or fourth year of life. Stern's chapter on adjectives (pp. 254–261) deals mostly with predicative adjectives.

[91] Cf. Grégoire p. 240. He calls attention to the fact that some standard languages do not use articles.

a mentioned in the Vocabulary are so doubtful that they can be disregarded. (Hildegard began to learn *a* at 2;1; but even then she used it rarely.) The lateness of attributive adjectives was charged to their pretonic position (476); this argument applies to the unstressed articles with even greater force.[92]

559. The use of nouns and pronouns in varying functions has been analyzed in sections 543 f. and 547 f. A glance was thrown at the types of nouns used (especially 543 f.). A word remains to be said about the types of pronouns which the child learned.[93]

Two personal pronouns, subject and object, appeared at 1;5 in the game cue *I see you*: but the sentence was imitated mechanically, without syntactic analysis, and remained unproductive for the learning of personal pronouns. *I* in isolation was also acquired at 1;5, but was nothing but a mechanical device to register a wish until 1;9.[94] When the

---

[92] Children differ greatly in the use of articles. Karla said *Ring the bell* M 1;11 sometimes with, sometimes without the article. She said *want a . . .* as a two-syllable form; but it was stereotyped and used where it did not agree with the standard practice: (*I*) *want a candy* E 1;11 instead of "I want candy" or "I want a piece of candy". A neighbor boy, age 1;6, playing with Hildegard, age 1;11, put ˀə before every noun. Talking about the same object, he would say "a bug" (or "the bug") and she would say "bug". Sully (p. 182) assigns the definite article to the third year. Smith (1933, p. 187), in statistics covering the intolerably wide range 1;6–2;5, states that 70% of the articles were omitted. Other languages are not easily comparable to English because the articles have often a little more phonetic weight. The time when articles began is given as 1;9 by Ament p. 171; as 1;11 by Grégoire p. 190; as 2;2–3 by Preyer pp. 164–168; as 2;8 by Cohen p. 120; as age 4 by Bergmann p. 243; cf. Decroly p. 210 f. Bulgarian, with articles as suffixes (Gheorgov pp. 273 ff., 373), is not comparable at all.

[93] For pronouns in general, cf. Decroly pp. 200–207, Gheorgov pp. 284 ff. and 385 ff., and Goodenough.

[94] This consideration shows that caution must be used in comparing the time when different children acquire the personal pronoun. 1;5 would be very early, but 1;10 is normal. Sully (p. 178 ff.) is too conservative. He establishes the first half of the third year as the time of the learning of "I" in favorable cases, considers 2;0–3 as normal, 2;5 as slow, and 1;8 as precocious, but registers one case as early as 1;4. Acquisition of "I" is reported for 1;7 by Idelberger (Gheorgov 1905, p. 392 ff.), by Stern (p. 273) for his third child, and by Gheorgov (1905, p. 359) for his second son, in spite of the fact that Bulgarian does not often use the pronoun with verbs. The month was 1;9 in the case studied by Nice. Bohn (p. 585) finds, surprisingly, that the girl whom he observed learned no less than six personal pronouns at 1;9, as many as "during all her previous life". The month was 1;10 for Cooley and Deville (Gheorgov 1905, p. 392 ff.); 1;11 for Gheorgov's first son and for Hogan (Gheorgov 1905, p. 392 ff.); 2;0 for Egger (p. 46 f.), Oltuszewski (Gheorgov 1905, p. 392 ff.), and Stern's second child (p. 293; forerunners 1;7 and 1;10); 2;1 for Ament (p. 167; ephemerally 1;8) and Stern's first child (p. 273; a single instance 1;10); 2;5 for Lindner (Preyer p. 244); 2;4–7 for Preyer (pp. 171–180); first half of third year for Trettien (p. 134); 2;5–8 for von Taube (Preyer p. 270; preceded by misuse of "ich" for "you" at 2;1–2, p. 268). Stern tabulates the findings of the older literature (pp. 275 and 277), with emphasis on the differences between first-born and younger children.

pronoun of the first person was really learned at 1;10, it did not take the form of standard *I*, but was based on *my*. *I* was learned at 1;11, in part still in a mechanical use, in the wish formula *I do*, but also in real sentences (*I spiel this*), rarely. (*I*, also still *my*, before verbs became more frequent at 2;1.) The pronoun "you" was not learned at all, either as a subject (until 2;1, and then only in the least regular standard way, with imperatives)[95] or as an object. The impersonal pronoun "es", "it" did not occur, except in the mechanically imitated sentence *Da ist es* *1;4. Its omission was sometimes striking, as in *Spiel house, knock (it) down* 1;11. Its place was sometimes taken by the more emphatic *this*. No other personal pronoun occurred. The pretonic subject pronoun of the third person before verbs[96] was omitted (476). The objective case of the first person pronoun, *me*, was learned at 1;11, but it was not its only form. Very often the form of the possessive, *my*, *mine*, took the place of the object and even more commonly that of the subject. It was the first form of the subject pronoun at 1;10 and remained more frequent than *I* during 1;11. From 1;10 it was used even before verbs.[97]

There is one instance in which the child used her name in place of a personal pronoun: *Katz, where Hildegard?* 1;11; but it was a fixed cue in a hiding game, quoted from me. Otherwise she was more circumspect than her parents in avoiding this misuse of names. (Another instance at 2;0 was followed immediately by a sentence with a better pronoun form: *Mama bite Hildegard, my naughty*.)[98] She never used "baby" in

---

[95] Most children learn the first person before the second, but exceptions occur, cf. Sully p. 178 ff., Trettien p. 134. Because of the shifting reference of pronouns, confusion between the first and second persons is often reported, cf. Bohn p. 585, Ament p. 167, Preyer pp. 268, 270 (von Taube case 2;2-8). No such confusion occurred in Hildegard's language, but Karla had difficulty with *you*.

[96] Cohen (p. 124) makes a distinction between heavy detached pronouns and short subject pronouns, linking the latter with verbal inflections. This distinction is clearer in standard French than in English and German, but applies also to the latter languages on account of stress conditions. Hildegard omitted the pretonic subject pronoun of the first person only rarely; (*I*) *bite Papa* 1;11 is the only example. There is no case like Karla's (*I*) *want a (piece of) candy* E 1;11.

[97] Kainz (p. 8) calls "das ungeschiedene Durcheinanderrinnen von Personal- und Possessivpronomen" a typical early condition, ontogenetically and phylogenetically. O'Shea (p. 80 f.), who observed several children (six?), found *my* to be used before *I* in every case. Sully (p. 181) emphasizes in the same connection that old forms are dropped gradually, continue to be used along with the new, improved forms, like Hildegard's *my* and *I* at 1;11. He reports a case of the opposite procedure, "me" used for "mine", and "us" for "ours". This seems to be exceptional. It did not occur in Hildegard's speech. "Me" is sometimes used before "I" (Sully p. 178 ff.). Preyer (pp. 171, 176, 180) reports "mir" 2;4-5 and "mich" 2;6 before "ich" 2;7. "My" instead of "I" occurs also in Pidgin English (Jespersen, p. 224).

[98] Karla used her name instead of "I" at M 1;11: (*May*) *Karla* (*get*) *all dirty? Oh no!* Gale's son (p. 47) used "Sammy" 1057 times in one day. Preyer's son used "Axel" instead of "ich" 2;3-6, both forms 2;7 and later (pp. 167, 171, 176, 180, 183). For name and pronoun, cf. Stern p. 274.

place of a pronoun to designate herself, because the adults did not do so.[99]

Mine as a possessive pronoun was learned at 1;6, at first as a game cue, but soon as a real possessive, from 1;9 in sentences of more than one word. Since Hildegard did not even separate *I* and *mine*, there was of course no separation of the pronoun *mine* from the adjective *my* (558). The form was the same for both, the final consonant of *mine* not being pronounced. The German forms *mein*, *meine*, and *meins* occurred ephemerally 1;7 and 1;11 as echoes, prematurely with representation of the sounds following the diphthong, but the first two for the adjective as well as the pronoun. No other possessive was acquired. ("Your" was missing until 2;1,[100] and so was "yours".) The ownership of other persons was indicated by means of names, nearly always without the standard possessive inflection (548).[101]

The only standard demonstrative pronoun was *this* 1;8. *That* was used only one day at 1;11 and discarded presumably as not sufficiently different in meaning. The demonstrative function was much older than 1;8; but before that time a primitive interjection and the adverbs *da* and *there* had been used, which are demonstratives, to be sure, but not pronouns. The functional difference in the child's language was not great, as the example *This (is a) big Buch, da!* at 1;9 shows. Yet, *this* was at once also employed as an adjective preceding a noun. Since Hildegard did not try to press *da* into the same function, we are justified in assuming that the standard meaning and functions of *this* were clear to her.

The indefinite pronoun *all* occurred only in the stereotype phrase *all aboard* 1;10 in the recital of a train trip. It cannot be assumed that it was analyzed as a pronoun.

---

[99] Other children use "baby" earlier than personal pronouns, cf. Sully p. 178 ff. The use of "baby" or a name instead of pronouns on the part of adults is due to the unconscious endeavor to spare the child the difficulty of shifters; cf. O'Shea p. 79, Preyer p. 268 (von Taube case) and p. 176, Stern p. 272. Several authors (e.g., Cooley, Gheorgov 1905, Trettien p. 134, Goodenough) connect the emergence of the pronoun of the first person with "a real advance towards the true self-consciousness". This consideration is much too mechanical. The use of "baby" or the child's name is psychologically no different from the use of the pronoun. In fact, it might well be argued that the self-centered attitude of the small child is more pronounced as long as no self-word is used, because nearly every utterance is related to the self as a matter of course and no need is felt to specify this reference. If the accent is on "consciousness", then the label goes too far. No real consciousness should be assumed. Sully's formulation (p. 180), "greater precision of the idea of 'self' ", is slightly better; but it is best to abstain from looking for philosophical implications; cf. Stern p. 271 f., Preyer p. 203.

[100] Ament (p. 168) records "dein" as late as E 2;9.

[101] Derivation of the possessive from the personal pronoun is reported occasionally; "she's" (Sully p. 181), "ichs" (Neugebauer 1915, p. 299; beginning of third year). Hildegard never used such analogical forms. Gheorgov's first son (p. 292) learned the first possessive pronoun at 2;7, his second son (p. 385 ff.) at 1;9.

Interrogative pronouns did not occur at all (until 2;1, when *what* was learned; cf. **530, 554**).

560. This leads us to a backward glance over the process of learning to formulate questions. We have seen that, from the one-word stage to the end of the second year, the intonation of the question was frequently used by the child to indicate a wish or request, and that, less frequently, factual questions of various types were also asked, likewise from the one-word stage on.

Interrogative intonation for the purpose of uttering a request for permission was used with single-word utterances from 1;3 to 1;8 (**513**). Two-word requests of the same type occurred from 1;8, first in the form of two related one-word questions, but also at once in the form of two words with a unified interrogative intonation (**521**). This form continued to 1;11. During the last month, three-word questions of the same character were uttered. One request consisted of three words as early as 1;8; but the three words then had still each its own interrogative intonation (**529**). All these questions were quite incomplete in comparison with standard formulations. None of them contained the explicit words "May I" or "Will you", which would be present in the nearest standard equivalent of wish questions. Hildegard did not learn modal auxiliaries in the first two years; but the personal pronoun subject was also suppressed. It occurred in a single example, *I spiel Nackedei?* 1;11. Once, in *Papa on me?* 1;11, the person to whom the request was addressed was named; but the name should be interpreted as a vocative (**529**).

With regard to factual questions, or questions in which the wish element did not predominate, it is a striking observation that Hildegard used practically no naming questions at all, questions of the type, "What is this?", "What do you call this?", questions which would have been very helpful in the process of learning to speak (**514, 530**).[102] The only questions which might be so interpreted were early in the one word stage, 1;5, and the words involved, *there* and *?ə*, were of an interjectional type and therefore no convincing bearers of intellectual meanings (**514**). No such questions were asked with two or more words, and the interrogative *what* did not emerge in any function until 2;1.[103]

Questions about place began at 1;6 in one-word form. The child would say *Mama* or the name of another person with interrogative intonation (**514**). The most natural interpretation is "Where is Mama?" Syntacti-

---

[102] Neugebauer (p. 145) reports such a question as the first question at 1;7. Hildegard began to ask such questions in profusion at 2;2 (**681**).

[103] Karla asked *What's that?* wa 'tæt? ephemerally at E 1;11, often during the first quarter of the third year. The same question, wa dɛ·t?, was used incessantly by Hildegard at 2;2 (**690**). Preyer (p. 184) records the first "was" at 2;6, not in a naming question, Snyder (p. 415) the first "what" at 2;8. Lindner observed a clear naming question, but without the interrogative, at 1;7, the first "was" at 1;9 (Preyer p. 244).

cally these utterances were amorphous,[104] but the intended meaning was clear, particularly in utterances of more than one word like *Mama? by-by?* 1;6 (522) and *Marion? Dodo? Da!* 1;9 (532), in which the addition confirmed the reference to place. At 1;11, finally, the interrogative adverb *where* was expressed (530).[105] In one example (540), a question with *where* was followed by an answer with *da* in parallel structure. This amounted to an application of the same question-and-answer pattern as in the earlier examples, but now in more explicit form. All place questions were static, pattern "Where is . . .", with the possible exception of *Mama? by-by?* Even here, the meaning may not be "Did Mama go out?", but "Is Mama gone?". *By-by* was too vague in meaning to prove a dynamic implication.[106]

Questions for confirmation[107] were rare. There are three instances, two in one-word form (514) and one in two-word form (522), scattered from 1;8 to 1;11. All amounted to "Is that what you mean?"

Questions which call for the answer "yes" or "no" were understood by Hildegard at 1;8 and answered quite haphazardly by either (522). She did not formulate such questions herself until 1;11 (530, 537). A forerunner of this type of question was the practice at 1;8 of asking questions and answering them herself: *This hat? Ja. This hat? No* (540). The purpose was exercise in the newly understood pattern, which took three months to be established as a functional device in real life situations.

The diary states for 1;11 that the child understood only questions referring to fact or to place, not those referring to time or cause or reason. Correspondingly she asked questions about facts and questions with *where*, never a question about time,[108] and *why* only as a single word for a few days at 1;10. *Why* was dropped again because it was not yet really understood (514).[109] (Three interrogatives were used at 2;1, *what*, *where*, and *why*. *Where* was still the most frequent one.)[110]

---

[104] Guillaume p. 216: "Where" missing 1;10, although space relations were understood early.

[105] Preyer (pp. 169–178): "Where" 2;3, the only interrogative until 2;6; Neugebauer (p. 146) E 1;8.

[106] Lindner found no semantic distinction between "wo" and "wohin" as late as the fourth year (Preyer p. 244).

[107] "Tentative statements", cf. Snyder p. 414.

[108] Preyer p. 184: "When" at end of third year, the last of the common interrogatives; Neugebauer p. 152: isolated time question E 2;5.

[109] Gheorgov's sons learned questions with "where" at 1;10, factual questions at 1;11, but with omission of the characteristic Bulgarian interrogative particle. "Why" is recorded for E 2;9 by Preyer (p. 183), for 2;4 by Neugebauer (p. 149), and assigned to the beginning of the third year by Decroly (p. 141). Concerning the different meanings of "why", cf. Sully p. 80, Decroly pp. 141–145.

[110] The first question of any kind is recorded, from observation and from the literature, for 1;7 by Neugebauer p. 145 (literature 1;1–1;11); for 1;10–2;3, generally third year, by Sully p. 75; for 2;3 by Preyer p. 169; for 2;5 by Ament p. 172.

561. Before we leave the simple sentence, a few remarks should be made about the word-order. On the whole, the words of Hildegard's brief sentences were arranged as in the standard languages.[111] The utterances in which the word-order differed from that which the adult speaker considers normal were exceptional.

Big June's dolly 1;8 looks as if it meant "June's big dolly". Actually, however, as explained in the Vocabulary under *big*, this word was not yet an adjective with an intellectual meaning, but a mere emotive. As such it did not need to follow the word-order rules for attributive adjectives. *Dicken Bauch wasch(en)* 1;10 is open to several interpretations (527). If the verb was not an imperative, but either an infinitive in the same function or an infinitive as complement of a suppressed modal auxiliary, the word-order corresponds to standard German practice. German, to be sure, was no longer the model for her speech in the last two months; but the possibility of a German pattern cannot be ruled out entirely. Otherwise, the placement of the object in first position must be explained as due to the desire to give the "psychological subject", the item of dominating interest, an emphatic position.

The latter is the explanation for most examples of irregular word-order. It is often observed in child-language.[112] *My shoe brush* 1;10, if it meant "Brush my show", is exactly parallel. So is *Mama wake up* 1;10, *Mama* being the object, not a vocative: "I am going to wake up Mama". The imperatives *Coat button* and *Nose blow* 1;11 are easily explained in the same manner. The fact that the addition of an object to the verb was not yet a fully familiar pattern (519, 527, 544) helps to account for the freedom of the word-order. *Dress me* was never expressed

---

Major (p. 281 f.) designates the last of 14 stages of language learning in the first three years as the questioning period. Sully (p. 75) assigns the advent of the questioning age also to the end of the third year, but states that the true age of inquisitiveness, with a rapid fire of questions, comes in the fourth year. This agrees with my experience with Karla, who has always asked questions much more freely than Hildegard. Ament (p. 172) makes the stage of exasperating questioning begin with the first question 2;5, undoubtedly overlooking a gap between the two stages. Boyd (p. 183) finds that very few questions are asked at age 2, but more than by adults at ages 3–8. For specialized articles on questions, cf. Bohn (1916), Davis, Lewis (1938), Neugebauer, Wallon.

[111] Cf. Stern p. 218. Moore (p. 135) even claims that the words were arranged "almost invariably in the proper sequence", but states an exception of doubtful validity for the prepositions "in" and "on", which were at first placed at the end. They may not have been prepositions. Her example "Monkey glasses on" would seem to be equivalent to "has glasses on"; but cf. Stern p. 218.

[112] Cf. Ament pp. 164, 173, Pavlovitch p. 151, Stern pp. 220–224 ("vorauseilende Aufmerksamkeit", p. 219), Boyd p. 189 (start with psychological subject frequent at age 2 and again at age 5). It should be noted that the child merely makes a freer use of a principle which operates with restrictions in the standard languages, in German more freely than in English, and in French more liberally than in either German or English, if we think of its regularized application to French questions with a noun subject.

with the same inversion. This confirms the explanation, because the reference to herself was taken as a matter of course by the child. The center of interest was the desired act. The addition of the personal reference had seemed superfluous earlier, and was now performed only in progressing adherence to a conventional pattern. *Papa, dies häng up* 1;11 placed the object *dies* in the emphatic position which is quite regular in German and possible in English, except with an imperative. At this stage the child had, of course, not learned to make such fine discriminations. In a few instances, the child combined the psychological word-order with the regular word-order by expressing an object twice:[113] *Stockings! Mama hangs up stockings; Wauwau! Meow bites Wauwau* 1;11. In the last example, a comment when she heard a dog barking, *meow* was thought to be the object. The word-order could then not be explained on the same basis, because obviously the interest was centered on *Wauwau*. But then, perhaps, only adults would assume that the dog must be biting a cat. Hildegard's idea may well have been that a cat was biting the dog, which made him bark.

There are only a few examples which cannot readily be explained by this psychological principle. *This on beads* 1;11, although said without a pause, doubtless meant "(Put) this on, (namely the) beads" (a chain of beads, therefore psychologically a singular); the word-order is then normal. *All pieces broken* 1;11, the climax of a story recapitulated in the form of question and answer, is not so easy to explain. Being based directly on the presentation, "all broken to pieces", the deviation in word-order is surprising. Perhaps the specification "to pieces" added to the familiar "broken" pushed itself into the foreground of her attention (cf. also 557). *Mama fixes Bett my* 1;11 looks like very irregular word-order if *my* is taken at face value; but since it often took the place of "I" and "me", the interpretation "for me" is plausible; this removes the irregularity of the word-order. *Mama sh mehr*, immediately corrected to *Mama mehr sh*, 1;11, seems to point to a feeling of uncertainty about the correct word-order. The example is difficult to judge. Although the rough meaning was clear, one cannot be sure which standard syntactic construction was the basis of the utterance. It may be that Hildegard used first the pattern for a statement of fact, "Mama schläft mehr", and then improved the utterance by using the pattern with a modal auxiliary expressing intention, "Mama will mehr schlafen", but with omission of the modal as always (531). The other possibility is that a shift from English to German syntax was involved, from "Mama (wants to) sleep more" to "Mama (will) mehr schlafen". Both explanations are based on the assumption that the child had assimilated the standard word-order in the patterns involved. It must be admitted that

---

[113] This device was frequent in Karla's speech for a while, 2;5, with adverbial expressions of time; cf. **984**.

the assumption is gratuitous. Hildegard may actually have been groping for an arrangement which was not stabilized in her memory. The assumption was induced by the fact that there were so few instances of irregular word-order. *Ja, Mama da bite* 1;11 (**532**) shows a position of the adverb which does not agree with the English pattern. The remark was an answer to a German question which meant "Have you been naughty?" It is conceivable that she used the German word-order of "Mama hat mich da geschlagen". One should be cautious, however, about assuming German patterns at the end of the second year, when Hildegard's language was developing energetically along English lines. Although the important point of the cheerfully volunteered information would seem to be the fact that her mother had punished her with a slap, it is entirely possible that the place in which the slap had been applied, underlined by the gesture of repeating the impressive performance, was more important to the child. This would bring the example in line with the psychological word-order discussed above. The fact that *da* did not precede the subject *Mama* might be taken as a compromise between psychological and standard word-order.

Watch bake cake Mama 1;11 shows unsuccessful arrangement of words in a new syntactic pattern. The sentence may be considered a fusion of two ideas, "I want to watch Mama" and "I want to watch the baking of a cake". This holds true, probably, for the standard construction as well; but it is not certain that the child's version resulted from imitation of the standard pattern, "Watch Mama bake a cake". At any rate, the standard word-order was not achieved. Very soon, however, this pattern fell in line with the corresponding standard one (**563**).[114]

562. Compound sentences existed only rudimentarily. Even if one counts sentences with two subjects or two objects as compound sentences, there are practically no examples.[115] During the preparatory

---

[114] For word-order in general, cf. Stern's sensible chapter, pp. 217–224. The arbitrariness of early word-order is emphasized by Gheorgov, by Jespersen p. 134 f. ("haphazard order"; but his examples seem to show regular or psychological sequence), by O'Shea p. 114 ("to a certain extent apparently a matter of chance"), by Deville vol. 24, p. 132 (good examples, some of which show psychological word-order clearly), by Bloch (1924) pp. 21, 41 ff. ("tout à fait arbitraire" at the stage of the two-word sentence), by Decroly pp. 158–161 (largely based on Bloch), by Sully p. 173. Bloch (p. 41 ff.) and Decroly (pp. 162–165, based on Stern) recognize that emphasis or emotional interest sometimes determine the irregular word-order. At times it is not the child's word-order but the adult's interpretation which is arbitrary. "Did Alec choke an apple?", reported by Sully for a boy at 2;3, may not mean "Did an apple choke Alec?" but "Did Alec choke on an apple?" His remark that children's arrangements of words "might suggest that our English order is not in certain cases the most natural one" shows that he dimly perceives the psychological principle of position.

[115] Decroly (p. 169) finds such in the literature as early as 1;6, but erroneously; cf. Stern p. 203, where the same example from Tögel is assigned not to 1;6 but to 1;1; this, in turn, is a misprint; in Stern's third edition (p. 186) the time is 1;11,

stage when two or more coördinated one-word sentences were uttered, they sometimes stood in a relation which the standard language would express by means of the conjunction "and". Hildegard said, for instance: *Marion? Dodo?* 1;6, which meant "Where are Marion and Dodo?" Sometimes she even added the name of her third cousin in coördination. Or she said *Mama? Papa?* 1;8, indicating by a gesture that she wanted both of us to come along. Although there was semantic coördination, it would not be justifiable to claim syntactic coördination. The paraphrase might just as well be "Where is Marion? Where is Dodo?" in the first case, and "Mama, will you come along? Papa, will you come along?" in the second. She came a little closer to syntactic coördination in examples like *Marion? Dodo? away!* 1;6 and *Marion? Dodo? da!* 1;9. The intonation given to each subject separately makes the inference inescapable, however, that no formal coördination had been achieved. *Marion—Joey—away* occurred without interrogative intonation 1;8, but it is not probable that the syntactic situation was different.

Eventually the subject and the object consisted often of two words, but never of two coördinated words (**543 f.**)

There are other instances in which two sentences separately expressed were semantically related. The absence of conjunctions makes it impossible to decide whether coördination on standard models was meant or the two sentences were placed side by side asyndetically. *My room, Taschentuch?* 1;11 consisted of two imperfectly formulated sentences. The meaning was "Shall I go to my room and get a handkerchief?" The unified intonation binding the whole utterance together into a single question makes it likely that we are here facing a real compound sentence, however defective its formal expression may be. Coördination is more likely than subordination ("to get"). *Spiel house, knock down* 1;11 may be considered as coördinated because the utterance linked together two successive acts of the game with building blocks which she was planning, on the pattern, "I want to play (build a) house and then knock it down". In *Ring, Mama* (**523**) and *Mary Alice eat, home* (**531**) 1;11, the connection between the two rudimentary clauses is so loose that one can hardly speak of syntactic coördination.

Antithetic statements (**540**) are more relevant, because the contrast expressed in them amounts to coördination with the conjunction "but", which was, however, omitted. In some of the earliest examples, like

---

which is correct, as the summary statement, "toward the end of the second year", in both Stern and Decroly confirms. The use of a double subject or object is not an elementary, but an advanced stage of syntax. At first the child will rather make a series of parallel statements, repeating the verb in each. Bloch (1924, pp. 37–39) describes this practice as typical of the middle of the third year, finds it still partly followed at 3;6, and explains it by the assumption that the child does not know how to generalize. Gheorgov makes the same observation. He finds the earliest conjunction, "and", first used between two complete sentences, at 2;0 and 1;10 respectively (pp. 319 ff., 415 ff.).

This hat? Ja. This hat? No 1;8, the contrast was present semantically, but not formally; the standard pattern, "I want to put on this hat, but not this hat" (choosing between two hats) was not yet the mold for expressing the idea; a more primitive form was chosen, in this example and others at the same time, to practice contrasts. In *Miau da, Miau not da* 1;11 the correlation was more intimate. It is clearest when the negative precedes: *No Mama's stocking, here Mama's stocking* 1;9; in such examples the adult would introduce the second statement by "but". The fact often observed that in the language of many children the negative statement stands in first place in antithetic couples,[116] means that these children were progressing toward compound sentences.

A different category consists of two sentences in which two things are distinguished, but the same statement is made about both of them (**538**): *This (shoe is) Dodo's, this (shoe is) Dodo's* 1;8; *This (is a) brush, this (is a) brush* 1;8. In such cases, "and" is the conjunction understood. (*This is) Dada's hat, this (one is) mine* 1;10 is intermediate between the two categories; either "and" or "but" would be fitting conjunctions. The close coördination between the two parts of these utterances was formally expressed by means of a contrasting intonation (**489**).

There is a single instance of an incomplete compound sentence with two objects linked by an adverb or coördinating conjunction: (*The cat) drinks milk, (eats) crackers too* E 1;10. (*Too* was the first conjunction learned 2;0, **663**. *And* was acquired 2;4, at the same time as the first subordinating conjunction, **700 f.**)[117]

563. There is even less to say about complex sentences. Hildegard did not achieve subordination of one clause to another. There is no point in examining utterances consisting of two or more sentences to see whether one of them is logically subordinated to another. Even the standard language, particularly in its colloquial form, often uses a paratactic construction in such a situation, that is, it places two sentences side by side, syndetically or asyndetically, leaving the logical relationship between them to be inferred by the listener. In other words, logical subordination need not be expressed by syntactic subordination. It would be futile to paraphrase *Ring, Mama* 1;11 by "This is a ring which Mama gave me" and claim subordination of the second idea. The paratactic paraphrase, "This is a ring; Mama gave it to me" describes the situation better, and even it represents a more elaborate

---

[116] Cf. Stern p. 207. He treats "chains of sentences" linked by their meaning as a step from simple to compound sentences, but does not make finer distinctions between successive independent sentences and the beginnings of coördination. Velten (p. 284) deals with a less mechanical type of contrasting statements built on the same pattern as a device for acquisition of vocabulary.

[117] Ament p. 171: "und" 2;9, a few days before the first subordinating conjunctions. O'Shea (p. 72) is "confident" that no conjunctions besides "and" were used before the fifth year. For other literature on conjunctions, cf. note to **555**. "Too" is usually called an adverb, but sometimes a conjunction in this use. Both classifications are justifiable.

analysis than is likely to have been present in the child's mind. *Mary Alice home, eat* 1;11 would naturally be paraphrased by "M.A. went home to eat", in which the infinitive is an abridged subordinate clause. The pause in the utterance makes the interpretation suspicious; *home* and *eat* were coördinated by the child: "M.A. went home; she is supposed to eat"; this is not even a compound sentence, but a set of two syntactically unconnected sentences (562), just like the variant *M.A. eat, home* 1;11, "M.A. must eat; she went home." *My room, Taschentuch?* 1;11 was really a compound sentence (562); as is commonly done in the colloquial standard, the second idea was not subordinated ("to get . . ."), but coördinated ("and get a handkerchief").

In two examples with the verb *ask* 1;11, it is probable that subordination was beginning to develop: *Ask Papa on* (528) and *Ask Mama this aus* (536). These utterances were made fluently, without a pause, and a paraphrase with a paratactic pattern cannot be made. The idea was "I am going to ask Papa to put this on", "I am going to ask Mama to take this off".

By the fact that the object of the verb *ask* was at the same time the subject of the subordinated verb, which, to be sure, was expressed only rudimentarily, this construction leads forward to the pattern, "Watch him go", "I want him to come", which is familiar from Latin (particularly in its use for indirect statements), common in English, and in restricted use in German. Hildegard learned it from English models, first with the verb *watch*. The only example before the two-year limit is *Watch bake cake Mama* 1;11, in which the word-order was not yet correct (561). (At 2;1, however, this construction became correct and frequent, always with the verb *watch;* the object was usually, but not always, *me;* 667). This pattern is easy because the standard dispenses with a formal expression of subordination. It is therefore suitable as a first approach to the complex sentence. In view of the fact that it was developing, it is possible to interpret *Dolly ride buggy* 1;11 as "I want the dolly to ride in the buggy" (528), and conceivably *This dolly up Bett* 1;11 (536) as "I want this dolly to go up to bed."

No subordinating conjunction occurred. (The first one was *when* 2;4, in mumbled phonetic form, 701.)[118]

---

[118] Dependent clauses, with or without conjunctions or relatives, usually begin in the third year, sometimes later. Stern, in a tabulation p. 210 f., finds in the literature only two examples before the third year, and these concern clauses without a conjunction, the peculiar dependent word-order in German giving a clue to subordination. Cf. Decroly p. 170, Ament p. 171 ff. ("dass" and "weil" 2;9; Lindner "wenn" 2;2, "weil" 2;5), Bloch (1924) p. 35 f. ("quand" 2;9–3;6); Preyer p. 180 ("wo" 2;7), Bergmann p. 243 ("ob" omitted 4;3 and middle of fourth year respectively), Cornioley p. 45 (2;3), K. Bühler p. 236; also Geissler p. 29 f. (bilingual conditions). Piaget (1928, p. 2), studying the use of conjunctions by children between the ages of 3 and 9, thinks that they are not interested in logical justification before age 7 and therefore use juxtaposition (parataxis, coördination) before that time. He is too hasty in identifying logical thinking with its linguistic expression, but there is a germ of truth in his observation. For further literature on conjunctions, coördinating and subordinating, cf. note to 555.

Morphology of the First Two Years

564. During the discussion of the development of syntax, side-glances have occasionally been cast at formal expressions of syntactic relationships by means of inflections or endings. Very few such formal signs existed. The accidence of Hildegard's language was rudimentary. Essentially her type of speech was isolating. Words were placed side by side without formal modifications, and the syntactic relationship between them had to be inferred by the listener.

This condition is reinforced by the fact that standard English has itself become partly isolating, and English was the mold of Hildegard's language during the later months, when inflections might have begun to develop. Yet English still has some inflections, and the German words which remained in her vocabulary might have shared in the fuller inflectional system of standard German.

It will be of interest to examine Hildegard's language as to its morphology, even though the results will be largely negative.

565. Before we go into details, we shall make a few general observations on the nature of morphological signs.

The fact that isolating languages, like Chinese, get along without formal indications of syntactic relationships, proves that they are not indispensable for the purposes of linguistic communication. The child, whose attention is at first drawn only to the major elements of the mechanism of communication, neglects the morphological devices for a considerable length of time. The elements affected by this neglect are not only morphological endings and other modifications of the word-stem, but also form-words, that is, small words like prepositions and auxiliary verbs used for the same purposes. They are subordinated in stress in the standard language because of their secondary importance, with the effect that semantic and phonetic reasons coincide in keeping the child's attention away from them.

Because of a growing conformation to the adults' language, which imposes itself relentlessly as an ideal on the child's speech, these formal elements are eventually added to the child-language as a refinement in clarity.[1]

This process is normally just beginning at the turn to the third year.[2]

---

[1] Nausester has devoted three treatises to his thesis that this refinement is a luxury as far as the spoken language is concerned. He advocates a stylistic model related to child-language and its idealized form, poetic language (1904, p. 35). Both types of language avoid constructions in which grammatical endings are of great importance (vol. 8, p. 232).

[2] Cf. Nausester (1906) p. 150 ff. Boyd (p. 190) states that grammatical inflections are known, but very often omitted at age 2, never at age 3, when mistakes are rare. K. Bühler (1926, p. 605) designates the acquisition of inflections, starting two to six months after the beginning of the stage of several words, as the last great step forward; conjugation, declension, and comparison begin almost simultaneously.

In fact, the absence of grammatical endings and stem-modifications contributes to the impossibility of distinguishing between classes of words in the earliest stage of speaking. In English, even the standard language often makes no formal distinction between nouns, verbs, and adjectives. In standard German the different word-classes are well differentiated by their endings. These endings, however, were regularly disregarded by the child.[3] Furthermore, syntactical distinctions between different forms of the verb were not marked by formal characteristics. In statements referring to the past, Hildegard used the same verb forms as in those referring to the present (586). In the case of weak verbs, the omission of the ending of the past tense, "-ed", might be charged to phonetic reasons (142). No such explanation fits strong verbs, and yet the child disregarded the standard change of the vowel to indicate tense distinctions with equal consistency.

566. Although the child does not use many formal signs of syntactic functions during the first two years, it is probable that, after the first stage of syntactically diffuse one-word utterances, the feeling for syntactic functions and for the discrimination between parts of speech grows clearer and clearer, as I have tried to show in the analysis of Hildegard's syntax.[4] As in the areas of vocabulary and sounds, it is reasonable to assume that the child progresses from a dim, diffuse perception of the material presented by the standard model to an ever clearer grasp of differences, from coarser contrasts to ever finer intermediate shades. The power of expression lags behind the understanding, until the full imitation of the model is eventually achieved. In the field of syntax, the morphological signs are the last stage, which in turn consists of a series of steps progressing from the learning of the most conspicuous and useful formal elements to the less essential ones.[5]

---

[3] Decroly p. 109: "Les flexions sont d'abord absentes; les substantifs sont au singulier (au nominatif dans les langues où il y a des déclinaisons), le verbe à l'infinitif, les adjectifs aussi sont sans déclinaison." This follows Stern p. 247. It cannot be decided with certainty whether Hildegard's monosyllabic German verb forms were in the pure stem-form, which is used in the standard imperative, or in the infinitive or present tense with phonetic omission of endings (151). In standard English most of these verb forms use the pure stem of the verb. Hildegard did not add the "-s" of the third person singular present. It is likely that in both languages only the stem-form as used in the important imperative impressed itself on the child. Cf. Delacroix p. 321 f. He quotes with approval from Cassirer, *Philosophie der symbolischen Formen*, p. 233: "ce n'est point 'Formlosigkeit', c'est 'Werden zur Form'." Descriptively this means nothing. The first stage is amorphous. The form develops later.

[4] Cohen p. 123 f.: "Il est vraisemblable que l'enfant distingue les catégories de mots même s'il est incapable d'exprimer cette distinction par des flexions". He makes the observation that nouns are commonly transferred to the function of actions, but verbs (and interjections) rarely designate things.

[5] K. Bühler (1922, p. 83) says about the acquisition of inflections: "Wir haben kaum die ersten Schritte in dies wundervolle Forschungsgebiet getan und warten

Unlike the learning of vocabulary and sounds, but like the learning of syntactical patterns, the acquisition of morphological elements proceeds not merely from imitation of tangible material presented directly and unchangingly in individual word units, but is subject to the grasping of a pattern, which is then applied to a large number of instances of parallel nature. To illustrate, when the child learns the word *cookie*, it imitates the word as a whole and at the same time each sound of which it is composed, progressing phonetically from a crude to a more faithful imitation. When, however, the z is added as a sign of the plural, this is not done for each noun individually by imitating the presentation *cookies* etc., but the child understands after a while that the added ending changes the function from singular to plural, and makes the addition independently from the presentation of individual plurals. Similarly, when the child realizes that verbs with the ending "-ed" refer to the past, he begins to add the same ending to many verbs for the same purpose. The child is then not imitating sequences of sounds, but a morphological pattern.[6]

That this is so is proved by the great number of examples in every child's speech in which the result is not sanctioned by standard usage. Many instances can be found in the Diary, particularly during the third year, when the learning of English inflections progressed rapidly; also later, when the process was repeated in the learning of German. The categories in the standard languages are not simple enough for the child to grasp at the beginning of the learning of inflections. There are several types of plural endings, especially in German, and several ways of forming the past tense. The child usually generalizes the most common device and extends its use to words in which the standard languages use a different pattern. The ability to distinguish between a variety of patterns belongs to a later stage of language learning.

Thus, some early instances of plural forms like *beads*, used also for the

---

auf den sprachwissenschaftlichen Fachmann, den Sprachvergleicher und Sprachtheoretiker, der mit dem weiten Blick des Historikers den biologisch-psychologischen Instinkt des Kinderforschers verbindet und die Sache mit sicherer Hand weiterführt." This challenge remains open. A study which restricts itself to the first two years and works predominantly with the comparatively amorphous English language cannot give the answers.

[6] The grasping of morphological and syntactic patterns is a task of enormous difficulty. The child is entitled to be presented with perfect models for imitation. Delacroix (1934, p. 6 f.) defends the use of nursery lingo, saying that it serves a useful purpose by linking the familiar (child speech) with the unfamiliar (adult speech). I would object that talking down to the child in his own forms does not help the child. He understands adult forms better than imitations of his own forms (cf. 681). Adapting vocabulary and grammar to the child's level of comprehension is one thing; using mutilated phonetic, morphological, and syntactic forms is quite another matter. It should not be indulged in to any considerable extent. Even with unmutilated adaptation the presentation should remain far ahead of the child's own stage; otherwise growth will be retarded.

singular, and of past tenses like *forgot*, for which no present form existed, prove that these forms were acquired by phonetic imitation and not by a grasp of a morphological device.[7] Conversely, the use of plural endings and past-tense endings attached to words which happen to operate with a different device in the standard, proves that the pattern is understood and that the form is not imitated as an individual unit.[8] All that remains to be learned is the restriction in the application of the chief pattern and the mastery of alternate patterns; this is a difficult process, to be sure, and takes years.

Some students see in such "false analogies" nothing but "errors" and imperfections, which they are, of course. Other observers justly emphasize that analogical formations show the child's ingenuity. Sully (p. 178) admires incorrect analogical forms, such as verbs with weak endings instead of strong ablaut formation, and says: "This last not only has the quality of originality, but shows the germ of a truly grammatical feeling for the general types or norms of the language." Karl Bühler (1926, p. 606) states that incorrect analogical formations show best the comprehension of structural principles.[9] Guillaume (p. 220) formulates the same conviction as follows: "Chose paradoxale, ce sont les fautes qui temoignent de la possession—incomplète—des lois de la langue."[10] Correspondingly, it has been found that retarded children have sometimes correcter speech than intelligent children because they lack the ability to operate with analogical abstractions.[11]

Such correctness is limited, of course, and impedes the further development of linguistic expression. Deduction of general patterns is needed for progress from phonetically imitated items of restricted usefulness to the development of a flexible instrument of expression able to serve more and more intricate purposes of communication. The mistakes which the language learner makes with the first steps into the realm of

---

[7] Guillaume (p. 220): "C'est un fait remarquable que l'enfant emploie depuis longtemps de nombreuses formes de verbes avant de commettre une seule faute; mais elles n'étaient correctes que parce qu'elles étaient des reproductions pures et simples; les fautes sont l'indice du début des constructions personelles; c'est seulement alors que commence au point de vue psychologique la véritable conjugaison." He records the first incorrect analogical inflection at 2;0.

[8] Cassirer (1944, p. 226) says concerning the use of incorrect analogical forms by the child: "In these he proves his ability to grasp the form of the language instead of merely reproducing its matter."

[9] Cf. also K. Bühler's book on child-development, p. 228. In spite of that, he does not accept Stern's tenet that the majority of forms are acquired by analogy. I disagree with him. Cf. Stern pp. 140 ff., 247–249; Nausester vol. 8, p. 224; Jespersen p. 128 f. Bergmann (p. 241 ff.) lists analogical verb forms 3;6–6;5.

[10] Tappolet's statement (p. 406) that the child is at the mercy ("der Spielball") of analogy does not do justice to the child's struggle. What he sees as a sign of impotence is the dawn of mastery.

[11] A. Collin, "L'enfance du débile intellectuel", Annales médico-psychologiques, 1919; cited by Delacroix (1930) p. 313, note 2.

morphological patterns are indeed an invaluable index of the growing powers of abstraction and the progress from fettered imitation to the freer handling of structural devices. The intellectual maturity needed for these first steps is normally not reached until the turn to the third year. The first signs of the awareness of morphological patterns in Hildegard's language before 2;0 will now be examined.

567. As to the inflection of nouns, we shall begin with the distinction between singular and plural.[12] The difference would seem to be easy and functionally useful. Both standard languages use endings for the plural, English in practically all nouns, German in most of them. Yet, throughout the second year, the distinction was not important enough to Hildegard to make her learn a consistently used morphological sign. To the end of the year, many nouns were used in plural function without a formal differentiation from the singular. Before the appearance of plural endings there is no way of telling whether the child even felt a functional distinction. After their appearance, the appreciation of the difference must have remained dim, because the use of nouns without a plural ending continued along with the sporadic use of nouns with a plural ending (even beyond the two-year limit).

The English plural endings z, əz, s were dropped for phonetic reasons during the greater part of the second year. Final s was not represented until 1;7 (172), final z not until 1;9 (150, 177). The substitute for both was ʃ.

Only after the representation was possible phonetically can we look for nouns with a plural ending. Among the numerous examples of words with final s there is not one in which it was a plural ending. Hildegard's word wiʃ 1;11, meaning *feet*, was tentatively explained as possibly coming from this etymon with the addition of an analogical plural s; but the hypothesis is improbable; her form is more easily explained as coming from the German synonym *Füsse*.[13]

The few plural forms which actually occurred had the ending z in the standard language. The earliest example with the ending represented by ʃ was *beads* 1;9; but this is an instance of non-functional use of the plural ending. The word usually designated a bead-necklace, which appeared to the child as a unified object. The word was imitated phonetically with the z, just like other words the stem of which ended in z. This became clear at 1;11 when, stringing up wooden beads, she needed a term for an individual bead and called it *ball-beads*, with the ending still present in the singular function. The distinguishing determination *ball* was undoubtedly added because Hildegard was conscious of the difference in shape, the wooden beads being much larger and more

---

[12] According to Stern p. 250, the distinction of numbers is much earlier than that of cases.

[13] Karla did use *feets* repeatedly at 3;7: *Papa, I see your feets.*

conspicuously spherical than the glass beads of her necklaces.[14] The doubtful word *stones*, used for one stone 1;11, may also belong here.

At 1;10 Hildegard used the plural form *cookies*, with the plural ending, phonetically improved with regard to the stressed vowel as well, along with an older reduplicative form lacking the plural ending. At 1;11, finally, a small number of nouns appeared with the plural ending, clearly distinguished from the corresponding singular form: *shoes, cookies, bobby-pins, balls* (2;0 *years;* 2;1 *toes, fishes*). The simple principle of the English plural formation had been recognized.

It was, however, not yet clearly enough established to be used consistently. Other nouns, and sometimes these same ones, continued to be used in plural function without a plural ending: *shoes, autos, stockings, all balls, nails, peas, hands, all babies* (even as late as 2;1, although less frequently at that time). A few of these plurals might be traced to their German synonyms, with the plural ending dropped phonetically: *Schuhe, Hände.* In view of the other examples, however, it is not necessary to resort to this explanation. It is implausible. If the simple and regular English plural formation was only beginning to be understood, the more complicated ways of forming the German plural as well as irregular English plural formations were undoubtedly still below the threshold.

The only irregular English plural which occurred was *feet* 1;10–11, but the singular "foot" was not used. Thus the item resulted from direct phonetic imitation without understanding of the morphological pattern involved.

German plurals occurred very rarely, and never with a distinctive plural form except for one word. *Schuhe* and *Hände* have already been mentioned as unconvincing prototypes. The compound *Handschuhe* was actually learned from presentation in the plural 1;10 (and was used as a substitute for the English plural "mittens" 2;1); but there was no difference between Hildegard's singular and plural forms and probably no awareness of the standard difference. *Blumen*, sporadically 1;0, 1;7, 1;11, occurred only in the plural, and the ending disappeared for phonetic reasons. *Autos*, although its plural formation is similar to English, lacked the plural ending.

The only German word with different forms for singular and plural was *Fuss, Füsse* 1;11. Although no misuse of either the singular or the plural form is reported, it is certain that the two forms resulted from phonetic imitation, because the singular was ʔutʃ and the plural wiʃ. The striking divergence can be explained phonetically (**125**), but not morphologically. It is reasonable to assume that it would not have been tolerated if a feeling of pattern had been present. If the alternative

---

[14] Karla used **bi**, *bead* 1;9. This would also have been Hildegard's phonetic representation of the singular.

hypothesis, that wiʃ goes back to *feet* + *s* rather than to *Füsse*, should be correct, it would prove the same thing: the vowel modification was not recognized as a morphological device to mark the difference between singular and plural.

Since articles were missing, the analytic German plural indication by means of their variable form was also not available.

In summary we find that the only pattern for distinguishing the plural which Hildegard learned was the addition of the ending z in the shape of substitute ʃ at 1;11;[15] but it was not yet used consistently.

The absence of the plural ending before the last month was not simply due to a phonetic deficiency, but to the fact that the functional device had not been recognized. The child felt no great need for the distinction because her attention was generally concentrated on a single object at a time. If an object consisted of many parts, like *Blumen* or *beads*, the aggregate unit was perceived rather than the component parts. In the rare cases when the attention was focused on individual items in succession rather than on the configuration of the whole, primitive devices had helped out earlier. *Light, mehr light, mehr, Mama* 1;8 might be interpreted, with imagination, as meaning "There are several lamps in this room; this one is Mama's"; but the child dissolved the plural idea into an enumeration of successive items in the singular. The same is true of such utterances as *This* (*is*) *Dodo's* (*and*) *this* (*is*) *Dodo's* 1;8 (**538**), which was her way of saying "These overshoes belong to Dodo".[16]

568. There is little to say about noun inflection apart from the plural. Most of the cases have no distinctive endings in the standard languages. Their function is indicated analytically, by means of prepositions in English, by means of inflected articles in German. Both types of unstressed words remained in abeyance. Thus the nouns used in object function (**544**) did not differ formally from those used as subjects (**543**) or predicate nouns (**547**). All objects were direct objects with the exception of one example, in which both a direct and an indirect object were used, if the criteria of standard syntax can be applied to the two-word statement involved. The indirect object was likewise not characterized formally. Datives of the plural, which usually have a distinctive ending in German, did not occur.

---

[15] Karla used the substitute t regularly: 2;3 kukit, *cookies*, like earlier nɔut, *nose*.

[16] Bohn (1914, p. 585) observed the plural at 1;7, Kenyeres (p. 202) at 1;5–8 (in Hungarian, where the plural formation is as simple as in English; but plurals were first used mechanically, incorrectly). Decroly (p. 187) observed it at 2; 3–4 (in French, where most plurals are indicated analytically, by means of the article). Holmes (p. 224) found no plural at 1;11. Smith (1935, p. 202) found that no plurals were used before 2;0 by the 220 children whose language she studied. Pavlovitch (p. 134) observed the plural from 1;10, but it was purely imitative, not productive.

The vocative is functionally important for the small child who likes attention. A common use of it was its combination with an interjection (**517**) or an imperative (**519, 527, 535**). The standard languages, however, use for it the same form as for the nominative without formal modification, except for increased emphasis in the shouted address and subordination in stress when it follows an interjection or an imperative.[17] Naturally, Hildegard's vocatives also were in the common, undifferentiated form.

There were certain instances in which I observed a formal distinction between the vocative and the subjective or objective case. At 1;10 she spoke of her kitten as *meow*, but called it with *kitty, kitty* in the falsetto voice which adults use for this vocative in a friendly, luring call. The term *kitty*, in spite of its strong emotional appeal, was only used sporadically throughout the second year. At B 1;11, the cat's name *Dasch (Katz)* served as a distinctive vocative for a while. These instances, however, in which different vocabulary items were used with distinctive functions, cannot be counted as illustrations of patterns of declension. Besides, these distinctions were fleeting.[18]

This leaves only the genitive in its common possessive function. This function developed early. From 1;6, one-word utterances sometimes stated ownership: *Mama*, "these are Mama's shoes"; *baby*, "this is the baby's toy, not mine."[19] It cannot be claimed, however, that the grammatical function of the possessive was developed in these amorphous utterances, much less the form.

From 1;8 Hildegard liked to dwell on statements of ownership. Two-word combinations often consisted of the designation of a thing and its owner: *June dolly* 1;8, *Mama shoe* 1;8, *baby dress* 1;9, *Joey kimona* 1;9, *Rita house* 1;11, even *Mary Alice Wehweh* 1;11 (**543, 544, 547**). There is one example of a predicate possessive (**548**) in the form of a simple noun: *This Dodo, this Dodo* 1;8 (stating the ownership of two overshoes). The possessive function was developed, but it lacked formal expression. Mere juxtaposition sufficed as a grammatical device. The owner was always a person, usually designated by a name (including *Mama, Papa*), sometimes by a generic term like *baby*. Only *Mama* and *Papa* eventually added the ending in the form of substitute ʃ at

---

[17] The addition of the interjection "oh" as a formal sign of the vocative is in German restricted to poetry, in colloquial English to the repetition of a shouted call to a person at a distance, when the first call has been ineffective ("Mary! Oh, Mary!"). Neither of these rare uses of "oh" occurred in Hildegard's language.

[18] Karla had similar examples. At 1;6 the name of the maid, *Vira*, had different phonetic form depending on whether she spoke of her or called her (vol. 1, p. 65, note 91). About 1;8, she used the shouted vocative *Vati* and the ordinary address, *Papa*.

[19] Egger p. 60: "*Papa* désigne non seulement le père de l'enfant, mais tous les objets qui appartiennent au père." He assesses this expression of ownership as a preliminary stage of vague association.

1;10, on the basis of either English or German, more likely the former.[20] Even these names did not have the ending consistently during 1;11. That the possessive function was implied in names without the ending is clearest in correlated statements like (*This is*) *Dada hat, this* (*is*) *mine* 1;10, *Papa pocket, my pocket* 1;10.[21]

When we compare the chronology of the plural ending and of the possessive ending, which are phonetically closely parallel, we find that the possessive was introduced one month earlier (1;10) than the plural (1;11). Neither was well established by the end of the year.[22]

569. Adjective inflections did not yet exist as morphological patterns. Since English leaves adjectives uninflected, the prevailingly English structure of Hildegard's language in the second half of the second year did not call for inflections. The adjective "this" has a distinctive plural, "these"; but she used only the singular (cf. end of **567**).

The attributive adjective in German is inflected, and from this source there are a few instances of inflected adjectives in Hildegard's language; but they were in every case immediate echoes of inflected forms which I had used. At 1;9 Hildegard showed me a white building block, after she had practiced selecting green ones. I identified the color for her, saying, "Das ist ein weisser". Immediately after, she brought another white block and said excitedly waɪʃə! This was the only time that she said the word in any form. At 1;10 she learned dɪkɛ baʊk as a fixed combination. The adjective ending was reduced to ə by 1;11. It may go back to the standard endings "-er" or "-en" and was used without distinction in subject and object function. There are certain indications that she

---

[20] woʃ might theoretically represent the possessive *Florence's* (177); but it is improbable, since other names were used without a possessive ending.

[21] Pidgin English, which we have sometimes had occasion to compare with the language of a small child, differs fundamentally in this respect. It uses an analytic possessive with a clear formal sign, the preposition "belong". Karla used unmistakable possessives as early as 1;8 (*Mama chair, Mama pencil*) and 1;9 (*Mama drink*, vol. 1, p. 73, note 114), many of them at 1;11 (*Hildegard dress*), all without an ending. At B 2;4 the ending was t, her regular substitute: dɛt mamat, *That* (*is*) *Mama's*.

[22] Time of acquisition varies considerably: Bohn 1;7 (1914, p. 581); Friedemann 1;8 (names; Preyer p. 246); Stern "very early", 2;1–4, but later than plural (p. 250 f.); cf. Decroly p. 187, Pavlovitch p. 130. Smith (1935, p. 202), in a study of 220 children ranging in age from 1;6 to 5;11, found that only four of the youngest children (2;0 and 2;5) used possessives of nouns. Preyer (p. 177) found "declension . . . as yet absolutely lacking" at 2;5, although plural endings and articles were used more frequently at the same time. Gheorgov's first son (p. 261 ff.) learned the analytic Bulgarian genitive early (1;10), although he omitted the same preposition in the dative, and the plural late; but his second son (p. 367) used the genitive very rarely and without the preposition, the dative more frequently, also without the preposition, and more plurals. Kenyeres (p. 201 ff.) emphasizes that the order of acquisition of the cases depends on the language. The Hungarian accusative is learned much earlier than the accusative of other languages.

learned to recognize the first part of the compound as an adjective; but
the ending was stereotyped. We cannot speak of a functional inflection.
When Hildegard played the teasing game which led to the learning of
the possessive *my, mine,* I played it with her in German, and as an
echo of the forms which I used, she occasionally used the adjective
meine with the feminine ending 1;7. This use was ephemeral, however.
For months after its occurrence, the word regularly lacked the ending
and even the final **n** of the German adjective. The ending had been used
imitatively without comprehension of its function.

There was no trace of a comparison of adjectives, not even in the form
of separate vocabulary items like "better, best".

In summary, no pattern of adjective inflection was acquired.[23]

570. There is even less to say about formal characteristics of the adverb. In German, the simple adverb either has the same form as the
corresponding adjective or is a separate vocabulary item not connected
with an adjective of the same meaning. In colloquial English the situation is essentially the same, since the adverbial ending "-ly" of the
literary standard is often omitted. At any rate Hildegard never used a
form ending in "-ly"; in fact, in the rather long list of adverbs in her
vocabulary there is none which would take this ending in the most
careful standard. The list consists of adverbs which supplement verbs
(like *away, down, in, on, up*), of sentence adverbs (*yes, no*), of adverbs
of place (like *far away, here, home, outside, there*), of adverbs of degree
or quantity (*much, more, too, way*), and the like, all of which are independent vocabulary items. The distribution in the shorter list of
German adverbs is the same. The adverb *schön,* not contrasted or coordinated with a corresponding adjective (*pretty* served in its place),
occurred once 1;1 in *danke schön;* but this was an isolated mechanical
imitation. Adverbs of manner, in which the ending "-ly" is used in
standard English, were missing, apart from this negligible German
example (**550–554, 557**).

There was no comparison of adverbs. *Mehr up* 1;7 in the meaning of
"up higher" can be called a vague comparative; but no formal comparison was performed. Not even the analytic comparison with *mehr*
and *more* was learned as a morphological pattern, although the former

---

[23] No examples of adjective inflection are given before the third year by Stern
p. 259, Decroly p. 193 f. Stern found the first endings from 2;0 on; but the rather
complicated German patterns were not learned until the fourth year. Decroly
(p. 194 f.) finds the earliest comparative in the literature at 1;11 (Kenyeres,
Hungarian); all other examples are from the fourth year. Stern (pp. 259–261)
registers the first use of "mehr", which must be interpreted with caution, in the
literature between 1;5 and 2;5, but no synthetic comparatives until the third year.
The superlative belongs to the fourth year. Cf. Gheorgov pp. 281 f., 379; O'Shea
p. 107 f.; Bergmann p. 241 ff.

was a frequent word in Hildegard's vocabulary. *Mehr* stood alone, or was combined with a noun or a verb, not with an adjective or adverb.[24] It was not contrasted with *much*. The two words remained completely separate vocabulary items.

571. Pronouns existed only in small numbers at the end of the second year. No inflections developed.

Personal pronouns can hardly be said to have an inflection in the standard languages. They operate with distinct vocabulary items for the distinctions of case and number. It has been shown **(559)** that the only pronoun of which Hildegard used two cases was that of the first person; but the difference had not yet become clear.[25] Although *I* was not used for the object, nor *me* for the subject, both of them were frequently replaced by *my, mine*. Thus, not even the difference between personal and possessive pronouns was clear. *You* occurred only in the mechanically imitated game sentence *I see you* *1;5. In *thank you* 1;3 there was a syllable for *you*, but it was a reduplication of the stressed syllable. Certainly it must be said that *you* was not acquired. Similarly, *es* had a representation in *da ist es* *1;5, but the imitation was likewise mechanical and unproductive. The pronoun of the third person was always omitted.

Other pronouns **(559)** were likewise not numerous. The only examples of inflections were German *meine, meins*, which occurred exceptionally as direct echoes. *Dies*, the German synonym of *this*, was used rarely and never inflected.

572. Interjections and most numerals do not belong in the accidence. They are vocabulary items, usually not subject to inflection. Interjections act as sentences. Some numerals can be inflected, especially in German, but none of the few which Hildegard used was. *Eins* occurred with and without a substitute for the final consonant, but the basis was the same, the unchangeable numeral as used in counting. Indefinite numeral adjectives did not occur, with the exception of *all*, which has no inflection (and *other, andere* if it be counted as such). There was no trace of such common words as "many", "some". *Much* was merely an adverb. *Mehr* did occur as an adjective, but could not be inflected. Ordinals were not used.

573. Real verbs come rather late in the child's linguistic development.[26] If we disregard the earlier months of speaking, during which words

---

[24] Cf. Stern p. 259 f.

[25] It was not clear at 2;7; cf. **727 f.**

[26] Bloch (1924, p. 22 f.) accounts for the fact that verbs are imitated later than nouns with psychological and linguistic reasons. His linguistic reason is that the noun, especially in French, has a more stable form than the verb with its many morphological variations, particularly in the most common verbs. He remarks that verbs continue to be omitted frequently, even after they are in the vocabulary, more frequently than nouns (p. 26 f.).

hover in a twilight zone between different classes of words, and consider only those words which are based on standard verbs, we discover
in Hildegard's case that she hardly used any verbs at all before 1;8
and that they did not become numerous until 1;11.[27] There are a few
earlier examples, which must be discounted. The stereotyped sentences
Da ist es 1;4 and *I see you* 1;5 contained verb forms; but we have often
emphasized that their imitation was mechanical and premature; if
taken at full value they falsify the picture of language acquisition.
Danke and *kiek* 1;1, *thank you* 1;3, *peekaboo* 1;4, and *bitte* 1;5 are verb
forms etymologically, but they have ceased to have the function of
verb forms in the standard languages themselves.

Real verbs began at 1;8. *Komm mit* (to be sure, with the verb proper
suppressed because of its pretonic position), *rollen, wischen, wash*
(*waschen*), *open, ride, rock, walk* were learned. Two of them, *snowing*
and *ironing*, even had an inflectional ending (578). From then on the
number increased slowly. (At the beginning of the third year the addition of verbs in complete sentences became striking.)[28]

574. The preceding chronological information serves merely as an introduction to the problem of verb inflection, which interests us here.

The verb in English and German is easier to learn than the verb in
the Romance languages, particularly French[29] and Spanish, because it
has fewer irregularities in the stem. In the present tense, which we shall
examine first, there are minor irregularities in German, hardly any in
English. In comparing child-language records from various languages,
this difference must be kept in mind.

On the other hand, the very fact that there is little formal difference
between the present tense, the infinitive, and the imperative in English
and German makes it difficult for the observer to decide which of these
forms the child is using. Of course, in German these forms are often
distinguished by different endings; but these endings may be dropped
by the small child for phonetic rather than morphological reasons.
Thus, if the child's form corresponds to the standard pure stem, it looks
like the imperative, which has in the singular usually no ending in the
colloquial model. It is difficult to tell, however, whether the child's
verb form was based on the standard imperative, or represented a present-tense form or infinitive with phonetically unrepresented ending.

---

[27] Karla's verbs also multiplied at 1;11; they were more numerous than Hildegard's. Among others she used *get, show, take* (unchanged in past tense), *see, look*
(these two only in the imperative), *haben* **ha:m** (for "Ich will das haben"), *have*
hæ·, hæt, hæ·tə (in *Karla have birthday cake?* for example).

[28] Concerning the distribution of word-classes, see Stern's summary of the
literature, pp. 244–247. Verbs are often found earlier than in Hildegard's case;
but one would need to examine how they were used. A great percentual increase
of verbs over nouns is noted for 1;5–2;5, a range which is too wide to be useful.
Bloch (1921, p. 711) reports the addition of verbs of action at 2;0 and 2;1.

[29] Cf. Guillaume p. 219.

In English there are even fewer clues, since the whole present tense with the exception of the third person singular of full verbs, the imperative, the infinitive, and in many cases even the corresponding noun, all have pure stem form;[30] and most of Hildegard's verbs were English, because she did not learn verbs until the switch to an English basis was rather complete as far as new words were concerned.

Theoretically it would seem plausible that the imperative should loom large in the child's experience, since many commands are addressed to him and he utters many wishes, the simplest form of which is the imperative (576). On the other hand, negative commands, warnings are also common in the child's experience, and they take in English the form "don't" or "you must not" followed by an infinitive; in fact, Hildegard learned to say the form with *don't* before the end of the second year. Also, we have assumed that many of her wishes were based on a formulation like "May I", "Will you", with the modal auxiliary unexpressed. In such cases the expressed verb was of course in the infinitive, if standard syntax applied. More important than the theoretical consideration is the testimony of observers studying children who learn inflected languages that the first stage of verbs is an infinitive stage.[31]

575. We have assumed the use of infinitives in all the sections (512, 520, 526, 528 f., 536) dealing with wishes in formulations which seemed based on standard expressions containing a modal auxiliary, provided a verb form was present. Since nearly all verbs were English, the infinitive had no formal characteristics, and the interpretation is inevitably speculative.

An infinitive seems clearly involved when a verb form was used after *don't*. There is no good example, however. As a rule, *don't* 1;11 was said alone, reflecting the unspecified warning which the child heard often addressed to herself, when the situation obviated the need for a more explicit formulation. The only example with a specifying verb was

---

[30] Sometimes it was actually doubtful whether Hildegard was using an English word as a verb or as a noun; cf. *brush* at 1;10 in vol. 1. A few times she used nouns with verb function (*Bauch* at 1;6–8) and verbs with noun function (*bathe* at 1;9, *bauen* at 1;9) in cases where the standard language did not allow this transfer.

[31] Stern p. 252; Decroly p. 188; Bergmann p. 243 (even infinitive in imperative function, which is possible in standard German, and, p. 241 ff., for the past participle, 2;11 to 4); Preyer pp. 159, 177 (2;1; almost always for imperative and past participle 2;5); Compayré p. 313 (based on Preyer 2;2 and Tiedemann 1;10); Guillaume p. 21 (frequency explained by imitation of sentences with a modal auxiliary or "aller"; but p. 23: imperative in meaning); Wundt p. 401 (same explanation); Meringer p. 156. Smith (1935, p. 201), on the other hand, although she finds the first infinitive at 1;11, claims that the infinitive was used by but nine two-year olds, that there were many "errors", and that it remained infrequent among the 220 children, aged 1;6–6;0, whom she studied. Since the language involved is English, mistakes in the evaluation of the uninflected verb forms may easily be involved. Kenyeres (p. 204) reports the infinitive as early as 1;6, although it is rarely used in Hungarian.

Don't spiel, with a German verb lacking the infinitive ending "-en". The latter may have been omitted for phonetic reasons, but we cannot be sure of that. It is entirely possible that Hildegard used the uninflected colloquial imperative for the purpose of a negative command, adding *don't* as a negative sign in a way not sanctioned by standard usage (as she did in the synonymous *No bite* as late as 2;1, **518**).[32]

In *Mama mehr sh* 1;11, *sh* was interpreted as an infinitive meaning "sleep" (**531**); but the verb was so primitive in form that it does not throw much light on the use of the infinitive. (At 2;1 it was used with the negative, *Don't sh*.)

The German infinitive has a distinctive ending and is easy to learn on account of its regularity.[33] In Hildegard's case the difficulty in tracing it in her speech is in part due to the fact that final syllabic n remained unrepresented in the earlier months of speaking (**151**). Later, it should have been represented by a vowel; but by that time, her linguistic stock was overwhelmingly English.

The only possible example of a German infinitive with the ending represented, is wɔə 1;8, an early experimental form of *rollen*, which I used in imperative function as a game cue. It is not certain, however, that ə stood for the ending; it could also render the final l (**151**). At any rate, it disappeared in the later history of the word, which may mean the abandonment of a morphological pattern for which the child was not yet ready, or a victory of the English synonym *roll*, which competed soon with the German word.

In view of the definite testimony of other observers in favor of an early use of the infinitive,[34] Hildegard's preference for the pure stem form of German verbs (assumed in **151** and throughout this study) might be explained by the prevailingly English pattern of her language, which did not promote the learning of a formal sign for the infinitive.[35]

---

[32] Colloquial English does the same in the loosely constructed expression exemplified by "Don't let's have another quarrel" (taken from the novel *Green Years* by A. J. Cronin, 1944, p. 270).

[33] Guillaume (p. 221 f.) emphasizes the fact that the German infinitive with its one ending is easy, whereas the French infinitive with its four different endings is difficult. He claims that the form is learned as soon as, or sooner than, the function when it is simple, and vice versa. He distinguishes correctly (p. 223) between morphological patterns and mechanical imitations, or, as he calls them, "personal constructions" and "reminiscences".

[34] Cf. note at end of 574. It should be noted, however, that "early" rarely means before 2;0 in the records cited there. Preyer (p. 172) reports that infinitives were frequent at 2;4, particularly in wish function, apparently with omission of a modal auxiliary.

[35] Karla used a German infinitive ending in one word from 1;10: she called me for dinner with the shouted word ʔɛtɛ, *essen*. Hildegard used the English synonym, *eat*, only, and there is no record of her calling me to the table with this word or any other formula. Meringer (p. 147) gives the reduplicated infinitive "baun-baun" as one child's first word at 1;7. The extensive vocabulary list of the same

576. I have assumed that the use of verbs in the form of the pure stem is to be charged primarily to the frequency of the imperative in the utterances addressed to the child and in the child's own wishful utterances (519, 527, 535). There is no proof for this hypothesis, because none of the imperatives which Hildegard used had an ending or other formal characteristic of its function. They could have no formal sign in English, because English uses invariably the pure stem for the imperative. German, however, has endings for imperatives other than the informal singular, can use an ending for the latter in most verbs (although the North German colloquial language usually omits it), and modifies the vowel in many strong verbs. Hildegard never used any but the familiar singular imperative in her German verbs, never added an ending,[36] and never modified the vowel. In fact, none of the few German verbs which she used in the imperative required the modification of the vowel; imperatives like "Iss!" "Sprich!" did not occur. Thus imperatives could only be recognized by their apparent function, not by their form.

Still, I have no doubt that the imperative was a frequent form of the verb, if not indeed the root of Hildegard's verb system.[37] Other students confirm that, next to the infinitive, the imperative is the most commonly used form of the verb.[38] The negative *Don't* 1;11 was undoubtedly based

---

child at 1;9, however, does not include this infinitive; instead, "bau-bau" appears in the illustrative sentences (p. 151). The representation of the ending is therefore dubious.

[36] *Backe* 1;11 is an imperative with an ending in the nursery rhyme, "Backe, backe Kuchen"; but its function is obscured even in the original. The imitation was mechanical. The imperative character of **hacke* 1;11 is even vaguer.

[37] H. Ammann, in *V⁰ Congrès* p. 5, calls the imperative the "Keimzelle des Verbums". Vendryes (English edition p. 137) says that the imperative is the verb form most appropriate for the language of action, the vehicle of wish and will, as is the vocative for the noun; a verbal expression like "Be quiet!", a noun like "Silence!", and an interjection like "sh!" serve the same purpose in the language of action.

[38] Many of the early infinitives have imperative function (see note at end of 574). Cf. Decroly p. 188; Lindner (Preyer p. 244: imperative most frequently heard by the child; first used; age 2); Stern p. 52 f. (finds, during the third year, a functional distinction between the old infinitive with imperative function and the new imperative); O'Shea p. 102 (no difficulty with the imperative; "The child's attitude in the early years is essentially mandatory."); Guillaume p. 23 f. (at 1;5–10 three quarters of all verbs are imperative in function); Hills p. 92 (at 2;0 the ratio of imperatives to indicatives is 10:1); Boyd p. 183 (percentage of commands high at age 2); Cornioley p. 25 (first imperative noted 1;8); Preyer pp. 171, 177 (infinitive with imperative function 2;4; the first example given, however, is really an infinitive with a modal auxiliary omitted); Pavlovitch p. 135 (imperative understood 1;3, later used for imperative and present indicative alike); Gheorgov pp. 249, 341 f. (imperative first of all; Bulgarian has no real infinitive, p. 260).

on an imperative (583). So are several other examples of 1;11 (527, 535).

577. Coming to the present indicative, we shall have very little to say about its morphology. Naturally, of all the tenses the present was the most commonly used. The great majority of the questions and statements can be assumed to have referred to a present situation and consequently to have been in the present tense functionally. The form of the verbs, however, was the invariable common form, which did not differ from the imperative and the infinitive. No personal endings were attached to it. As far as the verb is concerned, Hildegard was, at the end of the second year, still in the single-series, undifferentiated stage.

The forms which a small child would use most commonly are the first and third persons of the singular. The first person has no ending in English. In colloquial German the standard ending "-e" is usually omitted.[39] Hildegard could therefore not be expected to have an ending for the first person.

For the third person, however, both English and German have distinctive endings. Hildegard did not use them. In the earlier months they would have been omitted phonetically, sharing in the neglect of final consonants. English final z could be represented phonetically from 1;9 (178), final s from 1;7 (172, 174), German final t from 1;9 or 1;10 (141 f.).

There are a few instances in which I thought at first that the ending of the third person was used. At 1;11 the diary carries several entries in which I assumed its presence, with hesitation. In one of them, a German and an English example are given side by side, (the cat) bites me baits and (sie) pick-t flowers bɪt, and characterized as experiments with the ending of the third person. In the light of later experience and of the examination of the sound-system, this interpretation proved to be erroneous. In the first example the ts was no more than a faulty articulation of t (143), the more certainly so as final s was regularly rendered by ʃ. In the second example the t was a substitute for final k (218), not recognized as such at the time because Hildegard exchanged final stops rarely.

In the examination of her sounds, I have repeatedly faced the pos-

---

[39] Yesterday, helping Hildegard with her Latin home work (age 14;8), I utilized her knowledge of German to explain to her a difference between English and Latin usage. I asked her, in German, of course: "How would you say 'I am coming' in German?" Her answer was: "Ich komm'." This drove the fact of the colloquial pronunciation home to me; in a formal discussion of this kind I should say "Ich komme", but Hildegard is not familiar with formal German. The parallel helped her in Latin. It is interesting to see that an idiomatic difference which she has absorbed unconsciously in German, causes her difficulties in the conscious study of Latin.

sibility that English verbs used in the third person had the ending omitted for phonetic reasons: *fixes, washes, cries* 1;11 (**177**). Since these examples occurred long after final z could be represented (1;9), its omission is in all probability due to the fact that the morphological pattern had not been recognized by the child. She used the common, invariable verb form for the third person as for other functions.

The most convincing parallel is that of *reads* and *beads*. The verb was used at 1;11 in fluent three-word statements, in the form **wi**. The noun, which had plural form always, had a substitute for -z regularly from 1;9. This proves that the omission of -dz in the verb was not due to phonetic immaturity; the reason is morphological.

The tentative explanation of the troublesome nonce-word *steht* **deʃ** 1;11 as the German stem "steh-" with the English ending z (**141, 177**) loses all probability in the light of these findings. The meaning and the function of the verb were perfectly clear; the phonetic explanation remains in doubt.

Hängen was once 1;11 used indubitably in the third person; but Hildegard's form, which had no consonant after the vowel, should not be traced phonetically to the standard third person "hängt" (**142**), but to the common form without an ending. In *lutscht* 1;10 and *klappert* 1;11 there was also no trace of the ending in the child's forms.

Both in English and in German, the child's attention was not yet directed to the functional value of verb endings. No morphological pattern of conjugation was developed.[40] The verb lagged behind the noun, in which at least the beginnings of the categories of plural (**567**) and possessive (**568**) were discernible at the end of the second year.

578. The English progressive form of the verb (type "I am biting") did not gain a foothold in Hildegard's language before the end of the year.[41] Two words occurred in the form of the present participle, *ironing* 1;8–9 and *snowing* 1;8 and 1;10. Only the vowel of the ending was reproduced; the consonant was dropped phonetically. Both forms were echoes of the presentation the first time they were used. On the second occurrence their function was not clear, in both instances. *Dada ironing* 1;9 might have meant "Carolyn was (or is) ironing", but conceivably

---

[40] This is normal. Preyer (p. 177) says that conjugation and declension were "as yet absolutely lacking" at 2;5, although the validity of this statement is immediately restricted by examples showing the use of plurals, articles, and past participles. Two of the children whom Egger studied (p. 64 f.) began to conjugate the present tense at 2;4 and 2;7 respectively. Guillaume (p. 225) found the three persons of the singular to be frequent with children of age two to four; but this span is much too wide for the purpose, and besides the French verb has usually no phonetic distinction between these persons. Only Kenyeres (p. 204) records the first person singular at 1;6, and the third person early, in Hungarian.

[41] O'Shea (p. 99) found that the progressive form was not more difficult than the simple past, which he assigns to the third year (p. 98). This would seem to indicate that it was later than the simple present tense.

the gerund was used, "Carolyn does the ironing in our household". A statement of general validity was apparently intended, but it was grammatically amorphous; the name of the maid and one of her characteristic activities were simply placed side by side. It is more probable that the present participle of the progressive form was the prototype; but the grammatical structure was vague, since the progressive form is not an apt pattern for a general statement. The statement *Snowing, way up* 1;10 was obscure in meaning since there was no snow; thus it cannot be analyzed grammatically. Neither verb occurred without the ending.

At any rate, the standard construction was not learned. At 1;11 Hildegard said *Papa all through eat?* The question required standard "eating" (537), but the ending "-ing" was omitted. (At 2;1 statements of the type *I (am) going by-by* became frequent; *Carolyn (is) ironing* was again among the examples; 666).[42]

579. The verb "to be", as a full verb meaning "exist", "be located" and as a copula linking a subject, implied or expressed, with the real predication, was always omitted. The copula is phonetically unemphatic and semantically not essential. Many standard languages can do without it, Indo-European languages (Greek, for example) and non-Indo-European languages as well.[43]

Some instances of dissyllabic forms for *this* E 1;11 suggest the possibility that the vowel of their second syllable was based on the copula *is*. (The copula was still missing at 2;1; it was frequent at 2;5, 713.)[44]

The early sentence *Da ist es* 1;4–5, which contained a form of the full verb "to be", phonetically represented only by a vowel, must be discounted again. It was imitated mechanically, did not document a grasp of a pattern of conjugation, and did not pave the way for it. The phrase had long been discarded before the child began to learn patterns of conjugation.

580. The verb "to have" was also completely missing. As an auxiliary

---

[42] Karla used the construction often at M 1;11, omitting the copula and often also the subject: *(I am) walking, (I am) coming, Mama (is) coming.* The phonetic form of the ending was the same as Hildegard's. Karla used the present participle E 1;10-B 1;11 even in the function of the infinitive, *Playing?* meaning "Shall we play?" Thus the ending did not yet serve functional distinctions.

[43] Vendryes (p. 122 f., French original p. 144 f.) gives illustrations from Greek, Old Persian, Sanskrit, Russian, Old Irish, colloquial French, Chinese, Arabic, Hungarian, Swahili. For Finno-Ugric, cf. also Tihany p. 262 (summary of Zsirai's statement concerning characteristic syntactical phenomena of the Finno-Ugric languages).

[44] Lukens p. 457: "Perhaps among the very last words to be used in the sentence, at least by some children, is the little word *is* and its inflected forms—so important to logicians." Boyd p. 188: Copula omitted at age 2, rarely at age 3. Cf. Compayré pp. 256, 313, with references to Egger and Preyer; Bloch (1924) p. 24 f. Preyer p. 172: "ist" and "(ge)wesen" used at 2;4.

it could hardly be expected to exist. The compound tenses in which the standard languages use it were not learned until much later.

Even as a full verb it did not occur. As such it expresses possession, and possession became important to the child from 1;6. The idea of ownership was expressed predicatively from 1;8; but Hildegard chose the pattern of a predicate noun or pronoun in possessive function with omission of the copula (548) rather than "have" with an object.

A few times the latter pattern occurred, but the verb was suppressed. *My Wehweh* 1;10 is not an obvious illustration; but at that time *my* was the usual form of the personal pronoun. The utterance was taken to mean "I have a Wehweh (ache, sore, bruise)". Possibly the subject and the predication were placed side by side amorphously; but at this rather late stage it is more probable that a standard syntactical pattern was the basis, and "have" is the only plausible verb for it (523). *Papa apple* 1;8 is a clearer example. It could not mean "Papa is an apple". Obviously this more familiar pattern was not used. If the utterance was not quite amorphous (which is not impossible at this earlier stage), the conclusion is inescapable that the verb "has" was omitted, strikingly, unless it was the fuller verb "eats". *Meow oatmeal* 1;11 is parallel (523, 544). *Papa (has) my comb da* 1;11 (538) leaves no doubt about the verb to be supplied. ("Have" was still missing at 2;1, after a striking increase in verbs;[45] but the colloquial synonym *got* was acquired as a present tense, 586.)

581. The ideas expressed in standard languages by modal auxiliaries were very important in Hildegard's speaking. Although we have made it clear that by no means all of her utterances were wishes, the latter loomed large among her sentences, both declarative and interrogative. All the sections on requests in interrogative form imply the idea of "May I?" Wishes in declarative form usually implied "I want to".[46] They occurred so frequently that it was necessary to set aside special sections for utterances interpreted as lacking a modal auxiliary. Occasionally we have operated with other modal auxiliaries, "must" ("have to"), "should", in our tentative interpretations.

Most of these applications refer to the first person. Sometimes a third person was involved; not all utterances were egocentric.

Without exception, the modal auxiliary or equivalent verb ("let's" could be added to the list) existed only in the interpretation of adults on the basis of their own syntax. It is probable that the child was using these patterns of the presentation, omitting what was unimportant to her, the auxiliary and often also the subject. The probability that these

---

[45] Bloch (1924) p. 24 f.: Verbs like "have", "make", "go", "be" are often omitted to the end of the third year. Hildegard learned *make* and *go* at the end of the second year. Preyer p. 172: "haben" and "hat" frequent at 2;4.

[46] Concerning the classification of "want" as a modal auxiliary, cf. note to **520.**

interpretations are valid is heightened by the observation that the use of such patterns belonged to the latter half of the second year. *Hase Bett* 1;8, "I want the bunny to go to bed, too" or "the bunny should also go to bed" (**518**), may still be amorphous. More convincing examples belong to 1;9 (*Bau Haus*, "I want to build a house") and 1;10 (*Ride*, "I want to ride"). Most of them belong to the last month, when syntactic patterns were fairly well developed.

In all cases the inference is purely speculative. Not a single modal auxiliary was ever expressed by Hildegard. As far as formal expression is concerned, modal auxiliaries did not exist in her infant-language, a sign that a formal distinction between statements of fact and wishes had not yet become vital to her.

It may be worth noting that my interpretations never resorted to the modal auxiliaries "may", in its function of expressing possibility, and "can". "May", where used, referred to permission (German "darf"). "Shall" and "will" as auxiliaries of the future tense were also lacking (**587**).

582. This leaves only the auxiliary "do" to be considered, which is not used in standard German, but is important in English for questions and negative statements, and occurs also in emphatic positive statements. This auxiliary did exist in Hildegard's language. She learned it 1;11 in its positive form, in vicarious function for a full verb; but it was a mechanically imitated formula. Her aunt trained her to answer tempting challenges like "Who likes candy?" with the stereotyped phrase, *I do*. The playfully exaggerated intonation learned from the aunt continued to characterize the utterance as a part of a linguistic game when Hildegard used it in answer to other persons' questions of the same type. Thus the use of positive *do* did not reach the status of a syntactic pattern. "Does" did not occur, so that the acquisition of a morphological pattern is out of the question.

The learning of "do" as the auxiliary of questions can hardly be expected early. In rapid colloquial English it is commonly so much reduced phonetically that nothing but the consonant remains ("D'you want to . . .?"), or not even that. No trace of it was observed in Hildegard's speech.

Do as a full verb, apart from its vicarious use, was not learned (until 2;1, **666**; it was also used in the imperative at 2;1: *You do this*, **666**).

583. The negative *don't*, only used in this contracted form in easy colloquial language, was acquired at B 1;11. It occurred in negative imperatives and was readily combined with German verbs (*Don't spiel*, cf. **666**) as a convenient sign of interdiction, of which her young life was, passively, all too full. "Don't" was forever addressed to her when her own wishes came in conflict with the strange, yet powerful and fascinating conventions and convictions of the adults. Its important function together with its impressive phonetic form anchored this word firmly in her speech at the end of the second year. Previously non-verbal negatives like *no, no* had served the same purpose. It is not at all certain that the difference in grammatical character was appreciated by the child, since more primitive expressions (*No bite*, "Don't spank me", as late as 2;1) continued along with the better form. *Don't* is an auxiliary, however, which was formally expressed, and should be counted as the only auxiliary which Hildegard learned during the first two years. It did not occur in the indicative of the present tense, but only in the imperative, so that we can again not speak of a pattern of conjugation.

Don't approaches the character of a full verb when it is used elliptically, without a more specific verb. The unspecified interdiction *Don't!* is the first use which Hildegard learned 1;11, before she began to specify it by an added verb, which adults would take to be in the infinitive (574).

584. We have reached the end of the discussion of the present tense, in which most of Hildegard's utterances were made. The small child lives in a present world and is not much concerned with the past or the future.

This is not true, however, without restrictions. Sometimes the child does hark back to past experiences or looks forward to coming ones. The difference is not always so clear as it seems at first glance to the adult trained in logical thinking, trained by the grammatical demands of the developed language which he must use. Any statement of a fact observed by the child necessarily refers to a happening already past, or a condition which does not begin to exist at the exact moment of the utterance. Any wish or other forward-looking utterance points to a time subsequent to the time when it is made.

585. In examining the past tenses it is appropriate to begin with the past participles, which are often reported to be the first such forms used.[47]

Hildegard was apparently slow in beginning to use past participles. None appeared in German. This is not surprising, because by the time they might have been learned, her language had become essentially English, and most of her verbs were English. Even in English, however, there were no real past participles. The few forms which did occur did not have the character of verb forms, but acted as adjectives.[48] *Broken* 1;9 behaved exactly like the simultaneous German synonym *kaputt*. *Gone* 1;10 was the successor of *alle* 1;7 and a synonym of *weg* 1;10; it occurred only in the phrase *all gone*. *Closed* 1;11 was not only doubtful as to its etymon, but synonymous with German *zu*. For the former two, the common forms of the verbs, *break* 1;10 and *go* 1;10, were also in the

---

[47] Preyer p. 177 (2;5); Cornioley p. 44 (by 1;8 already distinct from infinitive); Decroly p. 190 (about 2;0); for infinitive forms used in past-participle function, see note at end of 574.

[48] Cf. O'Shea p. 95 (first participles "used adjectively", including present participles).

vocabulary; but there was no indication that the child learned to use the semantic relation and morphological distinction for grammatical purposes. In the case of *break, broken*, the semantic identity was felt, but the two forms were used without functional discrimination, exchangeably. In the other case, *go* acted as a verb, but *gone* did not. The two forms were distinguished functionally, but Hildegard obviously did not recognize the semantic connection between the two forms. It is also obscured in the standard use of *gone* which she adopted. They were two distinct words for her.

No past participles were used as verb forms.[49] Compound tenses, of which they might have formed part, did not exist even in budding form.[50]

586. For past events, the usual colloquial form is in German the perfect tense, consisting of the present tense of an auxiliary of time combined with the past participle of a full verb. Hildegard did not learn this pattern. English uses most commonly a simple past tense, distinguished from the present by an ending or a modification of the stem-vowel. Hildegard did not learn this scheme either.

For weak verbs there is the possibility that the ending of the past tense disappeared for purely phonetic reasons (**142, 148**). Final t was not represented until 1;10, and final d remained unrepresented throughout the second year (and even as late as 2;1). No phonetic reason explains the absence of past-tense forms of strong verbs. The phonetic explanation should therefore be rejected. Hildegard simply did not learn to make a formal distinction between present and past tenses.

One verb form based on a standard strong past tense did occur, *forgot* 1;11 (**532**). It lacked the pretonic syllable, but had the vowel of the past. This verb, however, was presented to Hildegard in the past ("Mama forgot the toothbrush"); it was imitated for two weeks only in this sentence, but later extended to other uses. It is most commonly used in the past tense by standard speakers on account of its meaning. The decisive point, however, is the fact that the child never used a form based on the present tense. There was no contrast of tense forms. The verb acted exactly like other verbs. The fact that its form was based on a different standard tense form has merely etymological interest. Func-

---

[49] Tappolet (p. 406) is right in his enthusiasm for incorrect, analogically formed past participles. They show better than correct forms that the category has taken hold in a child's language. The fact that Hildegard had none as yet is the best proof that she had not begun to learn the category. Guillaume (p. 221 f.) says that the German past participle is easier than the French. The difference between the two languages with regard to the ending is, however, not so great as in the case of the infinitive, and the pretonic prefix "ge-" is a phonetic difficulty lacking in French. Bergmann (p. 241 ff.) reports correct past participles with the prefix from 4;5 on.

[50] Cf. Decroly p. 190 (past perfect very late, end of third year or later, according to Stern, Lindner, Bergmann; present perfect earlier).

tionally there was no difference. (At 2;1 *got* was a parallel case. In the colloquial language, especially of children, "got" has come to be a present tense synonymous with "have".)[51]

The need for a distinctive past-tense form is not great in the undeveloped language. Most references to past events (**515, 523, 532, 539**) concerned the immediate past, happenings which had occurred just before the child spoke about them. Even the standard language extends the category of present tense to such situations. The span of memory was not long (**649**), or, more cautiously stated, the child's interest did not often linger on events long past;[52] there were some references to happenings of a day or a week before (**532**). When the need for distinctions of time awakens, the child might first resort to the addition of adverbs of time, which could be called an analytical pattern of tense-indication. Actually, even adverbs of time were missing in Hildegard's infant-language (**554**). She simply used the present-tense form unmodified for the past (and continued to do so at 2;1: *My eat too much; Lost mittens* in the story of the three little kittens contained a past-tense form, but in mechanical imitation; no contrasting present-tense form of the word was active).[53]

587. For the future, the use of the present tense is a less striking imperfection. In colloquial German it is much more common than the formal analytic future. In colloquial English the future auxiliary is usually inserted in the abridged form "'ll", which reduces it, particularly after personal pronouns, to a mere consonantal ending. Final consonantal l could be represented by a vowel in Hildegard's language from 1;9 (**203**); but no trace of it was ever observed in utterances which might contain the auxiliary of the future.[54] Hildegard used the unmodified present-tense form to point to the future, and no German influence need be assumed, because tense distinctions simply did not yet exist in her verb system.

---

[51] Cf. its use in uneducated popular speech: "All God's children got wings". It may be based on the past participle, "I (have) got," **666**.

[52] Lewis (1937) p. 44: The child frees itself gradually from the dominance of the present situation, second half of second year. Court: Memory 3-4 days at age 2.

[53] Cf. O'Shea p. 95 (at first present tense for all tenses); p. 98 (simple past tense, weak, mostly by third year); Decroly p. 189 (for a long time only present tense); p. 190 (imperfect, as rare in colloquial French as in colloquial German, late, 1;11, 2;11; Scupin 2;1, 4;0; Stern 2;6; Kenyeres, Hungarian, 1;5); Lewis (1937) pp. 49, 54 (first true references to past event 1;11-2;0, but in present-tense form). The difficulty of distinctions of time in the verb should be compared with the difficulty of adverbs of time (**554**). Karla had, during the third year, an analytic past tense which has no parallel in Hildegard's language, namely, the auxiliary *did* followed by the infinitive: *I did fall*, etc.; *It's raining—no, it stop—it did stop* 2;8 (the verb was phonetically *dᴐp* in both instances; the inadequacy of the first form was apparently felt).

[54] Lewis (1937) p. 55: infinitive only, first at 2;0.

The many utterances which expressed a wish or an intention of the child pointed forward to anticipated happenings in the future. The standard language itself, however, uses no formal expression of the future in such cases. "I want to . . ." emphasizes the present wish without giving formal expression to its future fulfillment. Intention can be indicated by "I am going to . . .", formally present tense, as well as by "I shall" (colloquially "I'll"), which acts as the form of the future. Actually Hildegard omitted this introduction to the announcement of her intentions, stating its content directly in a grammatically amorphous way. "I am going to lie down" was simply expressed by *Lie down* 1;11, which may have been the imperative addressed to herself.

There is no lack of evidence that she looked forward to events which had not yet taken place. *Mama? baden!* 1;8, anticipated that her mother was going to take a bath; but the utterance was not even one sentence; much less did it contain a formal expression of the future. In *Ask Papa (to put this) on* and *Ask Mama this aus* ("to take this off") 1;11 the verbs were completely omitted, and the standard language itself uses a neutral construction in which the future is not expressed. The wish *This outside* 1;9 was paraphrased by "This shall go outside", but the interpretation, while fitting the idea, was hardly the pattern underlying the utterance. If it was not entirely amorphous, the pattern might just as well have been "I want this outside", which agrees better with the structure of other utterances. In any case, "shall" is not an auxiliary of the future tense in the paraphrase.

Hildegard did operate with future time, but had no trace of a grammatical form for the future tense.[55] The auxiliaries of the future, "will" ("shall") and "werden" were completely absent.[56]

588. As long as not even the conjugation of the present tense and the

---

[55] First elliptic use of "will" 2;2 (690), transition from modal to temporal auxiliary. An indubitable future with "will" in the third person occurred at 2;4 (706; cf. 718).

[56] Karla had a method of indicating the future in the first half of 1;11. She added the adverb of time *soon* frequently: *Mammy, coming, soon* (531, 554, notes). It served obviously to avoid misunderstanding as present tense and may therefore be interpreted as an analytic future-tense form. I do not claim that the auxiliary "will" was understood; in fact the standard colloquial language itself can omit it and use the copula in the present tense with future function. The use of an adverb of time to indicate the future, the normal pattern of colloquial German, is often reported as the first form of the future (cf. Decroly p. 191, great variations in time; Gutzmann, p. 17 f., cites a statement, poorly formulated, by Goldammer to the same effect). In languages with a synthetic future, like French, the situation is different. There the future is often called easy and early (Feyeux p. 164; Perez 1895, chapter VI, p. 462: sense of time remains, however, very vague even at ages 5–7); but in Decroly's own case (p. 191) it was restricted to the verb "avoir" 2;11–4;8. English: O'Shea p. 100 f. ("shall" and "will" at age 2–3, at first mechanically; with understanding, age 3 or later; "shall" is rare even at age 10–11).

distinction of tense forms had begun to be learned, we cannot expect other, logically more difficult verb forms to be attempted.

There was no trace of passive constructions, which are a variant pattern of standard languages quite dispensable for simple thought expression. (The first passive was noted at 2;10, 736.)[57]

Subjunctive forms did not occur in any function. They belong to a much later stage of language development.[58]

589. The results of our examination of the verb are negative as far as its morphology is concerned. Even as vocabulary items verbs were late. Although Hildegard's words were based on standard verbs early, their function did not at first differ from items based on other classes of standard words. When her sentences began to be molded more and more in standard patterns, the verb continued to be omitted in many instances until the end of the period under consideration. It was not until the last month of the second year that verbs became more frequent as organic elements of sentences (and a striking increase did not come until the first weeks of the third year). It is no wonder then that formal discriminations for the varying functions of verbs were still beyond the child's power of grammatical analysis.[59]

590. In fact, in looking back over the whole chapter of morphology, we must clearly conclude that Hildegard had taken no more than the very first steps toward learning the morphological mechanism of language by the end of the second year. Standard grammatical functions were beginning to develop, but these functions were as yet tied to very few formal signs. Neither synthetic forms (endings, prefixes, modifications of the stem) nor analytic forms (use of form-words like articles, prepositions and auxiliary verbs) had been learned as systematic patterns of expression. Syntactic constructions were more advanced than the morphological devices to indicate them.

---

[57] Smith (1935) p. 201: The youngest of 220 children to use the passive was 34 months old. "Instead of the correct passive, the children used the verb 'got' or 'get' as 'it got made.' " (This construction should be counted as a real passive. It is a new passive pattern developing in the colloquial standard, much preferred by children to the literary pattern. Hildegard learned *got* in present-tense function at 2;1, but for the time being as a synonym of the full verb "have", active voice, 586.) Ament (p. 170) observed the first passive a month earlier, at 2;9; he adds an example from Sully, which he mistranslates from English. Decroly (p. 191) assigns the beginning of the passive to 2;6. He follows Stern (p. 254), whose children used the first passives between 2;3 and 2;7 and who culls the first examples from Preyer 2;7 and Lindner 2;7. The example which Decroly adds from his own observation (p. 192) at 2;5 is not clearly a real passive.

[58] Cf. Stern p. 251 f.; Preyer p. 244 (from Lindner's record). Karla began to learn hypothetical constructions in English at 3;3.

[59] Further references to tenses: Bohn (1914) p. 585 (future and past as early as 1;7); Bergmann p. 243 (tenses not until age 4 or shortly before, in German); Guillaume p. 225 (children 2–4 years old); Gheorgov pp. 248 f., 340 ff.

What we have found in the way of morphological devices amounts to no more than the following scanty items: a few plural endings 1;11 (567); genitive (possessive) endings attached to two names 1;10 (568); an experimental German infinitive ending 1;8, which was soon given up (575); the ending -*ing* attached to two verbs 1;8, without real learning of the present participle or gerund (573, 578); *don't* as the only auxiliary 1;11, without conjugation (583).

General Linguistic Problems of the First Two Years

591. Not all phenomena of infant language can conveniently be included in the traditional organization of grammar (vocabulary, sounds, syntax, morphology), which has been the guiding principle of all preceding discussions. The observer's attention is drawn to some problems of a more general nature, in which the linguist rubs shoulders with the psychologist and the philosopher. Without intending to encroach upon the fields of these other sciences, the linguist cannot afford to disregard the boundary regions. There should not be a no man's land between neighboring sciences. Exploration of the area from all the adjoining territories is preferable to blanks marked "Unexplored" on the map. Philosophers and psychologists use the field of language for the purposes of their studies, and they could not do otherwise, because language is basic to all aspects of human activity on any except the lowest plane. Linguists should likewise not confine their attention to the mechanics of language, but cast a glance at the purposes which they serve and the manner in which they do so.

These matters of principle are debated among present-day linguists. Those among them who wish to restrict the field of linguistics to the behavior of language directly accessible to observation should have found ample material in the preceding parts of this study, in which, I think, I have not strayed far from objective matters. They are invited to disregard the following chapter. Those whose convictions call for a less resigned attitude may wish to follow me further. I shall endeavor not to lose myself in matters which are beyond the linguist's competence.

592. The great field of semantics lies beyond the confines of the mechanics of language in the strictest sense; yet avowed mechanists include it in their consideration of language. For anybody but the most rigid behaviorist there is behind every word or combination of words an idea, which is expressed by these linguistic means. It is not easy to define an "idea". For the present purpose it may be sufficient to say that it is something which is different from ·the mere phonetic complex of the word, something for which the phonetic word serves as a tool. Words are instruments with which the speaking individual attempts to shape his inner and outer world in accordance with his needs and desires. They communicate to others the intellectual, emotional, and volitional stirrings within him, for practical or aesthetic reasons. I leave untouched the question whether words are created by "ideas", or "ideas" by words. I would say that the current flows in both directions; but this problem would lead us too deeply into purely theoretical considerations pertaining to the philosophy of language. At any rate, each individual utterance is preceded by happenings in the speaker's mind (or, for the mechanist, in the speaker's body) which have not yet been crystallized into the relatively sharp outlines of words. The speaker has a choice among a variety of forms of expression which are suitable to convey his experiences or urges to the hearer.[1] The phonetic word sums up a complex of experiences, which is called its meaning (or meanings).

593. The literature of child-language is full of discussions concerning the growth of concepts. Preyer made it the center of his careful factual record, and many writers since his time have debated the problem, arguing for or against him, or attacking the problem independently. Stern is one of those who have tried to come closer to a solution by establishing a hierarchy of concepts of different scope.[2]

Essentially this whole discussion is a fight about terms and their definitions. On the one hand there are indeed several different levels of concepts with varying degrees of abstractness and precision in the language of adults. Without entering into a definition of "concept", we must obviously expect the small child's concepts to be less abstract and less precise than the maturest concepts of adults; but it should also be emphasized that many of the working concepts of adults on an everyday level are imperfectly circumscribed and differ from a child's concepts only in degree of vagueness. On the other hand, the belief that any words have sharp, logical, unified, unvarying meanings in the developed language is a superstition which has been exposed for a long time, but which is slow to die. Erdmann showed nearly fifty years ago that the meaning of words, regarded descriptively, varies from situation to situation, and that there is hardly any word, even in the reaches of scholarly language, for which one definition is invariably correct. The school of descriptive ("general") semantics, which has recently succeeded in capturing the attention of educated laymen, has resumed the work of dispelling the fog of linguistic superstition by pointing out the haze of meaning in which words are enveloped; this part of its endeavor is a valuable contribution to a better appreciation of the language tool. The public is beginning to see that abstract words like "democracy", "individualism", "reactionary" have a diffused semantic content and appeal less definitely to the intellect than they seem to do at first glance. Erdmann

---

[1] Cf. Leopold (1932). I am conscious that my "definition" of "ideas" or meanings clears the haze only slightly. Many of the words used for it stand in need of definition themselves. Basically, however, that is true of all definitions. They define a word more clearly by providing more points of reference, but assume that the words used in the definition mean exactly the same thing to all users of the language. This assumption is gratuitous. Even the strictest definitions in the field of the most exact sciences cannot proceed to define the words used in the first definition, and so forth *ad infinitum*. Definitions are relative clarifications.

[2] Stern p. 195 f.: individual concepts, plural concepts, general generic concepts; the latter are learned during the fourth year; cf. Decroly p. 125.

makes it clear that this consideration applies as well to simpler words which are within the child's range of experience.[3]

594. Recognizing that the debate concerning the growth of children's concepts is essentially a debate about the definition of "concepts", and that it is not easy to establish a distinction between "concepts" and "meanings", I abstain from adding to the discussion about concepts and turn to the more directly accessible meanings of words.

Before I leave the concepts, however, I want to cast a glance at the bilingualism involved in Hildegard's language learning. As we have seen in the examination of the Vocabulary, there were many instances in which Hildegard used words from both languages for the same purpose, simultaneously or successively.[4] With regard to the crude linguistic system which she built up in the first two years, it would be quibbling to claim that such pairs of words did not cover exactly the same ground. She used *heiss* and *hot* exchangeably 1;8. She answered the challenge, "Say 'no more' ", instantly with *no mehr* 1;9, substituting an active German word for the passive English expression. She heard the remark, "Look at the cars", and reacted with the German word *"Auto"* 1;10, to show that she understood. She used *nass* and *all wet* as synonyms 1;10 and once uttered the hybrid phrase *all nass*. Although such amalgamations proved that her bilingualism had not reached the stage of putting two distinct language instruments at her disposal, they did show that something had developed behind her words which was not simply identical with their phonetic complex or indissolubly tied to it. In fact,

---

[3] Cf. Weisgerber (1929) pp. 62–66. Lewis (p. 220) stresses the fact that the categories of adults, like those of children, are practical, functional, rather than scientific. The fact that the meanings of simple words in the language of adults, or the concepts which they express, are likewise wavering and ill-defined, is not often faced in the discussion of children's concepts. A good passage from Winkler is cited by Köhler p. 202 f.; cf. Ament pp. 32 f., 149–151, 155. The views concerning children's concepts range from acceptance of a "great power of generalization" (Taine, according to Preyer p. 226; cf. Köhler p. 178) to denial of the existence of concepts until after several years; the application of one word to a variety of situations is then explained by the poverty of the vocabulary and the operation of vague associations (Wundt p. 301 f., Treitel p. 345, Conradi pp. 341–344). Many authors distinguish between child "representations" and adult "notions" (Cousinet p. 162) or recognize variations in the precision and scope of concepts. (Reumuth, Usnadze, Delacroix 1930, p. 299, Nausester vol. 8, p. 228, Meumann 1908). The growth of concepts beyond the range of active vocabulary is emphasized in Bloch (1923) p. 673 (discussion by Marcel Cohen), Preyer p. 92, Müller p. 117. The best summary of studies of children's concepts to 1929 is that of Köhler. Caution is certainly necessary. Hildegard and Karla both made excessive use of the word *pretty*, not because a strong power of abstraction allowed them to subsume a great number of impressions under one abstract concept, but because they lacked specific terms for many things and had to be satisfied with a vague emotional reaction. Karla dropped, Hildegard reduced the use of *pretty* when a more adequate vocabulary had been acquired. Cf. Erdmann pp. 196–198 on the distinction between abstracts of a lower order resulting from intellectual vagueness, and abstracts of a higher order resulting from intellectual discipline.

[4] Cf. vol. 1, pp. 176–179.

we shall find later, when we examine the various aspects of bilingualism, that this can be considered one of the advantages of bilingualism. The strict behaviorist would have to assume that the use of two different linguistic signs discloses a difference in the underlying linguistic situation or a difference in the purpose or functional value of the utterances. Such a conclusion would be manifestly absurd when applied to the bilingual elements in Hildegard's language. *Come on* meant exactly the same thing or served the same purpose as (*Komm*) *mit!*

Thus Hildegard disposed of meanings which could be detached from the phonetic words used to express them in one language and attached to different words taken from the other language. Such meanings, which were not indissolubly tied to fixed phonetic representations, may well be called concepts if we hold the definition of a concept for this purpose down to a level corresponding to the child's development.

595. We have cast a preliminary glance at the meanings of words in the examination of the vocabulary (vol. 1, pp. 169–171).[5] The classification according to the areas of the child's life will here be supplemented by a study of some of the categories which are of interest to the semanticist.

We shall leave aside the semantic implications of the formation of grammatical categories. Since the latter reflect forms of thinking they overlap with one of the domains of semantics, and a sharp line of demarcation cannot be drawn. The term "plural concepts", which has been used for the definition of one kind of noun concepts, reveals the contact which exists between grammatical and semantic categories. A concept which includes several individuals of the same kind in the semantic domain of a word is not far removed from a grammatical pattern which serves to distinguish between one and several individuals of the same kind. These matters, however, have been separated in this study and shall remain separated (cf. 624). The arbitrariness of this decision needs no excuse. It is inevitably inherent in any scientific analysis breaking up an indivisible whole into separate compartments for the purpose of close examination.

596. In re-examining Hildegard's vocabulary from the point of view of meaning, we shall keep in mind that meanings are necessarily hazy and vague at first, that the poverty of vocabulary compels the child to make use of words for purposes to which they are not adapted from the adult point of view, and that meanings become progressively sharper and closer to the standard. This process is parallel to the gradual refinement of the phonetic and syntactic systems, although the progress is less easily definable than the evolution of contrasting phonemic series (604; for contrast in meaning, cf. 625–627).

Take, for instance, the names of colors. Hildegard's first experience

---

[5] Meaning entered also into the discussion of blends (457). This aspect will not be resumed here, except in casual side-glances (602, 605).

with them came at 1;8. I called the last empty pages of a picture book "weiss", whereupon she reacted with *Schnee? No!* This shows that she understood the color name "white" to be associated with snow and apparently only with snow. She was puzzled that the word should be used for something that was obviously not snow. During 1;9 I often gave the names of colors to her, usually in pictures. I observed that she sometimes assorted her building-blocks by shape and color. On one occasion when she had assembled green blocks, I told her to add the remaining green ones. She did so and stated correctly that there were no more of this color (*alle!*). Then she showed me a white one and I named the color for her. At once she brought another one of the same color and shape and echoed excitedly *weisser!* This was the only name of a color which she said to the end of the year, and she did not use it again, spontaneously.[6] The only other words which might be considered color names were *light*, which she used once 1;10 as an adjective, *dunkel*, "dark", 1;8, and *dark* 1;10.

Thus categories of color had begun to develop, but their linguistic expression was in abeyance. She did not resort to emergency expressions. She used the classifying principle of colors in actions, but did not try to express it in words. She had grasped it by means of words presented to her, but it existed in her detached from any active phonetic forms. Her behavior proved the reality of a concept, or set of concepts, which was not indissolubly linked with a movement of the organs of articulation.

I have cautiously noted that her classification proceeded not only by identity of color, but also by identity of shape. It cannot be proved that shape was incidental and color the chief principle of selection. If it should be true that shape was equally important to her, this would only prove that her idea of color did not yet have the relative precision of the standard.[7] Some of the diary entries do not specify whether identity of shape was compulsory. I believe that on the occasion when Hildegard assembled all green blocks, shape was overruled and color dominated.[8]

597. Numerals are another category of an abstract nature; but in standard use it differs from that of colors by its intellectual preciseness.

Children usually learn to count early, but that does not mean that they master the meaning of numerals. A clear distinction must be made between the mechanical phonetic exercise of enumerating a set of numerals in conventional order, and the intelligent use of numbers with their standard logical meanings.

Hildegard learned to say the first numerals for counting at 1;10.

---

[6] Karla learned to name several colors B 1;10; cf. vol. 1, p. 129, note 273.

[7] "Relative precision", because the names of colors are among the least precise of standard meanings.

[8] For colors, cf. Stern pp. 257–259, Bateman ("Colors"). Bateman finds great variation in the time of learning colors; his findings, from previous research and from his own investigation, are not included in Stern's discussion and bibliography.

There was an earlier instance of counting without the standard numerals at 1;8, when she pointed to lamp after lamp saying *Light — mehr light — mehr — Mama*. The last word represented a break in the procedure. It stated that the third lamp to which she pointed was next to her mother's favorite chair, and therefore came close to a possessive, the function of which (though not the form) developed during that month (568). Up to that point, however, the intention of enumeration of like objects is unmistakable. The child was getting ready for the intellectual exercise of counting, although it was not yet counting in developed form.

Another instance, about a week earlier 1;8, confirms the use of *mehr* for this purpose. Hildegard said *mehr Ball* twice, until she had her three balls together. The fact that she did not continue to say it after she had the last one, indicates with some degree of convincingness that she knew how many balls she owned. In other words, she had a functional numeral concept "three", although she did not yet dispose of a linguistic expression for it. This is the more surprising as numerical concepts later lagged far behind numerical words.

At 1;10 she began to learn counting with specific words, not, however, with the purpose of establishing the quantity of like objects, but "one, two, three" as a signal of an impending action. When she was lifted down and the cue "one" was given by an adult, she continued *two, three*. When the cue was given in German, "eins", she continued *zwei, drei*. The German sequence came out as readily as the English although I was not conscious of having practiced it with her. Later during the same month the two series were amalgamated into one. Upon the challenge, "Count!", she would utter the fixed sequence *three, two, zwei, drei*. The initial numeral "one" and its German equivalent did not appear in the series because they had too often been the cue given by adults. In fact, "one" remained submerged, whereas *eins* was sometimes expressed 1;11 in counting *eins, zwei, drei*; more commonly it, too, was omitted. Once she said a series of three numerals which seemed to add the next unit of counting, "vier"; in the light of later experience, however, the sequence was actually the hybrid *zwei, drei, three* (*Vier* began to be learned at 2;1). Another one was, once, *three, drei, two*.

At the same time, early during 1;11, the numerical concept of "two" began to develop, with a garbled phonetic expression: *three two shoes*, once, with reference to two shoes; a little later in the month, *three two Auto*, with reference to two toy autos. The passive understanding of the meaning of the same numeral was aided at the same time. She had several cookies and I asked her: "Gib Papa zwei". She hesitated with the execution of the request, first tried to give me only one, but then added the second. Obviously, she had no clear idea what "zwei" meant; but the fact that I was not satisfied until she had given me two cookies must have contributed to the learning of its meaning.

Thus the numerical meaning of "one" was undeveloped; that of *two* was beginning to become clearer; but *three* was no more than a mechanical unit in a sequence, an unstable one at that, with no concept of any kind behind it.

Otherwise the last month brought no further progress. The announcement of an action like jumping made use of the same emphatic intonation which the adults used for the purpose, but settled into the fixed hybrid series *three, two, zwei*. (At 2;1 it was *three, two, zwei, drei*, which was also used once with the indefinite meaning of "many", with reference to many fishes in the Chicago Aquarium. The meaning of *two* was quite clear by that time. Cf. **669**. The distinction between numerals as phonetic words and numerical concepts has to be kept in mind in the later development. Counting as a mechanical exercise is learned early; but its application to the counting of objects is more difficult, and the learning of relative numerical meanings for the individual numerals is still another matter.[9])

598. Since numerals are abstracts[10], we proceed to the discussion of other examples of abstracts in Hildegard's vocabulary. Of course, an abstract is nearly as difficult to define as a concept. There are degrees of abstractness.[11] Also, the classifying principles of the standard language cannot simply be applied to the child's language. Hildegard's early word *hot* 1;4, for instance, should not be called an abstract during the first month of its life, when it was associated only with radiators in the apartment, for which she had no other name. Even the facial expression of caution, which accompanied it, gives no clue, since nouns could have heavy emotional components. Very soon, however, from B 1;5, the word was also used for the flame of a match, and as soon as it could be applied to a variety of hot things, its adjectival and abstract character was better established.[12] The degree of abstractness was low, because the controlling criterion for the application of the word was a sensory impression. Even then the child's power of abstraction was limited. At 1;10, when working on a picture (framing it?), I complained about the weather with

---

[9] As late as 3;3 and 3;5, Hildegard had clear numerical concepts no higher than two, although she threw around much higher numerals. Even "two" was not completely distinguished from indefinite plurality. Cf. **752, 756**. The situation was the same with Karla. When she received permission to take two pieces of candy, she would take a handful. She could count to ten at B 1;11, with preference for and better accuracy in the higher numerals of the series. For other observations concerning the learning of numerals, cf. Jespersen p. 119 f. (good comments on the learning of his son), Court, Perez (1895) p. 459 f., Neugebauer (1915) pp. 301–306, Beckmann (older children), Preyer pp. 160, 165, 247, Gheorgov pp. 282, 383 f., Nice. The results of most of these studies are closely parallel to mine.

[10] Perez calls them "abstractions numériques", and Jespersen warns that children from age 4 often think more abstractly with regard to numerals than educators assume (references in preceding note).

[11] Cf. note to **593**; Perez 1895; Kirkpatrick (1891) p. 175.

[12] Karla used the word for a greater variety of hot things from 1;4; cf. vol. 1, p. 88, note 158.

the sigh, "Es ist heiss". Although the German word for "hot" was just as familiar and intermittently used by her, Hildegard could not grasp its extension to the temperature of the air. She felt different parts of the picture before me to see if they were hot. The range of the adjective was restricted to tangible objects (not excluding the flame of a match!). The word was at first associated with one class of objects, radiators, then gained in range of applicability and abstractness, without reaching the full range and abstractness of standard usage. This is parallel to the learning of the color name "white", which was at first tied to snow and was not freed from this limitation without a struggle (596).

In the sense of applicability to a variety of things and situations, other descriptive adjectives might be called abstract, particularly those with intangible meaning like *naughty* 1;5, *new* 1;11. It cannot be denied, however, that this definition of abstractness is a wide one. Even the application of one noun to a variety of things of the same class is an abstraction in this sense, as has often been argued, correctly. Adverbs are abstract in the same sense, even adverbs of place.

If we use a more limited definition of abstract, as we usually do when we use this principle of classification, we must come to the conclusion that abstracts did not yet figure in Hildegard's language. Of course, negatives like *no* 1;6 and *not* 1;11 may be called abstracts when they figure in factual statements rather than in negative wishes, denying as they do a situation indicated by the other words of the utterance. On the other hand, we have found that adverbs of time, which are by their nature more definitely abstract than adverbs of place, remained below the threshold of speaking (554). The child's indifference to time distinctions in the use of verbs (584–589) points in the same direction.

Even the low degree of abstractness involved in indications of time was thus still beyond the grasp of the child.[13] It is therefore futile to look for abstracts of a higher degree. There were no abstract nouns in the more restricted sense in which the term is usually applied to the standard language of adults. The adjective *naughty* 1;5, which expressed a moral judgment, was perhaps the most abstract word which occurred. It had no positive counterpart ("good").

Hildegard's speaking was as yet tied closely to things present and accessible to sensual perception. At 1;10 she would tell long stories for the purpose of delaying her bed time. She took nearly all her clues from objects which she saw around her. Of course, a certain amount of detachment from the present situation was possible, speaking of things and persons not present, etc.[14] The span of memory (649) was at times a week long (1;9, 532). This detachment was better developed recep-

---

[13] Hildegard used *now* occasionally from 1;8, but only in the fixed phrase *now this*, in which it does not indicate abstract time, but succession of acts. This idea is also abstract, but on a lower plane. Its enumerative function takes it into the sphere of numerals.

[14] Cf. C. Bühler p. 148.

tively than productively. Also at 1;10, I once told her that her cat had sore eyes, when the cat was not there. A check in the form of questions and answers after ten minutes proved that she had understood perfectly. The very fact that we have to resort to the enumeration of such items in a section on abstracts shows that the power of abstraction was at a quite rudimentary stage of development.[15]

599. Leaving the discussion of categories of meanings expressed by conventional words, we turn to the problem of unconventional means of expression. The question whether or not children invent or create words is the subject of a lively discussion in the literature concerned with child-language.[16]

The first need in approaching this discussion is a definition of what is meant by "invention" or "original creation". For many writers the terms include all cases of free, unconventional handling of conventional linguistic elements, particularly the coining of derivatives and compounds not current in the standard language.[17] For others only the use of phonetic words without a prototype in the standard is covered by them.

Obviously these two matters are on an entirely different plane. In my opinion it would be a rare child who would be so unoriginal as to use exclusively the derivatives and compounds presented by the standard language. Such a child would not get very far in speaking. The purely imitative aspect of language learning is restricted to the acquisition of basic vocabulary items and the sounds of which they are composed. The learning of the more abstract patterns of language in syntax and morphology does not proceed by imitation of fixed phonetic material, but by application of abstract linguistic principles to variable phonetic material, that is, by analogy. In the analysis of the foregoing chapters we have made it a point to distinguish between grammatical inflections and syntactic constructions used in fixed phonetic sequences and those applied independently to varying phonetic materials. We have considered only the latter as proof of the acquisition of higher linguistic categories and emphasized that false analogies reveal better mastery than correct forms slavishly imitated.

---

[15] Neugebauer (1915, pp. 301–306) calls abstracts easy; but the examples which she gives involve only verbs like "scold", "wish", "understand", and belong to age 2;3–4. Preyer (p. 81) claims that abstractions are possible without words, but that higher abstractions presuppose language; cf. pp. 79, 83, 90. Lukens (p. 425) makes the point, based on the findings of speech pathology, that abstracts, in a wider sense, are learned latest, but retained longest; cf. Vendryes p. 135 f. (English edition).

[16] Compayré (p. 294) traces the theory of children's linguistic inventiveness back to Rousseau 1753 (*Discours sur l'origine de l'inégalité*) and other early French writers.

[17] Extension of meaning and other unconventional handling of imitative material are included, for example, by Bergmann (p. 238 ff.), Bateman (1915, p. 486), Grégoire (p. 265).

The patterns of word-formation stand midway between these two fields. Take as an example Hildegard's designation of an airplane at 1;9 as a *peep-peep-Auto*. It was a compound noun consisting of a designation of birds by a conventional reproduction of the sound which they make, and a conventional designation of a car. Both elements of the compound were learned by imitation of phonetic complexes presented to the child. Phonetically there was nothing original in the designation. On the other hand, no adult had spoken of an airplane as a "bird-auto". The process of combining two imitatively acquired phonetic words in order to create a compound in which the two elements restrict each other's meaning to form an expression for a new concept was original. The fact that the creative act was performed as an emergency solution to overcome a vocabulary deficiency takes nothing away from its originality. The principle of expressing a new meaning by combining two words was learned from standard practices. In cases like *egg-spoon*, *egg-ball* 1;11, which may or may not have been presented as compounds by adults, but which are entirely conventional in their formation, the acquisition of the principle of compounding is less clearly demonstrated. They may have been purely imitative. Again the unconventional compounds show the progress more clearly than the conventional ones. *Ei ball* 1;11, a hybrid compound of the same meaning, is a more clearly mature linguistic feat, since the adult speakers did not mix languages in their compounds. It proves that the principle of compounding nouns had been learned and was applied independently in a manner not sanctioned by the model.

Derivatives come at a later stage.[18] The principle operating in them is closely akin to compounding: imitatively acquired elements, word stems and prefixes or suffixes, are put together independently.

If we accept this view of word-formation, we shall not be tempted to call unconventional compounds and derivatives original inventions or creations. Originality is displayed in them, to be sure, but it amounts to no more than independent handling of procedures learned from standard speakers. It is exactly on a par with weak conjugations like "he speaked" instead of "he spoke", for which the third year brings many examples and which prejudiced observers call mistakes or errors rather than original inventions.

600. Noun compounds not taken over from the standard languages,

---

[18] Stern pp. 402, 407–416. Tappolet (p. 408) gives amusing examples of original word-formations not in agreement with standard ones. Karla called the hammer used in her "pounding game" obstinately a *pounder* at B 3;0. Hildegard's German noun *Trink*, which she used persistently in later years (vol. 1, p. 73, note 115), although neither a compound nor a derivative, would be an original word-formation for a monolingual child. Actually it was modeled on the common English noun *drink*, which had been in her vocabulary from 1;10. Preyer's example "messen" 2;2 meaning "to cut" is a back-formation from "Messer", "knife" (p. 162).

but formed independently by the child should therefore not be called original creations. Since the topic has been broached in this connection, Hildegard's coinages of this type will be examined here before we come to the subject of real inventions.

There is no need to discuss standard compounds learned by the child. They were treated phonetically like simple words of several syllables and learned by imitation. The only point of interest is the fact that sometimes Hildegard seemed later to become aware of the compound nature of such words, that is to say, she felt the connection between the elements and the corresponding simple words and adjusted their phonetic form to the latter. That could not happen with a word like *Bleistift* since neither element existed as a word by itself in her language. In fact, its simple, unified meaning ("pencil") prevents adult speakers from becoming conscious of its compound character unless they cease to use it naïvely and focus their attention on its formation. *Pocketbook* is different. From 1;8 the child's form consisted of two syllables, which reproduced the two stressed syllables of the standard. At 2;1 the unstressed middle syllable was also reproduced. Of course, the progress in phonetic imitation may be credited with this improvement; but the agreement in form with the simple words, both of which were in Hildegard's vocabulary, makes it likely that she had recognized the formation of the compound, in spite of the slight semantic connection (a pocketbook, a term for a lady's handbag, has little to do with either "pocket" or "book"; for that matter, it is no longer a "hand"-"bag" either).[19] The development of *toothbrush* (472) was similar.

The history of *Nackedei* is parallel. From 1;6 it had a garbled form. At the beginning of the third year it was suddenly phonetically perfect, without transition. The improvement was even more striking in this example; but, of course, it is not a compound, but a derivative.

Hildegard's first original compound was *Piep-piep-Auto* at 1;9.[20] This clever designation of an airplane, with its allusion to the two outstanding characteristics (599, 613), remained a nonce-word and the most independent of her formations. Of the later examples only one approaches it in originality: *bottle pieks*, *Wehweh* 1;11 for a medicine dropper, with reference to the material of which it was made, glass, and to its pointed shape, which recalled the pain produced by other pointed objects like pins; *Wehweh* was probably a pleonastic repetition of the idea expressed by the interjection *pieks*. This coinage can hardly be called a compound noun (601); as such it should have had *pieks* in first place, according to the rules of English and German noun composition.

---

[19] Karla reached a form E 1;11 which did not contain the middle syllable, but may have been based on an analysis of the compound just the same: ˈpˤaˑk buk.

[20] Stern (chapter 22) gives long lists of original compounds to 6;0 from the literature, but only three of the many authors represented report examples earlier than 2;0.

The ideas were strung up more loosely than in normal compounds, but the difference is not great psychologically.

Both of these examples were original circumventions of vocabulary exigencies. Other compounds were much more conventional. It is therefore not always possible to be sure that the child formed them herself. Some may have been heard from adults. The second example, *baby-bottle* 1;9, conventional as it is in its formation, was original. Her mother told her that she had used this bottle when she was a little baby. Thereupon she asked for it with the compound, into which she condensed the explanation. The compound, in fact, the whole four-word utterance in which it was contained, had level stress, which shows that the composition was not yet completely standard (**472**). *Oil-spoon* 1;9, about a week later, was judged to be an original compound coined to designate the spoon used for cod-liver oil. In it the second element had secondary stress. *Paper-ball* B 1;11 may have been an original compound. On the first occurrence it designated a ball of tin-foil, with a transfer of meaning induced by a gap in her vocabulary. The first element had secondary stress, the primary stress falling on the second. A few days later, Hildegard used the same compound with initial stress for a real paper-ball.[21] *A-a paper*, at about the same time, was definitely original. She saw a roll of toilet paper in a store and expressed the idea by using the German nursery term for the physiological function involved, shocking her mother, who was not at once conscious of the fact that it would not convey any meaning to English-speaking by-standers. Since "toilet" was not in her vocabulary, the compound was formed much like the standard one, but not based on it. *Egg ball* for an egg-shaped rubber ball had level stress and was therefore probably a self-formed compound not fully welded into one word. The adults took up the compound in English and German form ("Eiball"). Hildegard's blend *Ei ball* (**599**) was presumably not a mechanical bilingual blend, but a reconstruction of the compound with disregard for the language boundary. *Egg-spoon*, with secondary stress on *spoon*, seems conventional. *Ball-beads* for one spherical wooden bead must be original; it had level stress.

The most interesting compound is *Mann-Frau* 1;11 for "woman". It had no root in standard practice. The re-enacted etymology of the English word ("wife-man") in reversed order is, of course, an accidental similarity, though the parallelism is not without interest. Hildegard had long obstinately refused to separate "woman" from "man" (**609**). In pictures she called women *man* 1;5–2;1. Constantly corrected by me, she learned *Frau* 1;7; but four months later, the path from *Mann* to *Frau*, which we had often traveled together, led repeatedly to the

---

[21] Cf. **471**. I am no longer so sure that the compound was original. I have the impression that her mother sometimes stressed the second element, using "paper" like an adjective.

totally unconventional compound. Naturally, it could not maintain itself in her language. This was the only semantic blend which resulted in a compound.

601. Somewhat related to original compounds is the use of paraphrases to explain a meaning. In fact, a phrase like *bottle pieks, Wehweh* is really better described as a paraphrase than as a compound. At 1;10 Hildegard used ephemerally **dak** for a pencil. I misunderstood the word as "duck". She laughed and used her regular word **dadi**, *Bleistift*, to explain what she meant, but then returned to **dak** (*Stock?*), which disappeared from her language thereafter.[22] In *This on beads* 1;11, although said without a pause, the specific noun *beads* must be in apposition to the unspecified reference *this*, as an explanatory afterthought. When I misunderstood her statement **baɪ bu!** as "Der Ball ist kaputt" (a case of poor judgment on my part; neither word could have this phonetic form at that time, 1;11), she explained the second word ingeniously by *balloon way up*. (When, at 2;1, the mysterious word **daʃ**, probably *crash* with various extensions of meaning, was not understood, she explained it by *throw away*, **671.** She paraphrased the misunderstood word *peg-board* effectively by *put in hole(s)*, **671.**)

When a request of hers was refused with the words, "Nein, Papa muss arbeiten", she accepted the excuse and said *Papa read book* 1;11. This was her interpretation of the character of Papa's work. The conversation took place in the bathroom, thus without support from the situation.

602. Cases of child-etymology also belong in the neighborhood of compounds, because they often involve compounds or presumed compounds, or derivatives. These cases command special attention only because they reveal an etymologizing activity of the child with results unacceptable to standard speakers. Failures of this type are bound to happen on account of the restricted experience of small children; but they are based on the same activity as the more numerous instances of successful etymologizing. They prove what correct forms cannot prove: that the child does not proceed merely by imitation of individual items in learning words, but tries to establish semantic and formal connections between various items of the vocabulary,[23] and this is, of course, an important step in the process of language learning. The finding of such links facilitates greatly the acquisition of a more extensive and more flexible vocabulary, and failures by the way-side are markers of progress.

Blends **(457)** are early indications of the operation of this tendency.

---

[22] This example is not exactly a paraphrase; but the procedure of explaining a misunderstood word by another is related in character.

[23] H. Schuchardt (*Schuchardt-Brevier*[2] p. 426, quoted by Weisgerber, 1903, p. 151) emphasizes that man in general naturally strives for etymological connections. The record of Neugebauer (1915, pp. 301–306) reveals an unusually strong degree of etymological consciousness in her son during the third year.

In those instances in which semantic proximity of two words induced the child to evolve phonetically similar forms, we can assume that she had a feeling that similar meanings are expressed by similar forms. In Hildegard's case this feeling was strengthened by the fact that a great number of meanings had closely related forms in the two standard languages.

Now, cases of child-etymology originate in the conviction that similar forms must express similar meanings. This is generally true, but there are instances of misleading similarity, and at the early stage which is considered here, the formal similarity need not be very close. In Hildegard's case particularly, with many of her words based on two words in two standard languages, the disregarding of minor differences was encouraged. Thus we get the examples of child-etymology reviewed in **457:** *miau* analyzed as *mehr auf*, *Leona* as *mehr Oino*, *petticoat* as *pretty coat*. The deflection of the adverb *in* into a form corresponding to the interjection *ätsch* is a little different. Here the identity of the meaning in the child's conception induced identity of form, although it is true that the discrepancy between the forms of the two standard words must have seemed less great to the child than it does to adults.

The list of examples during the second year is short, because Hildegard did not yet imitate longer, more complicated words. More instances are bound to occur in the expansion of the vocabulary after the second year.[24]

603. Having removed several categories of deviations from standard usage which should not be called original inventions or spontaneous creations, we come to the only category to which these names should be applied, namely the creation of sound-sequences not based on standard words, but associated with definite, stable meanings.

Even with this restricted definition of the terms, observers disagree violently. Some claim that children do invent words; more are emphatic in denying it. "Why invent what exists?" says Delacroix.[25] To be sure, the child can find everything it needs for linguistic expression in the model language or languages and strives to imitate the model as faithfully as possible. Yet, there remains the possibility that on the long road to its acquisition the child may not always find the desired expression at once and may proceed independently to fill the gap, taking the risk of not being understood at once. This risk cannot loom large for the child since the same thing happens all too often with the phonetically crude imitations of standard words.

---

[24] All examples in Stern's last chapter are later than 1;11. Most of them belong to the fifth year. Sully (pp. 185–187) discusses child-etymology with some interesting examples (in the Lord's Prayer, "Harold be thy name"; neuralgia, "old ralgia"). Jespersen (p. 122) also gives some good examples from the literature.

[25] 1934, p. 3, within a general discussion of language learning. On p. 19, he refers restrictions on inventiveness to a general sociological frame. There is such a thing as invention, he grants (1924), but it does not go far and is not very original.

In examining the discussions of previous writers on the subject, it seems advisable to separate very early instances of invented words from later ones in children's lives.[26] At the time when the imitated language consists only of a few words, the temptation to invent should be much greater than at a later stage, when imitation has progressed to a more satisfying frame and when the capacity to imitate needed additional items has grown.

With regard to the earliest period, we need to examine the list of eight non-standard words with which the index to Hildegard's vocabulary (vol. 1, p. 140) begins. Six of them were very early, starting between 0;8 and 1;0. One of them was counted as the first "word" 0;8; several are among the earliest words (p. 151).

These items were carry-overs from babbling.[27] They were included in the vocabulary because definite meanings became attached to them, no doubt with a little passive aid of the environment. The adults were willing to understand them in the meaning which was associated with them. This kind of "invention" is likely to play a part in every child's linguistic development. The extent to which such "words" take root in a child's language depends on the reaction of the environment. It is natural for the family to take up such words, use them actively, and thereby reinforce them strongly, although the wisdom of this procedure is questionable. Hildegard's environment tried to avoid baby-talk, and consequently the babbling-words did not last long. The only one the life of which extended over more than a few months was a demonstrative interjection, which existed for at least ten months in variable phonetic form. It, too, was eventually replaced by standard words.

Two of such items began much later, in the stage of imitative language. The interjection kχ, indicating that something tasted bad, occurred twice 1;7 and 1;10. It was not learned from presentation, but seems to be a primitive reaction of wide-spread spontaneous occurrence.[28] Presumably it symbolizes gagging. It did not gain a foothold in Hildegard's language. The other item is bu:: as an imitation of the sound of thunder. It was recorded once 1;11. It looks like an original onomatopœia;

---

[26] Compayré, in his long, intelligent discussion (pp. 293–311), always has early babbling words in mind when he admits the existence of a limited amount of original invention.

[27] Karla had more babbling words than Hildegard. At 1;3 she said nəmə-nəmənəm, the vowel varying to ɪ, which meant that she wanted to be lifted up into a chair. At 1;4 this had the simplified form nɪ:. At 1;4 she uttered a threefold glottal stop followed by voice in the musical intonation high-low-high whenever she wanted to be taken to the basement. It referred primarily to her "horse", which was kept in the basement. The intonation might symbolize the up-and-down motion on the metal spring.

[28] I can add to the parallels in vol. 1, p. 96, note 182 the observation that her grandfather once used the same sound, much later, when he was offered a food which he disliked. I am convinced that neither influenced the other.

but it is not improbable that it was based on a standard interjection of a somewhat different nature (vol. 1, p. 60).

That is all. Among her imitative words were a few which were difficult to trace to a standard word. The most striking examples are daʃ for different kinds of rapid motions 1;10–2;2 and nuk for "coat" 1;10. The former was eventually traced, by examination of phonetic correspondences and elimination of less likely prototypes, to *crash*, and the latter to *Schnucks*. These derivations are far-fetched, I grant, but not inherently improbable. It must be admitted that the derivation remains speculative. My frantic search for standard bases proves that my experience had by that time convinced me that all of Hildegard's words proceeded from standard words. Students who approach the problem with the conviction that children do invent words will undoubtedly take these words as proof of their thesis.

It must be kept in mind, however, that it is very difficult to follow the child in all the often crooked ways of sound-imitation and semantic modification.[29] Observers who attempt this with less detailed care than is done in the present record are bound to miss connections which exist but are not quite obvious. Stern (p. 386 f.) has criticized the lack of linguistic imagination and psychological intuition displayed in the examples of earlier scholars. His summary of the problem and of the discussion in the previous literature (pp. 385–393) is sensible and exhaustive. With him, I would grant the possibility of invention as a result of the play instinct. I find some such examples even in Hildegard's language at a later stage,[30] in spite of her linguistic conservatism. Such coinages of momentary playfulness, however, do not become established unless accepted by a group of speakers.[31]

Onomatopœias, including the imitation of noises, belong to the category of original inventions if they are primary, not taken over from conventional forms presented by adults.[32] We have seen (**468**), however, that there were no certain primary onomatopœias in Hildegard's infant-language, and few doubtful ones, which include the abovementioned **bu::** for thunder.[33]

---

[29] Karla had a word **dam, damp** at 1;10, which changed to dʌmp E 1;10 and meant "I want it" or "Give it to me". It looks like a real word, but I was unable to find the etymon. "Jump" seems too far removed in meaning.

[30] Wundt (p. 297 f.) finds arbitrary names for things from the fifth year on.

[31] Grégoire (p. 264), who attacks Stern, agrees that enrichment of the standard language by children's words, if it occurred, would not be due to the speaking activity of the children, but to that of the parents, who save the word from eclipse.

[32] Stern (p. 385) wishes to exclude them from the category. I grant that they form a class by themselves and are on a different linguistic level. They are a form of imitation, but not imitation of standard words; cf. Compayré pp. 303, 308, Preyer p. 100. Their position is intermediate between original and imitative words. I prefer to confine the definition of imitative words to those imitated from standard speech.

[33] Examples of authors arguing in favor of word-invention: Stevenson p. 120,

604. In the preceding discussions we have looked at certain categories of meaning and the manner in which the child expressed them. In the following part of the analysis we shall reverse the process and examine phonetic words taken over from the standard language with regard to the meanings attached to them in the child's usage. Every observer notices that these meanings do not at once agree with those of standard speakers. Meanings are learned gradually, just as phonetic forms are (596).

Complete failures are rare, particularly in the case of a child like Hildegard, who was cautious in the use of new words and did not attempt to incorporate them in her vocabulary until she felt some assurance that she could cope with them phonetically and semantically. There is nearly always some agreement between the standard meaning and the child's meaning; but the outlines of the latter are often less sharp at first than those of the former, even considering the fact that standard meanings themselves are less stable than the naïve observer is inclined to think (593).

Chambers (p. 30 ff.) has a neat metaphor to illustrate the haziness of meaning and the growth in clarity. The child's intellectual landscape is like a meadow in a dense fog. Near-by objects are clear. Those next removed in distance are dim. Remote ones are in a light of mystery. Beyond that lies the great unknown. "The child unquestionably perceives the world through a mental fog. But as the sun of experience rises higher and higher these boundaries are beaten back". "The inexperienced user of a new word chops now on one side, now on the other side of the line."[34]

605. Several authors attempt to break down the growth of semantic precision into categories. One aspect of this process is the progress from predominantly emotional (affective) and volitional (conational) factors

---

Kirkpatrick (1891) p. 176, Jespersen pp. 150–154; against: Bloomfield p. 30, Compayré pp. 293–311 (especially pp. 301, 303: invention only at earliest stage), Feyeux p. 165 f. (but original word-formation), Meringer p. 220 (agreeing with Idelberger and Stern; but definitely new creations with external inspiration), Nausester (1904) p. 37 (but the inflections in language are a playful creation of children—a bold hypothesis), Preyer pp. 153, 186, 216, 252 (von Taube case, p. 263), Treitel p. 345 ("The fairy tale of children's word-invention"), Wundt p. 297 f. A middle ground (invention very limited) is taken by Delacroix (1930) p. 332 f. (at least neologisms, which do not persist, however), Lukens p. 438 ff. (inventions playful or early and ephemeral; good collection of examples), Tappolet p. 411. Neugebauer has a special study of original formations; the scope of her study is wider than the present topic, but the examples from the speech of her son, who was very independent in the handling of language, are interesting.

[34] The same article presents an interesting demonstration of the haziness and the growing clarity of the meanings of selected words at a later age. Of 2922 "children", age 5–27, 98% were "befogged" as to the meaning of the word "monk" at age 7, 82% at age 12, 24% at age 17 (p. 50). Cf. Macdougall p. 34: "The child's mind wanders at first in a fluid medium of relations which is potentially indefinite."

to clearer and clearer objective reference, which has perhaps been analyzed best by Lewis.[35] Much about this aspect has been incorporated in the discussion of syntactic growth (507–541).

Considering the types of words used rather than the purpose of the whole utterance, Bloch (1921, p. 706) makes the point that proper names are the first to have exact meaning.[36] That is to be expected, because the variability of reference of standard words holds least for names. Still, even in this domain, children's usage is not without vacillation. Bloch himself excepts "Papa" and "Mama", which are rather late in having exact meaning, not because the child recognizes the shifting reference of the words in standard usage, but because he extends their application for a while (Hildegard: *Papa* E 1;2–E 1;3) to all men and women regardless of their relationship to any other person. In Hildegard's case (list 4, p. 170, vol. 1), it is to be noted that the name *Rita* was for four months (1;5–9) also applied to Rita's friend Helen.[37]

No principles of semantic stratification in Hildegard's selection of vocabulary are discernible during the first two years.[38] The guiding principle is the interest and need of the speaking child, and it will not be easy to reduce individual variations to a common denominator.

One further item should be recalled in preparation for the semantic analysis which follows. The association between separate semantic units and corresponding separate phonetic combinations is much less close in child-language than it is in standard languages. The linguistic accident of homonymy is a restricted phenomenon in the latter, whereas it plays a considerable part in child-language (458 f.; cf. vol. 1, p. 172 f.). Unless the etymological history of each child-form is first established carefully, observers are likely to be misled by homonyms into assuming many more instances of unorthodox handling of meaning than necessary.[39] Many solutions remain problematic at best; witness the numerous instances of blends (457), in many of which an influence of meanings on

---

[35] Pp. 143 ff., 212, 221. The teleological (volitional) value of knowing the name of objects is emphasized by Decroly (p. 120 ff.), who attacks Stern's belief in the child's awareness of the symbolical value of words. Contrary to Stern, he thinks that the stage of language of action comes before the stage of objective reference and finds arguments supporting his position in Tracy and Kirkpatrick. Much of the disagreement is explainable by the pernicious practice of too many authors to take nouns at face value at too early a stage. Bloch (1921, p. 710) states correctly that nouns at the early stages cover not only objects, but all activities connected with them. Premature statistics about parts of speech falsify the general linguistic picture.

[36] Cf. Decroly p. 121.

[37] Cf. note to 609.

[38] Velten sees the problem and aims at establishing "lexical patterns"; but his child was so slow in learning to speak that the yield of his article is much more significant with regard to the growth of phonemic patterns than with regard to the problem at hand.

[39] Change of meaning and overlapping of homonyms must be kept apart in semantic analyses of standard words as well; cf. Sperber p. 87.

phonetic forms was assumed. Much that happens in children's language learning can only be surmised. It is one of the purposes of this study to show that casual references to child-language, usually delivered with naïve confidence, cannot be trusted. The processes of the acquisition of the speaking faculty, fruitful as their study is for general linguistics, are anything but simple and obvious.

606. The learning of standard meanings attached to phonetic words is a complicated process. Just as the child gropes for the exact phonetic form and learns to imitate it with growing exactness until the prototype is reached, he keeps on widening and restricting meanings until they coincide with the standard ideal, with many failures along the way. Semantic learning is much more difficult because the standard language itself is arbitrary in the range of applications which it allows for a certain word, and shifts meanings with the context, whereas the phonetic material of word-stems is fixed and tangible. It is more difficult, too, than the learning of morphological devices to express syntactic relationships, because these devices are few in number and phonetically rather simple. Yet, the learning of meanings begins much earlier, because words without meanings are useless for the purposes of communication. A primitive communication can be achieved without morphological elements, but not without meanings related to the standard ones.

The child learns a word as applied to a certain situation, but not, as a rule, from a single application. The word occurs again and again in situations which are similar, but not completely identical. When the child is able to grasp the similarity of a situation with one previously experienced, the word connected with it will eventually emerge from memory, first passively and later actively (**643–647**). In learning to group different situations under the same phonetic expression, the child tries to follow the same procedure as the standard speakers, but will not always succeed at once. "A child is often faced by some linguistic usage which obliges him again and again to change his notions, widen them, narrow them, till he succeeds in giving words the same range of meaning that his elders give them."[40] This process must be groping and the way beset with failures, caused not only by the lack of experience on the part of the child, but also—it cannot be said too often—by the arbitrary and accidental practices of the standard language.

Let us illustrate with a few examples. If a child hears the word "brush" applied to a hair brush, many repeated occurrences in the same function will bring about a firm association between the word and the object. The word is, however, also used for a clothes brush, for a shoe brush, and even for a tooth brush (without the distinguishing prefixes at least in the function of the corresponding verb, which, in English,

---

[40] Jespersen p. 117.

has the same form). The child must at first be puzzled by the use of the same word for so many objects or uses, when these objects differ greatly in shape, size, and even material (shoe brushes are often made of lamb's wool). Since each of these uses occurs many times, always linked with the same word, the child will learn to associate the word with all of them and will perhaps eventually understand that the similarity lies in the function. Let us assume, then, that the child sees a painter's brush for the first time, knows no word for it and calls it "brush", because the function seems again comparable and the shape immaterial. He has performed an extension of meaning, which will evoke no comment from the English-speaking observer, because his language does the same. Let a German-speaking child perform the same extension of meaning and the adults will laugh or think the utterance odd, because standard German calls the first-named objects "Bürste", but the painter's brush "Pinsel".[41] As a further step the disapproval of the adults will, of course, induce eventual correction of the misapplication; but the fault of the intermediate mistake is not the child's.

On the other hand, when the child uses one and the same word for a handkerchief, a towel, and a napkin, as Hildegard did, the adults do not approve, although the function of wiping parts of the body links these objects more closely than brushes are linked by their functions. In fact, in this case German can use one word, "Tuch", for all three of them ("Taschentuch", "Handtuch", sometimes "Mundtuch"). Shape and material offer no sufficient inducement for distinction. How is the child to realize at once that in this case the slight differences in function call for entirely different words?

The word "glass" is used for the material and for objects made of it: drinking glasses within the small child's range of experience, other objects (eye glasses, spy glasses, magnifying glasses, etc.) on higher levels. Yet, when Hildegard used the word "bottle" for several kinds of objects made of glass, the extension was wrong. She had to learn that this word does not designate the material alone, but the shape and function. In view of the fact that the shape of bottles varies greatly, the child cannot be expected to know that a vaseline jar is not called a bottle, but commands a separate word.

If the child used for each object the word which the standard speakers use for it, in close imitation, no semantic mistakes would occur; but the ability to speak would be greatly hampered. To simplify the learning process and to extend the range of expressible experiences, the child must form his own semantic clusters. Again, mistakes attest the independent linguistic operations of the child, which lead more rapidly to real speach than pure imitation, in spite of the lost motion of mistakes. To this extent originality can be claimed for the child's handling of

---

[41] Cf. **869.** A good example of similar import, based on an observation of Stern's, is given by Lewis, pp. 191 and 212.

meanings. As in the domains of morphology and of word-formation, all independent applications of standard principles the results of which happen not to coincide with standard usage, are doomed to eventual extinction, as the relentless corrective force of the standard-language ideal imposes itself on the child's speech.[42]

607. In child-language, processes of growth are condensed in time and circumscribed by the rigid model of the standard language, which is the goal of the development. What would be called descriptive semantics and historical semantics in standard languages coincide in child-language. Descriptive (synchronic, static) semantics studies the variability of meanings with the context, the situation, and the intentions of the speaker; this is what is at present popularly understood by "semantics" (**593**). Historical (diachronic, dynamic) semantics studies the change which generally accepted sets of meanings undergo in the course of time in a community or language; this is what linguistic scholars have primarily been interested in for several decades. Both approaches to meaning are valuable, and light falls on both aspects from child-language, in which the two methods move into immediate proximity of each other.

608. For the purpose of grouping the phenomena affecting the meaning of words, the tentative[43] classification which has long been used by historical semantics is serviceable. We shall therefore look at Hildegard's meanings under the headings "extension of meaning" and "restriction of meaning".[44] The category of "transfer of meaning" is, in child-language, usually too closely related to extension to be kept separate from it. We shall keep in mind that this grouping is a methodological one and will as such sometimes prove to be too rigid to do justice to the complexity of the processes of living speech. Sometimes we shall find an overlapping and interaction between these categories of "change of meaning".[45] The frame of reference for "change" is in our case prima-

---

[42] The term "analogy", in a wide sense, can be applied to the learning of meanings, as Cousinet does. His paper gives many interesting parallels between semantic operations of children and adults, debating the theories of previous writers and discussing representations, concepts, and notions, terms which I have deliberately avoided in the text above. Semantic learning is, of course, not limited to infant-language. For uncommon words it continues through life. Tappolet (p. 405) shows that the meaning of the relatively common verb "sell" was still too restricted in the usage of a six-year-old girl; she protested that houses cannot be sold because they cannot be carried away.

[43] Cf. Sperber p. 94.

[44] Wundt (p. 301 f.) claims that there is no extension or restriction of meaning and no formation of concepts until much later, but that on each occasion an individual concrete object is named by association. I cannot see an essential difference between the two processes. The question hinges on the definitions of concepts (**593**), and an overrating of the intellectual character of adult word concepts is probably involved.

[45] In fact, every extension of meaning in child-language calls of necessity for a later restriction, if it is not in conformity with standard usage. (The last two chapters of Lewis's book deal competently with these two phases.) This is the

rily the semantic system of the standard language with its relatively fixed complexes of meaning, not the older meaning, as in historical semantics. Otherwise expressed, the standard meaning of the day is, in child-language, both the point of departure and the end of the semantic development, because the child tries to imitate what standard speakers carry to him and because his unorthodox handling of meanings has no chance to survive the process of conformation to the standard ideal.

Acts by which the child tampers with meanings are usually caused by his lack of linguistic experience.[46] He lacks certain words which he needs, and gropes for substitutes; and the standard words acquired do not yet possess the relatively sharp semantic outlines of the prototypes. Obviously, these two deficiencies work hand in hand. The methods which the child uses in his semantic manipulations are the same as in standard changes of meaning; the great difference is that the results are temporary makeshifts bound for obliteration, comparable to individual and occasional meanings in standard languages, according to Hermann Paul's terminology.

---

essence of the process of refinement of meaning in children's language learning. The successive extension and restriction as it affects the word "papa" is described by Sully p. 167 and by E. B. Holt in an unpublished paper quoted at length by Latif p. 155 ff. Indeed, the restriction to the child's own father is likely to be the first and the third stage, to be followed by a renewed, limited extension when the "shifter" value of the word is discovered (613). Sully (p. 167 f.) also calls attention to the fact that an original compound like "eye-curtain" for "lid" combines an extension of the meaning of "curtain" with a specializing restriction of its meaning by the addition of "eye". For the opposite process, initial restriction of standard meanings, with ensuing extension to the standard scope, see 632.

[46] Delacroix (1930, p. 318 f.) emphasizes the "linguistic poverty" of the child as the cause of extensions of meaning. "Il faut bien se servir de ce que l'on a. Peut-être que l'enfant qui dit ôter la peau du crayon pour tailler le crayon, ne fait pas une comparaison, mais s'exprime comme il peut." Surely; but that does not take away from the fact that the child performs a semantic extension of the word "skin", an act which is closely related to comparisons or metaphors of the standard language. Bloch (1921, p. 707) speaks of poverty of vocabulary and lack of experience. The two are on the same level. Both authors speak of generalization of meanings. The intellectual ring of this term is misleading. The child's early words have a vague meaning rather than a general one. This brings us back to the distinction made by Erdmann and referred to in 593, note. Cousinet (p. 159 f.) stresses that lack of words is not the only reason for extension of meanings. Children perform it, too, when they know the correct words. This should be admitted. Children proceed exactly as adults do, as Cousinet emphasizes, with references to the earlier literature. The distinction which he makes (p. 171) between the early naïve "analogies" and the consciously playful transfers performed in games of imagination at a later stage, is worth noting. A good explanation for the extended use of the few words of the earliest stage is given by Cohen, p. 116; he refers to Pavlovitch p. 116, where, however, the objectionable word "generalization" is used. Cohen's own formulation (p. 118) is better: "il n'y a pas lieu d'en conclure que l'enfant constitue une seule catégorie avec tous les objets voisins; mais les premiers mots acquis servent a désigner les objets contigus."

Instead of "change of meaning", we shall sometimes say "change of application" or "change of reference". These are more cautious expressions, which state linguistic facts without commitment concerning the underlying thought processes. Wherever the traditional terms are used, they should be understood in the same manner. "Extension of meaning" is the use of an old word for a new object, situation, or experience.

609. The most common phenomenon with regard to the use of words with a meaning different from the standard, is extension of meaning. The child subsumes experiences under standard words, the range of which has narrower boundaries in standard usage; or, expressed more cautiously, the child applies these words to situations in which the standard language does not permit their use.[47]

The arbitrariness of the limits is often that of the standard language. Before Hildegard acquired the word *Frau* (1;7), she had no word for "woman" and did not feel the need for one. Women played a much greater part in her life than men; but just for that reason they were individualized and had each their own name. Most of the names of persons in her vocabulary (vol. 1, p. 170, item 4) were female names, some of adults, some of children, and they were in much more frequent use than the few male names, nearly all designating children, many of which occurred only once or a few times.

Men in the street were called *Papa* E 1;2-E 1;3,[48] but later this ex-

---

[47] Sully (p. 161 f.) says that a child's extension of meaning "must not be taken to mean that he goes through a process of comparing things which he perceives to be distinct, and discovering a likeness in these"; cf. Kirkpatrick (1891), p. 175. On the other hand, Moore (p. 123 f.), who gives striking examples of extensions of meaning, emphasizes that use of the same word for a variety of things did not mean confusion of the things referred to; her boy called all girls Dorothy (as Hildegard called two girls *Rita*, 605) and referred to cats and cows by the word "bird", although he knew the difference between them very well (no such striking case existed in Hildegard's language). Sully (p. 163), citing an example from Taine, characterizes a bold extension of meaning as involving "plainly a rudimentary process of classification. Any point of likeness, provided it is of sufficient interest to strike the attention, may thus serve as a basis of childish classification". This should be admitted, and it should be added that the result is often different from adult procedure, but not necessarily so; standard meanings likewise embrace very different things; the boldness of extension is no childish prerogative; cf. Jespersen p. 115. Kenyeres (p. 199 f.) says that extension of meaning really amounts to associations evoked by some faint similarity of the objects or situations. Standard extensions proceed often by the same principle. It is a semantic fallacy to assume that for every standard word a definition must be found which embraces all its applications. That is why so many of the Indo-European roots reconstructed by comparative linguistics are supposed to have vague and general meanings.

[48] The fact that the name *Opa* for the German grandfather, 1;0-1, did not take root in Hildegard's language, but was replaced by *Papa*, may reflect the lesser need for individualization of men. *Papa* was on the way towards becoming the forerunner of the word *man;* but the semantic development was stopped by the protests of the environment. If this explanation is correct, the uses of *Papa* for

tension was rescinded, doubtless because of the critical reaction of the adults. By 1;5 the need for a general word for "man" was felt when she was describing pictures. (She had pointed out men and women in pictures since 1;4, but without a word.) She learned the standard word *Mann, man* for this purpose and transferred it correctly to living men from 1;6. The only thing which was wrong with her greeting to a neighbor, *Hello, Mann!* 1;10, was the fact that standard usage, arbitrarily, does not allow the biologically correct descriptive term to be used for social purposes. Meanwhile the word continued to be used for men in pictures, but also, persistently (to 2;1), for women in pictures.

Here is the chief point which I wish to make in this connection. In Hildegard's conception, the word "man" could be applied to men and women in pictures alike. Its range of applicability was that of "person" or German "Mensch".[49] In fact, English "man" can have the same range in the standard language ("Man is mortal"). Hildegard's only mistake was to perform the same extension of meaning on a level of everyday conversation, on which standard English does not admit it. Obviously, the arbitrariness is in the standard language. The great jump from men in pictures to living men met with the approval of the environment; but the slight extension from men in pictures to other persons in pictures was rejected. This, at the same time, serves as an illustration of the great intellectual labor which the child must perform to assimilate the semantic outlines of standard words. It is not always a question of mature logical thinking, but of following the vagaries of the standard language in its demarcation of meanings.

Hildegard did learn the German word *Frau* at 1;7, because I would correct her, "Nein, das ist eine Frau"; but it did not become a fully active word in her vocabulary (600). She used it only when I rejected the word *Mann*. It served only for women in pictures. To the end of the second year she did not feel the need of a general term for living women. That is probably the reason why *man* was never extended to women in real life. She would not have hesitated to do so, as she did with *Oino* (from *Onkel*), which, in actual usage, covered nearly the same range as "man", and was extended by her to grown-up women. Cf. the early use of *Papa* for *Mama*, 1;2; the difficulty in learning the word *Mama* was not phonetic, but semantic.

The distinction between adults and children was more vital to her than that between men and women. *Man* covered adults, *baby* meant children of any age, much to the disgust of older children who heard themselves thus described.

"Opa" need not be interpreted as reduplications of the second syllable of *Opa* (as was done vol. 1, p. 118).

[49] Cf. the early use of *Bild* (vol. 1, p. 54), which seemed at times reserved for pictures of persons. It went out of use before the word *man* was learned and may have been semantically its predecessor.

This discussion shows the coarseness of semantic contrasts which still prevailed at the end of the second year. The rough distinction between children and adults was appreciated. The finer subdivisions within these two categories were not yet well developed. *Frau* made hesitating inroads into the field covered by *Mann*. Similarly, *boy* was used, infrequently, from 1;8, after instruction, but *girl* did not appear until just after the turn of the year. In general the undifferentiated term *baby* sufficed.

610. Another illustration of gradual extension of meaning is the word *tick-tock*. We can leave aside the fact that this is originally an onomatopoetic term imitating the sound which a clock makes, presumably a pendulum clock. The word is used by standard speakers of nursery language with reference to any kind of time-piece. In fact, it was presented to Hildegard as a noun applied to my wrist-watch. These extensions are pre-historical as far as Hildegard is concerned.

Hildegard used *tick-tock* from 0;11, first with reference to my wrist-watch, soon also for a wall-clock. At B 1;0 she applied it to four or five watches and clocks which differed considerably in appearance, location, etc. Since the time-telling function of the instruments meant nothing to her, of course, the basis for grouping them together with regard to the application of the term must have been the fact that she heard the adults call all of them *tick-tock* or *Uhr*. The only possible clue in her own experience supporting this grouping is the sound which they all made (there were no electric clocks in her range of experience at that time). The sounds produced by a wrist-watch and a wall-clock are so different, however, that she would probably not have grouped them together linguistically without the inducement of standard practice.

Up to this point the extension of the meaning had followed standard usage. At 1;0 I showed her a gas meter, naming it in German, "Gasuhr". She said *tick-tock*. It is not easy to decide whether this was a purely linguistic reaction to the word "Uhr" or an association with time-pieces by the shape of the instrument. The word "Uhr" had not been presented often; at least in speaking to her, the nursery word "Ticktack" was favored. On the other hand this particular gas meter had round shape, whereas my wrist-watch and the other familiar time-pieces were square or rectangular.

Still, the round shape must have become characteristic of a *tick-tock* at some time, perhaps because some of the time-pieces, although angular in frame, had a round dial. At 1;2, on the ocean boat, she was greatly interested in a fire hose wound on a red spool, which she greeted again and again enthusiastically as *tick-tock*. The adult can see no other point of contact but the round shape. She certainly did not hear this object called "Uhr". At 1;3 she called a bathroom scale *tick-tock*, again on account of its round dial.

Roundness was not the only criterion, however. By 1;4 she identified clocks in the street, whether round or square. She was groping in more than one direction for making her use of the word identical with the baffling extensions and restrictions of the standard language. The example is particularly illuminating, because the unifying criterion in standard speech is the time-keeping function, and this function was bound to remain obscure to the child for a long time to come, since she had no sense of time (586). Thus she continued to attach the word to varying objects upon clues which did not satisfy the adult speakers: at 1;4 to the drawing or photograph of a machine, because a control-disc was the only part of it which evoked a memory in her, namely that of a clock-dial; at 1;9 to a round eraser for typewriter use. Roundness apparently remained an important criterion. On the last occasion she even held the eraser to her ear. I would hesitate to conclude that she mistook it for a watch. I prefer this analysis: the shape summoned up the word *tick-tock*, which she had often applied to circular objects. The saying of it evoked the memory of holding an object to which it was applied to her ear, and she did so mechanically. She did not really expect it to tick, and felt foolish for yielding mechanically to an impulse which was obviously out of place. Her facial expression revealed this feeling, or at least a doubt as to the correctness of the identification, if we insist on interpreting the behavior as indicating a logical operation rather than an acquired reflex.

The story of the word *tick-tock* shows a constant extension of its field of application. Some of these extensions found the approval of the environment, those to a variety of time-pieces. Others were indulgently admitted, those referring to discs of dial shape. Others were rejected: the hose spool, the eraser. In the latter half of the second year, Hildegard used the word most frequently correctly; but she could not be expected to achieve the correct limitation until time meant more to her.

611. From circular objects it is only one step to spherical ones. Balls are naturally the first object through which children become acquainted with spheres. Hildegard learned the word *ball* 1;0 in German form, 1;9 in English form. She applied it at first to her toy balls, of which she owned three at the time, one being crocheted. Historically, the standard use of the word for this purpose is probably a restriction of a more general meaning; but descriptively, I suspect that for most standard speakers it has become the basic meaning, the numerous other uses of the word "ball" being felt as extensions of it. At any rate, that is the situation for the child.

Hildegard used it at 1;4 to ask for a toy balloon, repeating the process which has taken place in the standard language, because "balloon" is ultimately derived from "ball", but violating standard semantic lines of demarcation, because a balloon can no longer be designated as a ball. She applied the same word to a ball of yarn. So does standard English, but with a consciousness of metaphorical use, which need not have been present in Hildegard's use. The similarity with her crocheted ball was great, and the functional difference may have been vague to her.

More strikingly she said it twice when she saw the dome of the observatory on the campus 1;8. She undoubtedly did not mistake it for a ball to play with. I also refuse to interpret the designation as the result of an intellectual operation of the type: "This object is approximately spherical as my balls are; therefore it should be named the same". The process is undoubtedly more primitive: the shape recalled that of the balls, and this recollection brought up the word *Ball*. It could be paraphrased: "When I see this object, I am reminded of my ball". Underlying this extension is, nevertheless, an incipient classification by the spherical shape, which the standard language performs in many instances with the designation "ball", but does not happen to permit in this instance.

Later extensions 1;11 were less adventurous. *Paper-ball* is standard; the spherical shape is rather imperfect, but the function often coincides. Both the form and the function of game balls are the bridges to extended meanings, in the standard language as well as in child-language. Hildegard did not learn the word "marbles", although the German equivalent "Marmeln" sounds similar. *Balls* sufficed. She did not yet feel the need of specification. The name is logically adequate, but the standard language prefers to emphasize the functional distinction rather than the similarity in shape. She did have a separate word for *beads*, which meant necklaces composed of beads, and wooden beads for stringing up. She needed it, because both the ornaments and the toy were important to her, and particularly because the beads were not always spherical. The classification by function outweighed that by shape in importance. For a wooden bead in spherical form she did coin the compound *ball-beads* once, which shows that the shape could emerge to secondary importance at times. The compounds *egg-ball*, and, in hybrid form, *Ei-ball*, were taken over from standard speakers. Adults and children can waive the emphasis on the shape in favor of the function. The solid rubber ball, which was shaped and colored like an Easter egg, served the same purpose as ordinary balls, with pleasantly surprising variations in bouncing effects, but differed in shape. If shape were the invariable classifying principle for balls, the designation "egg-ball" would contain a contradiction in terms. This shifting of the semantic link shows again how difficult it is for the child to learn the logically unreliable semantic system of the standard language. The child's procedure is no more haphazard than that of standard languages; but his performances have no chance to stand up against the authority of the standard language.

The material from which balls are made does not enter into consideration for the standard language: hollow rubber, solid rubber, wool, paper. The child did not need, on that account, to feel any hesitation in applying the word "ball" to the dome of the observatory or to glass marbles.[50] On other occasions, the material is the primary concern of the standard language and of the child, as has been shown for glass (606). When Hildegard used *paper-ball* for tin-foil rolled into a ball, the designation was not acceptable to standard speakers; but the distinction between paper and paper-thin tin-foil belongs to those finer distinctions which are not yet within the capacity of a small child.

612. An example of how material can be prominent in the child's attempts at classification in defiance of standard usage is the nursery word *Wauwau*, which reproduces the barking of a dog in conventionalized form and can therefore be applied as a noun only to dogs. Dogs differ greatly in looks, and they do not always bark. On the whole, this difficulty seems not to bother children much. Dogs are interesting enough, so that the classification becomes soon perfected by experience. Errors of judgment do occur. Hildegard called a stone lion *Wauwau* 1;1. She probably took it for the image of a dog, which is not surprising in view of the great variation in the appearance of dogs. Later on she used the word for a great variety of animals, real ones, sculptures, and pictures: horses (bronze book-ends 1;3, pictures 1;4, live horses 1;6, although she understood "Pferd"), an elephant (porcelain) 1;6, a sloth (picture) 1;8, an Easter lamb (made of cake with sugar frosting) 1;9. At that stage she presumably mistook them no longer for dogs, but she used the name of the most familiar animal for any animal. She had a number of other words for animals (vol. 1, p. 170, item 3); but many of these were conventional imitations of their voices learned by drill. Only birds seem to have been set off from quadrupeds early. Of the latter, the cat was the first to be added to *Wauwau* at 1;8, and cats were never called *Wauwau*;[51] before that, the call *kitty* had been imitated 1;3, but did not become established. No other animal name came to rival those of dogs and cats in importance. The mature word *dog*, with the diminutive *doggie*, did not make its appearance until 1;11. Apparently the single designation *Wauwau* was satisfactory for any mammal during the greater part of the second year. Although animals and their voices are of great interest to children, the break-down into species proceeded slowly and was not carried into great detail.

Aside from animals, the word was used for objects which were not animals, and this brings us to the topic of transfer of application by similarity of material. At 1;3 Hildegard used it for her toy dog, which was made of soft material, and for her soft house slippers, which had decorations simulating a face on them; they could be taken for a dog's face as easily as for any other kind of face. The transition to the emphasis on material is clearly discernible here. It should be stressed,

---

[50] But cf. **680.** Standard "glass marbles" shows how a designation can start out from a material and end up with a function, in complete oblivion of the origin.

[51] Karla did call cats *Wauwau* 1;4 (vol. 1, p. 131, note 278).

however, that the material was not the only bridge of extension. In the examples first discussed, material was entirely disregarded in favor of more essential characteristics. In objects which she handled regularly, the feel of rugged softness was quite likely to push itself into the foreground of attention. She had probably touched dogs and noticed the similarity of the feel of fur.

The example which shows this branch of semantic extension most clearly was observed at 1;4, when she saw an advertisement containing the picture of an old man clothed in furs. Her reaction to it did not mean that she took it for the picture of a dog, but that the shaggy furs brought dog's fur to her mind, that of real dogs or, more likely, that of her toy dog or her slippers.

Other extensions of the same word do not concern material, but proceed on similar paths of association. As early as 1;1 Hildegard asked for her picture book by "barking". In a sense, *Wauwau* meant then "picture book"; it was a linguistic device to induce the environment to produce it for her. To say that the meaning of the word was extended to include the picture book, is, however, a somewhat mechanical way of describing the process. What actually happened must be this. Wanting the book, she recalled primarily the pictures of dogs in it, and this imaginary stimulus produced the accustomed linguistic reaction.[52] The explanation is similar for her use of this word, at 1;7, for her own baby pictures, simply because on one of them she held a toy dog in her arm. The emotionally appealing incidental feature called forth the associated linguistic reaction. Perhaps this case could be called a "transfer of meaning". If the bridge, the dog visible in one picture, had remained unrecognized, the observer would consider the case puzzling.

The occasional meanings of *Wauwau* which strayed too far from the domain of the word in standard usage, receded as the vocabulary grew and made standardizing restrictions possible (630). In fact, for her baby pictures, the rival term *baby* was already in existence, and the general term *Bild* was applied to them at least after immediately preceding presentation. Since the use of *Wauwau* for her picture found no support in the language of standard speakers, it had no chance to maintain itself

613. The picking out of an incidental feature, like the dog held in a baby picture or the control disc in a multigraphing machine (610), was, of course, not the child's regular procedure. Many other machines were designated by a word which characterized them as machines. No such relatively abstract term was presented to the child; each machine was given its own individual name. This specification was, however,

---

[52] I have similarly assumed the operation of an associatively recalled visual stimulus in the episode, in which she said *pretty* at 1;4 upon feeling a necklace without seeing it (vol. 1, p. 120).

still beyond the child's power. For all but the most familiar machines, special names were not yet learned. When the need arose to name a machine, the memory of the most familiar machine, the automobile, came to Hildegard's mind. She said German *Auto* or English *auto* for all sorts of contrivances which she assuredly did not confuse with motor cars. Not a conscious, intellectual, but a subconscious, associative, emotional category "machine" was undoubtedly operating in this linguistic behavior. The choice as to what to call a machine was, of course, arbitrary; in fact, adults would find it difficult to define a machine beyond the obvious cases.

The predecessor of the word *Auto* was the interjection *sch*, which Hildegard learned at 1;0 as an accompaniment to railroad games. It did not refer at first to machines, but to sounds (the interjection was meant to imitate the sound of an engine), extended to the sound of music 1;0, but also to motions and moving objects 1;4, cars, elevated trains, chairs which she pushed around the room. The next step was to apply it to objects capable of motion, but not moving, a wrecked car, cars in pictures, a toy wheelbarrow (which acquired its own name, not yet permanently, at 1;10 and 1;11), a picture of an old-time carriage.

This primitive word had to do service for six months, until more specific words were learned. The most important progress was the splitting off of the verbal idea of moving by means of the verb *ride* 1;8. *Auto* 1;5 and *choo-choo* 1;7 took over the noun functions, hardly with any advance in specification.

The word *Auto*, with which the English *auto* competed from the beginning, was learned for pictures of cars 1;5, for real cars 1;8. It was once applied at 1;8 to a toy duck on wheels, which was otherwise called *duck* on account of its similarity to the bird—again a case of an incidental feature (wheels, rolling motion) coming to the foreground of attention, in this case merely as an occasional designation. It is not impossible to assume that *my Auto* as applied to the duck is comparable to metaphors of standard languages.

Up to this point the rolling motion on wheels furnished, presumably, the inducement to use the word *Auto*. At 1;9 however, she reacted to the illustration of a complicated instrument for use in psychological laboratories first with *choo-choo*, then with *Auto*. The only point of resemblance with either a train or a car was that it could also be regarded as a machine. *Piep-piep-Auto* 1;9 for a flying airplane showed that the wheels could recede from the focus of attention, leaving only the machine-like characteristics. The kind of motion emphasized by her was the flying motion, indicated by the nursery word for bird. The ingenious compound represented, as such (**600**), a great step forward. The double designation enabled the hearer to rule out much of the vast semantic area covered by each of the elements and understand the utterance as a reference to the limited field in which their meanings could meet.

The electric mangle in the kitchen was called *Auto* at 1;10. It had, to be sure, a revolving drum; but this would hardly have called up the memory picture of wheels. I think it is safe to say that the slowly rotating part of the ironing machine was disregarded, except in so far as it contributed to creating the impression of a machine.[53]

The other examples of 1;10–11 all involve cars, real ones and toy autos. The meaning of the word was in process of being restricted to usages in closer conformity with the standard meaning. The more formal word *automobile*, rare in the presentation, was learned at the same stage of semantic maturation, 1;11.

A side-light is thrown on the semantic vagueness of *Auto* by the original compound *Auto-noise* 1;10. It was formed in recollection of an experience in which a real auto had made a frightening noise close to her. The emotional component of fear, however, had been distilled out of the word by the time of its first appearance, although a fear of autos, without linguistic expression, persisted. It was used for noises of any provenience, including cars, but not at all confined to them. Not even great intensity was invariably a requirement; a sucking sound produced while drinking was enough. The semantic accent was on *noise*. The genetically obsolete qualification could cling to it because the former vagueness of *Auto* did not forbid it. The extension of meaning went so far that *Auto* was in this compound almost completely divested of meaning.

614. In the preceding discussion the word *choo-choo* was mentioned several times, because it competed with *Auto* for the designation of objects which recalled each other through a vague resemblance subsumable under the standard term "machine". It was learned two months later than *Auto*, at 1;7. In accord with the presentation, it referred at first to trains. Rather naturally, because *sch* had been learned in connection with railroad games, it fell soon into the grooves of meaning prepared by this interjection. The illustration of a piece of psychological apparatus, already referred to, was first "called" (reacted to by) *choo-choo*, then *Auto* 1;9, which showed that the two words were synonymous as well as vague in meaning; perhaps it also showed that the former was not fully satisfactory. Aside from trains, *choo-choo* was used for an airplane 1;10, a wheelbarrow 1;10, a street-car 1;11, a trunk 1;11. All these items had their own names before the end of the second year, except "trunk", which differs from the other cases. Motion is involved in all three of them, motion on wheels in two. Together with the apparatus of 1;9, they might all be classified as "machines" by

---

[53] In popular usage, the automobile is sometimes simply called the "machine", with a restricted, specific meaning of the word. In the remote jungles of Costa Rica, I had the experience of hearing an adult, uneducated wilderness dweller ask, upon seeing a photographic camera for the first time in his life: "¿Qué máquina es ésta?" Karla called a camera *choo-choo* at 1;3.

mature speakers. A trunk does not fit in this classification on any count. The word was evoked by the fact that the sight of it recalled to Hildegard her traveling experiences, by association. This instance could hardly be called an extension of meaning; it is a transfer of meaning, or better, a transfer of reference.

Choo-choo showed less inclination to become restricted to the proper meaning. The extended applications continued longer than in the case of *Auto*. The latter seems to have emerged from the semantic haze a little sooner. Still, there was a nucleus of semantic distinction in spite of the overlapping of the two terms. Cars were never called *choo-choo*. Trains were never called *Auto*. Half a month before the end of the year, the standard nursery compound *choo-choo train* was learned. It led over to the maturer word *train*, which she had understood for several months. Doubtless the child was ready to add this specific term only because the semantic fog around the word *choo-choo* was beginning to clear away. The emergence into active use of the words *airplane, street-car,* and *wheelbarrow,*[54] all at 1;11, confirms the assumption. The case illustrates the breaking up of large, ill-defined areas of meaning and designation into smaller ones with sharper outlines.

615. It seems that functional considerations determine the extended use of words quite frequently. I give a few more examples of this category.

She learned *boat* at 1;10 and used it at once for a toy sailboat, although she was not familiar with sailboats. She recognized the similarity of function. This transfer was anchored in her language because it agreed with standard usage. At 1;11 she applied the same word to the picture of an airship, again recognizing the similarity of the function and disregarding the difference in the medium of locomotion, as the standard language does. Of course, English and German happen not to have chosen "air-boat", but "air-ship"; but the transfer involved is the same. "Ship" was not in her vocabulary. Even the ocean liner, which must have dominated her experience in this area long after the transatlantic trip, had usually been called "boat". If German had maintained a stronger position in her speech, "Schiff" might well have become the key word in this area of meaning, and then the transfer would have resulted, no less accidentally, in a designation comparable to the correct one, "air-ship".

The word *cake* had an early occurrence at 1;6, in which it served to designate candy. Later, when it really became active, from 1;9, it was used in close agreement with standard practice for real cakes and fic-

---

[54] The first more specific term for a wheelbarrow was *wheel*, used only once 1;10 for this purpose, with extension of meaning; *wheel* had been used since 1;8 in the proper sense. This seems to confirm that the wheel was the salient part of the apparatus. The full word *wheelbarrow* was learned at 1;11. *Wheel* was, in addition to its correct use, also extended to include a toy wagon and a ring 1;11.

titious sand-cakes. She learned *candy* at 1;10, but used it also for cherries 1;11. Anything sweet to eat apart from the regular meals fell into the same semantic classification, or, stated more cautiously, called forth the word belonging to a similar object. Specification proceeded rapidly on account of the strong emotional importance of sweets. Candy and cake were already kept apart at 1;10; for the latter, the German synonym, *Kuchen*, was in active use at the same time, 1;10–11. "Cherry", however, was not learned. It is all right to say that the poverty of the vocabulary made it necessary to use semantically related words. It is just as correct, and perhaps more significant, to take the reverse view: specific words were not learned until it became important to break down a hazy semantic area into finer sub-divisions. There is no indication that Hildegard felt her earlier indiscriminate use of words as inadequate.

Bobby-pin 1;7, which designates a hairpin of special shape, was used for hairpins of any shape. The child did not understand the specification by shape and disregarded it, extending the use of the word to all pins of similar function.

616. A few more examples in which the material furnished the bridge will also be given.

Hildegard learned *oil* 1;6 for cod-liver oil. She used the same word independently for oily preparations used on her skin and in her nose and found herself in full agreement with standard usage. Of course, she used it also for vaseline. This is objectively an oil derivative, but the standard language does not choose to call it an oil, on account of its slightly different consistency.

Milk bottle 1;10 was used correctly, but once for a bottle filled with white tooth-powder. I doubt that she mistook it for a bottle filled with milk. Its shape was different, and the utterance must have been made in the bathroom, where milk bottles did not belong. The white color simply reminded her of milk-filled bottles, and this called forth the verbal response associated with them. Color can perhaps be included among material properties, or at least physical characteristics.

617. In all the examples of extended meaning, we have found that one object or experience called up another which seemed similar to the child in some respect. It should not surprise us that the points of similarity seem to the adult sometimes far-fetched. The emphases of the child need not be the same as those of the adult. New impressions cluster around established ones, and the association brings about the same linguistic response, until the progress in speaking leads to the breakdown of complexes into smaller units and thereby to a refinement of the semantic system.

In some cases the association[55] was quite loose, being based on mere

---

[55] I am conscious of the fact that modern psychologists avoid the term "association". It seems to describe the underlying facts adequately, however. I use it, leaving it to the reader to substitute other terms which may suit him better.

contiguity or on a functional link which was not close enough to allow the adult to use the same unmodified word.

Sandbox was learned 1;10, but was at 1;11 also used for sand, not only sand in the box, but sand accumulated in her shoes and pockets from playing in the sandbox. The sand was, of course, far more important to her than the container. One might say that the semantic accent was so decidedly on the sand that the *box* part was submerged in her consciousness, although the word existed independently, with clear meaning, in her vocabulary. On account of the latter fact it may, however, be better to assume that the functional link between the sand and the sandbox was felt to be so intimate that no lexical distinction was needed yet. This situation would have been much less striking if Hildegard has used "sand" for both purposes, as adults might well do ("Play in the sand" instead of "Play in the sandbox"); but she did not learn the simple word "sand" before 2;0.

Piano was used at 1;11 also for the piano bench, the real one and her toy piano bench. Rather than to state that the piano assembly including the bench formed one undivided conceptual complex in her mind, I would say that seeing the bench recalled the piano by functional contiguity. The difference between these two ways of looking at the situation is not very great; but the latter view may be genetically more adequate. If Hildegard had called another musical instrument *piano*, it would have been an extension of meaning of a more conventional kind.

The use of the word for the piano bench is perhaps better called a transfer of meaning from the point of view of traditional semantics. Genetically the process is very similar. An association with another object somehow related calls forth the corresponding linguistic response.

Another transfer would seem much more pardonable to adults. Hildegard used the word *sun-suit*, which she learned at the very end of the year, also for my bathing-suit. The similarity in material, in cut (this was still the time of full-length bathing suits for men) and even in function, was so great that the transfer does not offend.[56] The child may well have noticed the differences in all three respects, but did not feel them to be important enough to make a linguistic distinction, particularly, to learn a new word in order to emphasize it. (Even a year later, she still used the word for any bathing-suit. She did not feel the need for narrowing the semantic sphere of *sun-suit* to provide for the slight difference of function, this being all that was left of the distinction, since material and cut must have been recognized as nondistinctive by the time she had seen a variety of sun-suits and bathing-suits.)

618. In the whole preceding discussion we have examined nouns.

---

[56] Cf. this newspaper gag: "When they're hanging together on the washline, who can say which is junior's sun suit and which mother's bathing suit?" Arnold Glasow in "The Wake of the News", Chicago Daily Tribune, July 25, 1945.

Extension and transfer of meaning were not restricted to nouns, however. They were also performed with other classes of words.

Adverbs were often involved. *Up* 1;4 was used in a variety of situations. Few of the uses differed greatly from standard practice. That makes the extensions less striking, but the semantic process is the same. When the result does not differ from standard usage, it is impossible to decide whether the child has performed original extensions which happen to agree with standard usage, or imitated standard expressions which make use of the same word. More likely, the former hypothesis is correct, the standard example serving merely as a confirming and anchoring device.

Hildegard learned *up* for the wish to be lifted up on the davenport, but the word did not remain restricted to this situation. On the first evening she uttered it as a reaction to my command "aufstehen". This was in all likelihood an independent extension. In English the same word is used in the latter situation ("get up, stand up"), but in German it would not be possible to use exactly the same adverb. In other words, the same extension performed with a German vocabulary item would have resulted in an unacceptable version. (The history of *auf* 1;6 in vol. 1, p. 38, may be compared; but it is complicated by the fact that it was a homonym of *aus, out.*)

Disregarding, for the moment, the use of *up* for the opposite wish 1;4, which we reserve for a separate section (**625**), we come to its use for the wish to have the lid of a box taken off, 1;6. "Off" is the word which adults would use for this purpose, but the child may have thought of the upward motion which the lid was to perform. During the following months, *up* served wishes to have an upward motion performed with her own person, another person, or an object. Some of them undoubtedly were independent extensions, although others may have been influenced by standard "get up". From 1;8, the ingredient of wish subsided, factual statements of motion or position being made with the word. The extension to static position is possible in colloquial English ("It is up in the bedroom"). In German, again, it would have overstepped the semantic limits ("oben" vs. "hinauf"). There are limits to the static use in English. Hildegard's use of *up* for "I am upstairs" was not standard; but how was she to know? Adults who objected to such a misuse might as well have objected to the arbitrariness of the colloquial standard. Such instances show that the widening of the realm of applicability of an adverb does not proceed by docile imitation alone. On the other hand, the learning of a compound verb like *cover up* 1;11, in which the local meaning of the adverb has faded out, is definitely due to the standard example. Other compounds like *pick up* 1;10, *roll up, hang up* 1;11, in which a more or less faint remnant of the local meaning survives, helped the child to go the same semantic way as the standard language has gone. The process was facilitated by the fact that the child

expressed, by that time, also the verb, which then took over the semantic accent. From 1;7, *up* was commonly used in the phrase *way up*,
just like its opposite, *way down*. Both phrases occurred in a similar
variety of uses (cf. vol. 1, p. 133).

619. The German adverb[57] *alle* meaning "all gone" 1;7 furnishes good
illustrations of extended use. In colloquial German it is used only for
exhausted supplies, occasionally for an exhausted person. The latter
meaning, which approaches slang, did not occur. Hildegard used the
word at first in the standard meaning, as a substitute for her earlier
English *all* 1;5 with the same meaning, based on standard "all gone".
It was at once extended to the meaning "(a person is) gone": *Mama
alle* 1;7. The English version shows how small this step is. Standard
German, however, does not allow the word to be applied to persons in
this sense. Hildegard, undoubtedly, was not translating the English
"gone" into German *alle*, but extending its meaning slightly, as standard
English does (although the process is, historically, the reverse in English:
"gone" fits persons primarily, things metaphorically). *Bath alle, bathe
alle* 1;9, meaning "I have finished bathing", contains another slight
extension, to an action. Neither German "alle" nor English "gone"
happens to fit here. *All gone* was learned in full 1;11, but *alle* continued
to be the favorite expression (until 2;1, when the English synonym swept
it away). It was still used for persons, even when no action preceded
which resulted in the disappearance, as is required for standard "alle"
and "gone". It amounted then to "not there". This is again a slight
shift of the meaning, the bridge being the negative idea contained in
the word, which she sometimes underscored by shaking her head with
the utterance. *Wehweh alle* 1;11 offends less; again, English says "a
pain is gone", although German does not admit "alle" in this situation.

This example is illuminating, because all the extensions are slight,
most of them even permissible for the English equivalent, but not for
the German word. They show that the child was operating independently in widening the semantic sphere. The result might have been
correct, and the process would then have been much less easily observ-
able. As it was, Hildegard's uses of the word covered a wider territory
than in the standard language. Its meaning was vaguer, although no
vaguer than that of many standard words; this particular one happens
to have unusually narrow limits of applicability. The vagueness made it
more useful in the early stages of speaking. Later, it would have needed
narrowing down to standard outlines, if it had survived. Perhaps, the
sporadic use of the synonym *weg* from 1;10 was the forerunner of this
refinement. It fits many of the situations in which *alle* was not standard.

620. The word *by-by* has two realms of application in nursery standard, as a good-by greeting, customarily accompanied by waving the

---

[57] On account of its meaning "exhausted", *alle* can also be classified as an adjective (**549**, especially last note). It is similar to "fort", "weg".

hand, and, by extension, in the phrase "go by-by" for "go for a walk, for a ride". The German equivalent for the former usage is "winke, winke"; but this expression, by its nature, does not lend itself to the same extension as in English. If Hildegard had learned the German term, or if the English one had not undergone the extension in standard usage, she might well have performed it herself, because this is a typical extension in child-language. In fact, the English extension is probably based on children's usage; adults would not easily coin the phrase "go good-by" for this purpose.

The use of this word starts early and with a strong emotional component. Children like to be taken outdoors, at any rate Hildegard did. She learned to understand the word as early as 0;11 as a clue for waving good-by, one of those little drills which are performed with all children. When she said it herself, from E 1;3, the other meaning seems to have prevailed at once. Hearing the cue "by-by" or the German equivalent "ausgehen", she would repeat *by-by* 1;4 and run into the other room, where her coat, hat, and stroller were kept, instruments for implementing the fulfillment of the wish and therefore associated with it. Consequently, she said *by-by* spontaneously, later 1;4, with reference to articles of clothing which she wore on expeditions into a wider world. The wish to go out, usually present, could disappear on such occasions, but not the pleasant memories associated with these articles. Still, a progressing intellectualization can be discerned in such instances. The vague reference was sufficient at a time when the need for naming the articles individually and specifically was not yet felt.

At E 1;4 she said *by-by* with falling intonation, with a considerable pitch interval between the two syllables. She had learned the device by which the farewell greeting is distinguished in standard speech from its application in the phrase.

The later history of the word in the two-word stage shows the clearing of the fog which originally enveloped the vague term. At 1;8 she often specified, *by-by Auto, by-by choo-choo*. At 1;9 another kind of specification became desirable. Once she was disappointed because the wish *by-by* was fulfilled by her being placed on the balcony of the apartment, which did not satisfy her. She invented then the specifying phrase *big by-by*. Although the content of *big* was not so intellectually clear as it is in the language of adults (where it is also relative, but refers more definitely to size), it sufficed to convey the desired idea.

At 1;10 Hildegard once pointed to the window and stated *By-by dunkel*, which meant "It is dark outside". This utterance is interesting because the first word was divested of its usual component of wish or pleasure and the second of its component of fear. It was an objective statement of fact. It is also interesting because it was syntactically crude. *Dunkel* was a predicate. *By-by* was psychologically the subject, but grammatically it cannot be assigned to any standard part of speech.

It was used in a vague associational way. The utterance was clear enough to convey the desired meaning, but cannot be subjected to conventional grammatical analysis. The adverb *outside*, which might be a synonym if *by-by* was meant as a static adverb, had occurred once at 1;9, but was not yet really active. Thus no organized manner of expressing the idea was at her disposal.

During 1;11 Hildegard used again the specified form of statement, *By-by street-car*, this time as a factual report of a past event. More important, she said once *By-by, go by-by*, adding the verb, which meant a great step forward in grammatical analysis.

621. In the field of adjectives, *dunkel*, "dark", 1;8 furnishes an illustration of fluctuating reference. I introduced the word, showing her dark rooms and halls in the apartment. It is doubtful how far the idea which she connected with the rather abstract word corresponded to the relatively clear meaning it has in the standard language. At 1;10 Hildegard had a brief period during which she was afraid of the dark, and the word *dunkel*, perhaps now clearer in intellectual meaning, became the vehicle of this emotional component. This fear complex subsided, but the word continued to be the carrier of the emotion of fear, transferred to other media. For a few days she was afraid of rolling window-shades and referred to them by *dunkel*. She also called thunder *dunkel*, but with a glance at the shades. It is possible that the window, for which she had no word, furnished the bridge between these varying meanings. She observed sometimes through the window that it was dark outside (*by-by dunkel* 1;10); the shades were on the window; and the lightning which accompanied the thunder was visible through the window. Certainly, however, *dunkel* did not mean "window". It expressed fear. With progressing intellectualization, she found less emotional paraphrases for shades and for thunder, and *dunkel* was divested of its emotional emphasis.

The situation with regard to the adjective *big* 1;8 was similar. The factual meaning of size was sometimes present, but more often the word was used as an emotive in connections which do not correspond to standard usage (**518**). The extension of meaning concerns here the emotional overtones, which are often present in standard speech, but subordinated to the factual content.

Descriptive adjectives in attributive position were rare (**558**). In predicative position (**549**), most meanings deviated little from the standard, except in early one-word utterances, for which the classification by standard parts of speech is misleading.

Some words, like *mehr* and *no*, hovered on the boundary line between adjectives and adverbs (**558**). The grammatical uncertainty is a consequence of their use with extended meanings. Functional distinctions were not understood well enough to prevent extensions of meaning from crossing such boundaries (**624**). The same consideration applies to personal and possessive pronouns, two categories which overlapped in the form *my*.

622. Verbs, although late, did not escape extensions of meaning. *Bite* 1;10 had the standard meaning frequently, but was soon 1;11 made to cover situations in which the standard language uses "spank", "slap", and "pinch", words which were lacking in Hildegard's vocabulary. The vague meaning of the verb might be defined by the adult as "cause pain by physical interference". The standard restriction to the use of teeth, without emphasis on pain, was a form of specification for which the child did not yet feel a need. Instead of saying that the poverty of the vocabulary forced the assumption of related meanings by this verb, it is better to say that the related verbs were not learned because no finer specifications were yet required by the child. The distinction is important. It means that the child, in using "bite" for nonstandard purposes, did not perform a metaphorical extension, but failed to grasp the limitations of the standard definition. The term "extension of meaning" is fitting only from the point of view of the standard language. Genetically, "lack of limitation of meaning" would be a more adequate description.

The difficulties involved in learning the limits within which the standard language allows a verb to be used can be illustrated negatively by the verb *roll* 1;8. Hildegard learned the word as a cue, in its German form, for the game of rolling on the floor. At 1;9 she transferred it spontaneously to rolling a glass. At 1;11 she said *roll up* for rolling up stockings in the hand. These are three quite different rolling motions. Yet, in this case, the standard language permits the use of the same verb for all three motions. If it insisted on the same degree of specification as with the verb *bite*, the transfer of 1;9 would appear as an extension of meaning. Genetically the situation is the same. The child's procedure was identical, but the result differs, because the standard language defines this verb as loosely as the child did in the preceding case. It is not easy for a child to learn that some words have a wide range, whereas others are restricted in their applicability. The wide range, the loose definition are the natural condition of a child's early vocabulary. Limitation of definition, if required by the standard, is not primarily a consequence of increased vocabulary; rather, the vocabulary increases because the need for greater specification is felt as the child grasps more and more of the finer semantic discriminations made by the adult speakers of the environment.

The verb *wash* 1;8 was used in a variety of meanings: to wash clothes; to wash parts of the body; and, as a noun, for wearing apparel subjected to the process of washing. All these uses were correct because the standard allows great latitude in the application of the word. In such cases we cannot decide whether the child performed spontaneous extensions or learned each application by imitation. As in the chapter on morphology, mistakes show independent handling of imitated material more clearly than items which happen to be correct, that is, in agreement with standard practice.

Crash, the hypothetical etymon of a puzzling word in Hildegard's vocabulary 1;10, agreed fairly well with the standard meaning in only one application, at 2;1: throwing away a broken glass. If the etymology is correct, the other instances involve extended meanings: letting herself fall into my lap, the most common meaning 1;10–2;2, and running around fast in the garden 1;11. Rapid, surprising motion is a vague definition, which is adequate for this stage of semantic development. In the last-mentioned application the surprise element would have faded out. This is possible, just as the element of accompanying sound, which belongs to the standard meaning, was suppressed. The standard meaning was much too specific to be assimilated by the child in all its precision at once.

The verb *buy*, which had a precarious existence 1;11, was used in connection with a toy balloon brought home from a shopping expedition. The fact that the balloon was not actually bought, but given as a favor with a purchase, was, of course, beyond the powers of discrimination of the child. The example illustrates clearly why early meanings must be vague. The meaning "acquired in a store" was remarkably precise as it was, in view of the fact that not even a general verb "receive, get" existed in Hildegard's vocabulary. It was too specialized to be incorporated firmly in her speech (it is marked as ephemeral in the Vocabulary). She used it once or twice because her mother had used it, with satisfactory comprehension; but it did not yet fill a real need of the young speaker.

The reason why more verbs did not undergo extensions of meaning is twofold. In the first place, many of Hildegard's early verbs were such as could be applied to a great variety of situations in the standard language, like *put, fix, make*, also *spielen*. Vague as their standard meaning is, they were used infrequently (until 2;0), because just for this reason they could still be dispensed with. On the other hand, most verbs were not learned until the last month of the second year, and by that time the powers of specification had already grown sufficiently to enable the child to grasp more specific meanings accurately enough and to use the verbs correctly. Thus we have the queer situation that the primacy of vague words is, in the case of verbs, hidden by the fact that verbs were not yet necessary syntactic ingredients of sentences and were omitted when they added nothing essential to the utterance, whereas they were used when they were the carriers of essential elements of the idea to be expressed. To illustrate: "wash ears," "watch Mama," or "The duck bites me" could not well be expressed without the verbs; but "Jack has the measles", "This is wet", "I want this", "Fix my hair", "Make wet", or "Put this bell on" could still do without the verbs as long as the feeling for syntactically complete sentences was not well developed.

Sometimes the evidence is misleading. The verb *wake up* 1;10 appears only in situations in which it was used correctly, in the first two months. This was accidental. The diary shows (681) that the meaning was not yet sharply defined; the later evidence proves that it was not well separated from that of "get up".

623. Extensions and transfers of application in the case of interjections need no detailed discussion. Words which serve primarily the expression of an emotional reaction are used in a variety of situations in which the reaction is the same or similar. For illustrations, see the range over which the primitive interjection *ʔə̃*? 0;8–1;6 was used (vol. 1, p. 81),[58] or the various transfers of reference in connection with the interjection *sch* 1;0–6 (vol. 1, p. 121), together with the specific terms superseding it at the stage of growing refinement of vocabulary. The latter example shows at the same time how an interjection can be utilized as the bearer of rather intellectual, objective references, designating as it did a variety of vehicles rolling on wheels, even though they stood still or were merely pictured, and objects which could be pushed (613). Another case is the interjection *hello* 1;5 (vol. 1, p. 95), which was used for hailing persons, but more commonly on the telephone. At 1;8 it took on the function of the verb, "to telephone", and at 1;9 that of the noun, the telephone as an instrument.

624. These last examples show incidentally that extensions of meaning do not halt at functional boundary lines (cf. 621). Words pass easily from one part of speech to another without change in form. The English standard frequently allows this, but the child went much further. The lack of morphological development and the meager syntactic organization allowed greater freedom in the handling of words. Functional vagueness and semantic vagueness are not the same from the point of view of the standard language (595), but for the child they go hand in hand as aspects of the hazy outlines of words.

When the negative adverb *not* was acquired 1;11, its negative meaning was clear enough to Hildegard. She practiced it especially in the phrase *not da*, "not there", meaning "not present", and contrasted it consciously with the corresponding positive statement: *Meow da—meow not da*, with emphasis on the negative. During the same month, however, she also said *no*, *not* as a reinforced sentence adverb; that is to say, the functional difference between the negative which takes the place of a

---

[58] Extended applications can even be found for expressive gestures. Hildegard had a gesture to call attention to music 1;0–4, with isolated recurrences 1;8 and 1;11. It is mentioned under *radio* (vol. 1, p. 134). She used the same gesture 1;2 on the ocean boat when she heard the agonized sounds produced by a victim of sea sickness. Their identification with music was offensive to adults, but it cannot be denied that there was a modicum of resemblance. She beat time with her index finger when she passed the door of the social hall where she had previously heard a trio play. She did it also at the second door, from which she could not have seen the musicians. The gesture had been transferred, by association, to the room (640).

sentence and the negative which is inserted into a sentence was not yet understood. For the same reason, *no* used as an adjective before a noun is suspicious in correct examples like *no book*, *no A-a* 1;11. Possibly the functional extension was correct only because the standard language seems to allow the same transfer (does allow it, speaking descriptively). When Hildegard used the same word in a negative imperative (*no bite* 2;1 for "don't bite"), her usage was at variance with the standard; yet, the process of extension behind this case was in all likelihood the same. The three English negatives, *not*, *no*, and *don't*, all in her vocabulary by the end of the year, were semantically clear, but functionally not well distinguished (554).

The case of *bauen* 1;9 is comparable. It was basically a verb, but functional limitations were not clear to the child. In *big Bau* 1;9 it looked like a noun, but must have been functionally indistinct; *big*, likewise, was not clearly an adjective, but a vague emotive. In *Papa make Bau* 1;11, in a syntactically rather advanced construction, the grammatical object takes the place of a noun with less room for doubt. Since, however, such a noun had not been presented to the child, the inference is inescapable that Hildegard performed a functional transfer which might have been permissible with an English stem, but usually does not work out in German. Of course, there is such a noun as "Bau", but it does not belong to the colloquial level of speech, certainly not of small children's speech.

I shall not multiply the examples of functional extension. They appear often in the record, but belong in the semantic analysis only by way of a side-glance.

625. The designation of logical opposites by the same word is a striking special case of extension of meaning.[59] It puzzles the adult that children use the same word for "up" and "down", for "warm" and "cold",[60] even for "no" and "yes".[61] This procedure seems more radical than the extensions discussed up to this point. Of course, designation of opposites by the same word is not unknown in standard languages.[62] German "leihen", and similarly, English colloquial "to loan", is said both of the lender and of the borrower; the syntactic context or the situation must be consulted to determine the exact meaning in each individual instance. An apartment is "rented" both by the landlord and by the tenant.[63] This example, even more than the preceding one, gives rise to

---

[59] Sully (p. 164 f.) states that association with the opposite is related to extension of meaning by association and explains it as due to the difficulty of abstract relations. Stern deals with "Gegensinn" on pp. 239–241 and 256.

[60] Cf. Jespersen p. 120.

[61] Preyer p. 82, on the basis of Lindner's observations at 0;9; cf. Preyer p. 100. Preyer himself (pp. 151, 173, 182) noticed affirmation instead of denial at 1;11; at 2;4 and 2;7: "too much" instead of "too little", "never" instead of "always".

[62] Cf. Egger p. 44 f., Ament p. 134.

[63] These examples are better than that given by Ogden, p. 66: a "screw-driver"

occasional misunderstandings, and yet the language is not seriously inconvenienced by the ambiguity. Other examples might be added: "a book sells", "a book is sold", etc. They all go to show that logical opposites are not always clearly distinguished in linguistic expression.

There are few cases of the kind in Hildegard's record. The typical example, "hot" for "cold", occurred once 1;7. Touching a plate with ice cream, she said *heiss*. The psychological explanation is obvious: considerable deviations from average temperatures were covered by the same word. This represents a two-phase discrimination among temperatures: normal and not normal. The next step is a three-phase distinction: cold, normal, and hot. Hildegard reached this phase as late as E 1;10, when *cold* was added to the vocabulary. The series was not subdivided further. "Warm", for instance, was included in *hot*. Since normal temperatures were not commented on and no word existed for them, the vocabulary progressed, speaking linguistically rather than psychologically, from a one-word phase (*hot* 1;4 and its synonym from the other language, *heiss* 1;5) to a two-word phase (*cold* E 1;10). The reason why *hot* preceded *cold* is that the child had more experiences in the household with hot and warm objects than with cold ones. The words remained attached to concrete objects, radiators, flaming matches, etc. There is an instance on record that she did not understand my statement, "Es ist heiss," referring to the weather; she examined the objects before me for their temperature, 1;10 (598).

Up was used 1;4–5 for both "up" and "down". One word covered the wish for a change from the present position.[64] To be sure, she learned *down* also at 1;4, but said it for some time only mechanically upon request, whereas *up* was used spontaneously in situations in which the adults expected "down". In this case the one-word phase was overcome rapidly and early. The bilingual situation enters into the picture by the fact that *up* had a German synonym, *auf* 1;6. It was, however, not applied to a change of her own position until 1;11, and seemed to be based on a standard separated prefix rather than on an independent adverb.

There is a case of undistinguished uses of "light on" and "light out". Operating the light-switch was a fascinating experience. She said *light out* at 1;8, and *aus* in the same situation 1;10. She used *an*, from the German presentation "Licht an", at 1;10 correctly, but also for the opposite operation, switching the light off. "On" and "out" were used correctly in many examples. They are opposites only in this one special

---

gets screws in and out. This is a case of linguistic economy; "screw-driver and -puller" would be too cumbersome. German selects the other aspect, for the same reason: "Schraubenzieher".

[64] In Karla's case it even included the wish to be taken out of her play-pen. Her first word was *down* 1;1, and the one-word phase lasted much longer. *Up* was not added to the vocabulary until 1;7.

application, even more clearly in German than in English, where "off" may take the place of "out"; "off", however, was not learned. We find that *out* was used in this function two months before *an*, and yet the distinction between *aus*, its synonym, and *an* was not clear by 1;10. The explanation is that the first use of *light out* 1;8 was an echo of the presentation. At 1;10 the adverbs were used without the noun, more independently. *An* was the stronger and could cover the two opposite operations. *Aus* existed as a vocabulary item, but was not yet distinguished semantically from *an*. Undoubtedly, the distinction was learned soon thereafter. For the time being, either word could be used as a signal for operating the switch, without consideration for the specific effect of the operation.

626. These are the clearest instances of exact logical opposites covered at times by the same word. In all of them, the explanation is that the child used a single word to indicate a deviation from a normal condition in any direction.[65] Specifying the direction represented a later semantic stage, into which Hildegard was entering already without as yet reaching clear differentiation.

It is doubtful whether cases like *man* for "woman", *Onkel* for "Tante" (**609**) should be included. They are in complementary rather than contrasting relation.

In the remaining cases, the merging of opposites was apparent rather than real, because the intellectual semantic content of the words involved was much fainter for the child than for adults.

At first glance it seems striking that the adjective *big* was firmly established in Hildegard's vocabulary from 1;8, whereas the opposite, "small, little" was missing until 2;0. *Big* was applied in a great variety of situations. Sometimes it was connected with objects which adults would definitely call small (a small egg-shaped solid-rubber ball), sometimes with words to which a consideration of size cannot easily be applied (*by-by*, *A-a*). It might be argued that size is relative, that objects may appear large to a child, small to an adult. One might also think that here, as in other instances, any deviation from indifferent size was expressed by the same word. In so far as the child referred to size at all (and this intellectual semantic component was not always completely suppressed), the explanation may be correct; but it does not serve for the instances in which size was not a consideration. It is more satisfactory to say that the emotional component of the word (admiration, awe), which adults often attach to it by intonation, especially when speaking to small children, was singled out by the child and made

---

[65] Thus Jespersen p. 120, Stern p. 240 f. Preyer's explanation (Ament p. 134) amounts to the same. Bloch (1921, p. 707) makes the point that the sensations "cold" and "hot" are precise, but not so the words, which means that the linguistic situation differs from the psychological conditions. Stern (pp. 254–256) emphasizes the emotional value of all early adjectives.

its chief content. *Big* was primarily an emotive and only secondarily a designation of size.

A different explanation applies to misuses of *danke, thank you*. In addition to correct uses, **dada** was also said when she handed things to others, E 1;4–5. This usage may hide a case of homonymy; the word may be a reduplication of German "da", which is standard for this purpose (she learned the corresponding English *here* at 1;9). It may, however, also be a confusion with regard to the domain of a social formula which was learned rather mechanically, by social training. Hildegard learned *thank you* as early as E 1;3, but during the first month it was a mechanical response to a request, really without meaning. Because of the constantly repeated demand, the use of the social formula gradually became better established and clearer; but it did not reach the vitality of the antonym *please*, more commonly in German, *bitte*.

Bitte was learned E 1;5 as the successor of an expressive non-linguistic gesture, hand-clapping; *please* at 1;9. Both were used frequently and much more spontaneously, because they served the interests of the child more effectively. They produced results. They were necessary to procure things and services which she coveted. Nothing was gained by the standardized expression of gratitude after the desired result had been obtained, except the satisfaction of a social demand with which she would be importuned if she did not comply, and this urge was naturally much weaker. When she did not produce the conventional reaction, the adults would remind her by the question, "What do you say?" Sometimes she would then answer *bitte* at 1;7 and produce *thank you* only when the first answer was rejected. This is not surprising, because the adults asked the same question when she forgot to put a request in the proper social formulation. She knew that a social pattern had to be satisfied when she heard the question. The semantic value of this linguistic luxury to her was slight. The stronger formula was likely to come up first in her mind.

Naturally, the frequency with which both formulas occurred in daily life and the insistence of the adults on the choice of the proper one produced the correct distinction early.

627. In the later months of the second year, confusion of opposites (or rather, what appears to adults as confusion) was observed less frequently. In fact, from 1;9 a predilection for antithetical statements became conspicuous (**540, 562**). This frequently observed phenomenon[66] is an indication that the child is progressing to a two-phase stage of meaning, and is in full harmony with the postulated principle of contrast. At 1;9 Hildegard uttered negative and positive statements of the same structure in sharp opposition. *No Mama's stocking—this Mama's stocking* is the example given in the diary, with the remark that she

---

[66] Cf. further, Sully p. 174 f.

liked to make such antithetical utterances.[67] Correspondingly, the familiar phrase *way up* sprouted, at 1;10, the opposite *way down*, not in direct imitation, but by independent replacement of the adverb of place in the phrase by its opposite. It was applied first to the slide in the neighbors' backyard, then, in our new house, to the wish to go down the stairs, two situations in which adults would hardly use the phrase "way down".

Also at 1;10, possessive relationships were practiced in antithetical statements of ownership: (*This is*) *Dada's hat—this* (*is*) *mine; Papa's pocket—my pocket.*

At 1;11, the contrast pattern was extended to a matter of syntax: *Where my ball?—Da my ball.* The interrogative adverb of place was learned in the contrast between question and answer. *Meow da—meow not da*, with a strong emphasis on *not*, toward the end of the year, shows that the negative adverb, in perfected form and independent use, was learned and practiced in contrast patterns.

628. The preceding excursion into the field of antithetical statements was necessary to show that the progress to logical disquisitions belongs to a later stage of language learning. It is part of the gradual intellectualization of speech, which has of necessity considerable bearing on the sharpening of meanings and therefore on the scope of semantic extensions.

As the vocabulary grows, each item needs to embrace less and less semantic territory; or, expressed in reverse, as meanings become more sharply defined, more and more words are needed to express the meanings now excluded from the semantic domain of words in the earlier, limited vocabulary. Addition to the vocabulary and reduction of individual semantic complexes are two facets of one process. Both are features of the progressive mastery of the standard model. It is best not to assign priority to either of them.

This consideration implies that the later months necessarily show the process of semantic restriction in operation. The early vagueness of semantic categories, which goes together with the need for a very limited vocabulary, results in extensions of meaning from the standard, as has been shown in the preceding sections. In the following, a comparison of Hildegard's earlier meanings with those in her later, more developed language will demonstrate how wide semantic complexes were broken down, with the aid of added vocabulary items, into narrower ones, which involves a narrowing or restriction of the meanings of the older words.

629. Examples of secondary restrictions of meaning have been given incidentally in the foregoing discussion of semantic extensions, to demon-

---

[67] Concerning antithetical negative and positive statements, cf. Bloch (1924), p. 39; K. Bühler p. 234 f., with reference to Stern's examples, p. 204 ff.

strate by contrast the earlier diffuseness of reference. In this context it is necessary to remind the reader of some of these examples. Sometimes extensions and restrictions were intertwined. We should not expect the child to progress always in a straight line.

A complicated example is the history of the word *baby*, in which the interplay of the two semantic processes began even before Hildegard said the word herself (1;2). She understood it E 0;8, when the question, "Where is the baby?" made her look at her own baby picture. The restriction of meaning involved was induced by the adults. Two weeks later she began to distinguish between this baby picture and other pictures, reacting correctly to "Wo ist das Bild?", which meant pictures on the wall other than the favorite one. At B 1;0 she understood "baby" to refer to her likeness in the mirror and to other children, a twofold extension which may have been spontaneous (the diary gives no exact information; the semantic problem was not fully appreciated at the time of writing). At B 1;2 she expressed her interest in a little girl by saying, for the first time, *baby*. In the following months, the double meaning combined in "baby picture" split into two meanings of *baby*, "child" and "picture", but the meaning "child" gained ground. At 1;4 she was able to give different words for magazine pictures according to the objects which they represented. The term *baby* was now reserved for children's pictures, a restriction which brought its meaning closer to the standard. To the end of the second year, the meaning of *baby* remained extended to that of standard "child".[68] She did not learn the latter word. The distinction between children and adults, which was important for her, was achieved; but only a beginning was made toward a further break-down of both categories by age or sex (609).

630. Another good example for the gradual restriction of an overextended meaning is the very common word *Wauwau*. In standard nursery usage it stands for the barking of a dog, which it imitates onomatopoetically, and, by extension, for "dog". Hildegard's first use (E 1;1) was for barking, but also, by original extension, as a sign that she wanted her picture book, in which pictures of dogs were obviously important. This extension incorporates the standard extension. It is doubtful whether the reference by this sign to a stone monument representing a lion was an extension of meaning. It may also have been a mistaken identification. The difference between these two explanations is not great linguistically. Anything that reminded her of dogs brought up the associated response (612): her soft toy dog (an extension sanctioned by standard usage), her slippers with a simulated dog face on them, book-

---

[68] It is interesting to note as a parallel that "baby", according to the Oxford dictionary, meant formerly a child of any age; that a reflected image of oneself (although of a restricted kind) was a meaning which existed to the end of the seventeenth century; and that the plural meant pictures in books, and still does in northern dialects.

ends in the form of bronze horses, and real dogs (1;3), other real animals, a picture of an old man in furs (1;4); real horses, an ash tray shaped like an elephant (1;6); a porcelain dog (standard extension), a porcelain elephant (original extension), her own baby pictures, because she held a toy dog in one of them (1;7); the picture of a sloth (1;8); an Easter lamb of cake with white frosting (1;9).

Thereafter the use of the word for non-standard purposes ceased. A number of words had been learned which could be used for more satisfactory designations of objects involved in these extensions: *baby* 1;2 (which was used for baby pictures, **629**), *Bild*, sporadically 0;9–1;8, *man* 1;5, *book* and *shoe* 1;6, *cake* 1;9, *hottey* (*horsey*) 1;10. The progressive approximation to standard usage restricted the scope of applicability of this word as of many others. The growing refinement of classifications made the wild extension in all directions less and less satisfactory. It must be understood that the extensions in the child's usage do not mean a widening of the definition of the word to embrace all its occasional uses. The core of meaning is from the beginning similar to the standard; but at first there is a hazy semantic aura around it, into which references can be extended. This haze clears away in the course of time, and only extensions allowed by the standard language (toy dogs, dog pictures) remain eventually in use.

Progress in maturity of vocabulary kept pace with the intellectualization of meaning. The more grown-up synonym *doggie* made inroads into the semantic area of *Wauwau* at 1;11, and even the adult word *dog* began to be used.

631. Other examples can be treated more briefly. *Papa* 1;0 meant also "Mama" and "Opa" in the first months, and for one month beginning E 1;2 any man in the street. By E 1;3 the unorthodox meanings had been given up and *Papa* had been restricted again to its original function, a name for one individual. *Mama* had been learned B 1;3; "Opa" had fallen into disuse because the person so named was no longer around; the generic term *man* was in abeyance until 1;5, but potentially present from this time. The extended use of *papa* with shifting reference to various person's fathers was not learned; but *mama* occurred as a shifter 1;11.

Man itself included women to the end of the second year. Restriction by addition of the word *Frau* began at 1;7; but conforming to the standard semantic distinction was a laborious process, which was not completed during the period under consideration (**609**).

Food and hunger were referred to by the spontaneous interjection *m* from 1;0. By the end of the month, the meaning was extended to include the judgment of value, "it tastes good", a conventional gesture being added to set off the new meaning. The interjection became a word, clearly so by E 1;8, when it was used like a verb, with a subject, *Frau m*, "the woman (in the picture) is eating". The child was ready to learn the standard verb; *eat* was added to the vocabulary 1;10. The old term *m*, however, continued. It was henceforth restricted to the standard meaning of nursery language, "it tastes good".

In so far as *m* served as a forerunner of nouns designating food, its semantic sphere was restricted progressively by each standard noun from the same semantic area which the child added to her vocabulary. The first one, after five months, was *apple*. Each following month brought additions (see the list, vol. 1, p. 170), in increasing numbers, swiftly enough to preclude the necessity of pressing *m* into the function of a noun in sentences.

With each of the specific terms replacing it, the process of reducing wider areas of coverage to narrower ones went on apace. The word for *cookie* referred to cookies and crackers at 1;6. *Cracker* was learned at 1;7 and its sphere of reference cut off from that of *cookie*, the extension of reference of the latter word being rescinded in the direction of standard usage. *Cake*, tried 1;6, really learned 1;9, cut down the semantic sphere of *cookie* again. In its first use, 1;6, *cake* referred actually to candy. *Candy* was learned 1;10, but at 1;11 it still included cherries. The process of splitting off areas of reference went on beyond the second year.

The interjection *sch* 1;0–6, which served for a variety of motions and vehicles, was replaced, in its various functions, by more specific terms like *Auto* 1;5, *choo-choo* 1;7, *ride* 1;7, *wheel* 1;8 (for "wheelbarrow" 1;10; the word *wheelbarrow* 1;11). In this case the restriction went to the point of disappearance of the infantile word. An incidental benefit was that the homonymous interjection *sh* 1;6 for "sleep" could continue undisturbed. It served in the function of the verb from 1;8 (to 2;1). No need for a more specific use of the interjection or for a more mature form of the verb was felt, because the meaning was clear enough.

Choo-choo itself was for a long time a vague term applicable to divers kinds of machinery (**614**). At the end of the year it was expanded to *choo-choo train*. It is safe to assume that by this time the meaning was becoming restricted to the standard one, new words having been learned previously to designate objects which had formerly fallen in its sphere. *Auto* (**613**), at first almost a synonym, must have become relatively clear when the full form, *automobile*, was learned 1;11.

632. In most of the preceding instances, the child began by giving words a wider range of meaning than the standard model allowed. This range was reduced later, with growing linguistic experience, toward the standard range.

The process of restriction of meaning has another aspect. In some instances the child began with a restricted application, which later had to be extended to the wider standard range. An example is the inability to transfer the familiar word *hot* from concrete objects to the weather (**625**). A more striking instance is the association of the color name "weiss" with snow 1;8. To be sure, snow is the most impressive demonstration of the color, but there were enough other white objects within Hildegard's range of experience. The transfer to white paper in a book obviously presented difficulties. At 1;9 she learned to distinguish colors well and said *weisser* once; but the principle of classification by color did not go any farther linguistically (596).

Other instances concern the attempt to differentiate between synonyms which were acquired early, before the child was able to grasp their semantic range clearly. For a while 1;8, the German affirmative *ja* was used only with interrogative intonation for the purpose of requesting permission. Consent was given with the newly learned expression *all right*. She often asked the question and extended permission to herself in immediate succession: *Ja? All right!* The new term was expected to be semantically different from the old one and restricted the function of the latter. By 1;9 the typical over-use of the new word had worn off and *ja* resumed its wider affirmative meaning.

At 1;10 German *weg* was learned. Its negative idea competed with that of the firmly rooted word *alle*, which indicated, in Hildegard's language, not only an exhausted supply, but also the absence of things and persons. The new word might have been useful for reducing the inflated semantic scope of *alle*; but Hildegard did not succeed in making the correct differentiation. She used *weg* exclusively in requests, "Put it away". In this meaning, however, it competed with the established English synonym *away* and did not make headway against it. Its use remained sporadic.

Sometimes a differentiation between bilingual synonyms was attempted, resulting in a restriction of the standard meaning of both. At 1;10 it was observed that *bitte* was used for spontaneous wishes, *please* only as a conventional addition to requests upon demand. The latter was said in compliance with social training, whereas the former, older and better established, had been found to be a useful concomitant of wishes, which augured well for their fulfillment. In fact, *bitte* went back to the one-word stage 1;5, during which it was the exclusive linguistic expression of a wish, to which the content of the wish had later been added by a second word. The younger *please* 1;9, on the other hand, was nearly always a functionally less important addition to another word, at first even to *bitte* itself.

German *rollen* and English *roll* 1;8 seemed later to be differentiated. I taught her the German word as a cue for the game of rolling (herself) on the floor. It stuck to this game and was transferred only to the rolling of a drinking glass around its axis, a similar motion. Other rolling motions, like rolling up stockings into a ball, were designated by a phonetic variant form which went back to the English model. Glass-rolling, which was intermediate between these kinds of motion, participated in both sets of forms.

Several words, English and German, were used with reference to the cat: *meow* (*Miau*), *kitty*, and *Dasch*; the latter, based on German "Katz" (a colloquial variant of "Katze"), had developed into the name of the cat, the adults using the word with Hildegard's phonetic substitutions for this purpose. *Kitty* was only a sporadic echo for calling cats, 1;3, 1;10, 1;11; it did not really become active (at 2;1, in the poem of the three little kittens, this ɲoun was in each instance replaced by *meow*). *Meow* was at first 1;8 the imitation of the cat's voice and remained that. In addition it also became the generic term for "cat" as early as 1;8 (and as late as 2;1), but in a phonetically different form. These two meanings and forms of the word were in force at B 1;11, and *Dasch* was used to call her cat. Later the generic form served also for calling. At the end of the year, the doublets based on *meow* merged into one form with two meanings, which was the condition of the nursery standard. Naturally, *Dasch* remained separated as the name of her cat, because the adults had accepted this restriction of meaning.

633. The last example leads over to Hildegard's attempts to introduce formal distinctions for semantic differences, which did not exist in the standard model. Such observations were made rather frequently in the early months of speaking.

At E 1;0 she used a double interjection, ʔa ʔa, to speak to dogs. At B 1;1 she learned the nursery term *A-a*, which has the same standard pronunciation; but she pronounced it at first without vowels, as a double glottal stop followed by voice. Whether this unusual substitution reflected a subconscious wish to distinguish the new word from the old or not, is impossible to decide. By E 1;3 the new word had the vowels, but the old interjection had disappeared.

Wauwau had at 1;3 the form **wuwuwu**, probably based on a variant presentation of mine to imitate the barking of dogs. It was used especially for her soft slippers, which reminded her of her soft toy dog. She addressed two bronze horses with the same phonetic word, but in falsetto voice. The distinction, if any was intended, presumably did not concern a difference of reference so much as a difference of function, the latter form being a greeting of more or less interjectional nature.

At 1;1, whispered **ba-ba** could have three meanings: *Papa*, *Opa*, and *Ball* (the German word, reduplicated). A week later, it was pronounced with voice in the meaning *Papa*. Again, at 1;3, **baba** with voice meant *Papa*, the same form whispered meant *by-by*. At B 1;4, this distinction continued, although *by-by* had slightly improved form, which alone might have been sufficient to distinguish it from *Papa*. At the same time, **dada** with voice meant Carolyn, whereas the same word whispered meant *thank you*—again it was the person whose name was said aloud. A little later, **dadaɪ** whispered meant *thank you*; the same form, with or without the final ɪ, was said when handing things to another person, which was either a reduplication of German *da*, or a misuse of *thank you*, but apparently with a functional distinction between receiving and giving.

At the time of observation, I sought semantic intentions in the use of words with or without voice. In view of the great number of homonyms which were later found to coexist in Hildegard's language (459), I am no longer certain that such distinctions were more than accidental. The possibility, however, remains that, at the stage of few words, a subconscious urge to distinguish their forms existed. We need more studies of whispered articulation (359).

After the passing of the stage of whispered pronunciation, and concurrently with it, some homonyms with full vowels seemed to utilize other devices for semantic distinction. At E 1;3 *da* with the rising intonation of the question indicated a wish; the same German word in an even high pitch meant a more objective interest in the things pointed to, without the wish to have them. At 1;4 **da** was the form for both *da* and the new word *down*; both could have a short or a long vowel, but the former had falling, the latter rising intonation. Much later, at 1;11, both occurred in the same sentence, twice, both times with the same difference in the quantity of the vowels; but this may well have been accidental.

At 1;10 the word *dunkel* was used in a variety of situations to which the standard meaning "dark" applied only remotely (621). It seemed to me then that the form **dukɔ** applied to roller shades, **duko** to thunder. This, however, is almost certainly a case of finding a distinction where there was none. The slight variation of the tongue position in the unstressed syllable was without significance (192, 349 f.).

At 1;11, when *no* was used both as a sentence adverb and as an adjective, it seemed as if the phonetic form **nɔ** was preferred in the former function, **no** in the latter. Again, however, the cleavage was not clear-cut. The difference was probably accidental.

None of these examples is absolutely convincing. The observer had his eyes, or rather, his ears open for possible phonetic reflections of semantic distinctions, but the result of the examination is negative. At this early stage of language development, there was no minute coördination of semantic differences with phonetic differences. Both systems were still too coarse to approach the degree of coördination which exists in the standard languages, and it is imperfect even in the latter (606). It is implausible that the child developed distinctions of her own, which did not exist in the model. This consideration leaves untouched the hypothesis that the whispered articulation of the earliest speaking stage made an unconscious distinction between the first imitated words and the older voiced babbling combinations (359).

634. Looking back over the process of learning meaning, we find that sometimes the child used standard words in a more restricted application, which was later extended to the standard range. More commonly,

words were used in a variety of applications which the standard did not allow. The process of learning to conform to standard usage then required a later reduction of the scope of applicability. Sometimes these two processes were intertwined, and progress was not always steady in the direction of standard practice. The standard usage was the ideal, however, which imposed itself relentlessly on the child's speech and was bound to obliterate all deviations eventually.

We saw the reason for extended application in the vagueness of principles of classification, which is natural for an inexperienced small child. We emphasized the fact that the arbitrariness in applying one word to different experiences is not always a sign of the child's immaturity, but that the standard languages themselves are guilty of arbitrariness in many instances. The principles underlying standard classifications are not always logically superior to those of the child; but the child recognizes the authority of the standard language and yields to it step by step. The limitations of the child's early vocabulary required the use of few words for many purposes; but the opposite aspect of the situation should not be overlooked. The child learned additional words as soon as she felt the need for more specific terms. At early stages, rough classifications sufficed. With advancing maturity, finer subdivisions were needed and new words were learned to express them.

The process is parallel, in its general outlines, to the learning of sounds, grammatical forms, and syntactic constructions. The material to be learned is taken over in an organization which reproduces at first only the crudest outlines of the standard organization. Little by little, finer classifications of the standard are recognized and reproduced. This requires the addition of more and more items of vocabulary, which cover less and less semantic territory. The outlines of the areas to which each word is applicable, become more and more distinct and coincide progressively with standard practice.

The tangible progress from one phase to two contrasting phases and later to finer subdivisions applies less clearly to semantics than it does to sounds and syntax. The only semantic area in which we could definitely follow it was that of opposites (625), in which the standard languages themselves show a sharp logical cleavage by contrast. The child's appreciation of the principle of semantic contrast was shown to be relatively late and to be paralleled by a liking for antithetical statements in the field of syntax (627).

635. We are at the end of the examination of infant semantics as it applies to our case. The learning of meaning is an important segment of the language-learning process. Its outlines are comparatively sharp. It could be lifted out of the texture of the whole without cutting off too many vital strands. Nevertheless, semantic learning is only one aspect of language learning. In the following we shall turn our attention to other processes of a still more general nature, with which it is inter-

woven. Their consideration will lead us farther into regions in which linguists and psychologists join hands; but we shall try to keep the linguistic approach in the foreground.

636. At the outset, it is worthwhile to emphasize again (cf. 491) the difficulty of the task which the small child faces in learning to speak, and the greatness of the achievement, by quoting several authors. Delacroix (1930, p. 300) throws light on the complexity of the process in a sentence of 16 printed lines, which leaves the reader, symbolically, almost in the same bewilderment as the small child: "Analyser la continuité sonore du discours entendu, décomposer la phrase, des flexions et des morphèmes, déduire les relations logiques, retenir dans une appréhension simultanée cette mélodie évanescente et qui se construit à mesure qu'elle s'évanouit, construire au fur et à mesure un ensemble sur des éléments qui disparaissent au fur et à mesure, faire une synthèse en même temps qu'une analyse, attendre en sachant ce qu'on attend, imaginer, prévoir, interpréter, aller de l'intelligence de l'ensemble à l'intelligence des éléments et *vice versa*, tel est le jeu d'opérations fort complexes . . . qu'à partir d'un certain degré et sous une certaine forme la compréhension du langage met inévitablement en œuvre . . ."

This statement takes into account only the difficulty of learning to understand spoken language. It does not touch the task of learning to speak and omits the concomitant need of learning to create order in a world which presents many more problems than merely those of language. Macdougall (p. 34) mentions the latter fact along with language: "The adult is prone to lose sight of the complexity of the problem by which the child is faced in learning speech. . . . In the case of the young child all this synthesizing is yet to take place, and the whole system of correspondences must be established point by point in a world which at the outset is a practical and intellectual chaos."

Sully (p. 183) says: "If we are to judge by the effort required we might say that the child does as much in deciphering his mother-tongue as an Oriental scholar in deciphering a system of hieroglyphics". This is, of course, an understatement. The scholar starts in possession of at least one fully developed language system, which he can use for leverage, not to speak of the system of thought and the classification of the world of phenomena associated with it.

K. Bühler (p. 62), speaking as a psychologist, has the strongest statement concerning the achievement: "Die grossen Menschheitsschritte der geistigen Entwicklung fallen in die ersten Lebensjahre, auf die sich darum für immer das Hauptinteresse unserer Wissenschaft konzentrieren wird."

Delacroix uses ever varied metaphors and comparisons to characterize the difficulty of language learning: the child gropes about in the vast domain of the language of adults (1930, p. 298); "L'enfant baigne, pour ainsi dire, dans le langage. . . . La trame du langage recouvre la trame de la vie. Le mot paraît en même temps que l'émotion et que le fait. Toute la vie passe dans le langage" (p. 227); "Ils sont dans la même situation que celui qui voyage dans un pays étranger dont il sait mal la langue; il peut saisir et comprendre des mots isolés ou des phrases qui lui sont addressées, mais une conversation entre indigènes lui échappe totalement" (p. 317). Apart from the important new point that the child learns more from speech addressed to him than from speech of adults passing before him, the last quotation suffers from the same inadequacy as Sully's above.

Gutzmann (p. 24) emphasizes that merely to learn a word requires hearing, attention, repetition, and reproduction.

637. The learning proceeds by imitation of the language which is presented to the child by the environment. This whole study endeavors to show how one child proceeded, step by step, to acquire the languages to which she was exposed.

Nevertheless, it must not be forgotten in this consideration that imitation is by no means a passive process. The preceding section has shown that imitation of language is anything but a mechanical problem, that it requires the most active coöperation of the child and the exercise of all the capacities which develop apace with it. More than that, the child remains the arbiter of what to imitate. He makes a selection from the vast linguistic material offered by the environment and determines the order of its acquisition, often enough resisting efforts to teach specific items when such efforts are made. "Sans doute son génie personnel ne s'efface jamais; . . . il est le maître et non l'esclave des instruments dont il joue."[69] Any record of child language must confine itself to items which the child imitates, disregarding the presented items which he fails to reproduce.[70] A note regarding vocabulary which would seem useful to a child and which, nevertheless, was not acquired in the first two years, was given in vol. 1, p. 168 f. The material which the child does not imitate is much larger than that which he learns early. He makes his own selection. In our case, the history of the important word *Mama* showed how the child refused to learn a word until she was ready for it.

The selectiveness of the procedure is the feature which helps us guard against a misinterpretation of imitation as a passive attitude. The transmission of a language is not like the filling of an empty barrel. It is a guided re-creation of a complex instrument.[71]

On the other hand, the objective nature of the standard language which the child learns must also not be exaggerated. The child learns

---

[69] Delacroix (1934), p. 73. Cf. Vendryes p. 166 (French edition p. 198) for the same principle of selection as applied to the historical development of languages.

[70] Cf. vol. 1, p. XII, note 19.

[71] Cf. Cassirer (1933), p. 34. Piaget (1929, p. 31) says that the child is to be regarded "not as a being of pure imitation, but as an organism which assimilates things to itself, selects them and digests them according to its own structure. In this way even what is influenced by the adult may still be original."

the language of a community; but a community is composed of individuals, and the language of a community manifests itself only in the speech of individuals.[72] For the child who is learning to speak, the number of individuals is small. The speech differences which exist between them reduce the unity and objectivity of the model to be imitated. It was seriously impaired in the case of Hildegard, who was spoken to in two different languages. In such a situation, a child will eventually understand that two separate instruments of expression and communication must be acquired. We have seen that Hildegard availed herself, during the first two years, of her prerogative of free selection from both languages without separation.

In spite of these reservations, the dominating power of the model remains a reality. A child would undoubtedly evolve a sort of language with a few companions, without an adult model; but it would be a scanty instrument, like everything that does not rest on a foundation of tradition.[73]

638. Regarding the motivation for learning to speak, there can be no quarrel with the explanation that the child aims at establishing communication with the environment. In a rudimentary fashion, communication is begun in the crying stage. The child succeeds by crying in making its wants known and having its needs satisfied. This type of communication, however, is too crude to remain satisfactory for long. The child discovers that the organs of articulation, with which it has been playing in the exercises of the babbling stage, can be used for more effective expression and achieve more satisfying specific results. It is at this stage that some babbling combinations turn into words with meaning. The growing powers of observation then enable the child to find out that the adults have certain set ways of using the organs of articulation for very specific purposes. The superior functional efficiency of the adult instrument of communication impresses itself on the child. The first steps in imitation bring experience in the effectiveness of the newly tried tool, and this experience gives encouragement to continue on the road of imitation, which yields satisfying results. The imitation becomes ever more faithful by dint of strenuous efforts at discrimination and reproduction, because every step forward carries its rewards in improved communication resulting in greater satisfaction. "It requires less energy to talk than it does to perform handling reactions," as A. P. Weiss says (p. 302), and, more important, it leads to the satisfaction of more specific wants. Learning to speak is a labor saving device, but it is more than that.

Very soon, these wants are not all utilitarian, as Bohn emphasizes.[74]

---

[72] Jespersen (1927), especially p. 581.
[73] Delacroix (1934), p. 12.
[74] Bohn (1914), especially p. 586 f.

There is an element of pure enjoyment in self-expression, and communication with others does not only serve practical ends, but is enjoyed in itself.[75] Self-expression can be viewed as the polar opposite of communication; but the distinction is theoretical rather than real. Self-expression is enjoyed more when it produces an echo, and communication communes about something which arises in the self.

A similar consideration applies to the question whether the child's early speech is primarily egocentric or social; in fact, this polarity amounts to the same as the one just discussed. Piaget is the extreme exponent of the thesis of egocentrism, in language and otherwise. He has been taken to task by many writers for his exaggeration, especially by Delacroix.[76] Speaking serves egoistic purposes of various kinds, indeed; if we interpret egoism in a very wide sense, the same can be claimed for the speech of adults. On the other hand, the very purpose of speaking is social; its aim is to bend the environment to the wishes of the speaking individual, or at least to enhance individual reactions by sharing them with others. Pure, unsocial individualism would be a bar to the acquisition of language.[77] Even if it were true that children speak primarily to express their own feelings, the aim would be to enrich the experience by giving it a social extension. Conversation between adults can also degenerate into an exchange of monologs[78]; yet it is more enjoyable to the participants than silent thoughts because of the social feature of communication.

The important questions whether objects or actions attract the child's interest first, and whether emotions, volitions, or objective statements dominate the early speaking,[79] have been given much attention in previous parts of this study,[80] and will not be resumed here. It has been shown that the discussion of many writers is distorted by the fact that they take parts of speech at face value at too early a stage (506), and we have found that emotional and volitional utterances are very soon supplemented by statements of facts. Exclusive emphasis on one or the other aspect should be avoided by anyone who wishes to arrive at a true picture of child speech.

639. Gestures are not a linguistic phenomenon. Since they precede[81] and supplement articulate speech, they deserve a few words in passing.

---

[75] Trettien (p. 135), in less effective formulation, speaks of the fundamental impulses of expression and imitation.

[76] Delacroix (1934), pp. 52–57, 73, 99; cf. (1930), p. 322 f.; Stern p. 146 ff.

[77] Delacroix (1934), p. 52.

[78] Delacroix (1930), p. 323.

[79] Kenyeres pp. 194–199, with polemics against Stern, Koffka, Reumuth.

[80] Cf. especially the last sections of vol. 2, and the Syntax of this volume.

[81] Wundt p. 309; Compayré p. 290, note 1 (quotation from Romanes). In Hildegard's case, gestures are actually not recorded before speaking; both began at the same time. Theoretically, the genetic priority of gestures should however be conceded.

Pointing to objects on the part of the adults is an important aid in the child's early steps towards learning to classify the welter of phenomena and towards the linguistic reflection of the classification. Before the child is able to imitate words, it is natural, therefore, that he will learn the easier muscular coördination needed for pointing with the hand, later, with improved muscular control, with the finger. These gestures do not cease abruptly when the method of linguistic pointing is learned. Gestures continue to accompany words, in fact, they do so through life, because the reference is more direct and impressive by means of the gesture.[82] It should be understood that my term "linguistic pointing" is not restricted to adverbs of place; words based on nouns and verbs have also a pointing function.[83]

Pointing gestures are not the only ones to be considered, but they are genetically first, and will be taken up first.

The first pointing gesture recorded in the diary came at 0;10. Hildegard would point at a picture with her hand, saying *pretty* or *there* at the same time. Before that, she had fixed her eyes on objects, from 0;3, and, when she began to understand questions, had turned around to look at the object referred to, from 0;8. These reactions should not be called gestures. *There* was always accompanied by pointing with the right hand, usually at pictures; *pretty* often shared the same gesture, to the end of the first year. These were the only real words at 0;10, apart from *Bild*; *Bild* was likewise often accompanied by pointing.

General demonstratives were developed early. In addition to *there*, 0;10–1;0 (and again 1;5), there were ʔə in varying phonetic forms, 0;8–1;6, *da*, from B 1;0; later *this* 1;8. Naturally, they were frequently accompanied by pointing, in the case of *da* to the end of the second year. *Da* called for pointing naturally, in all uses except in the meaning "present": *Meow da—Miau not da* 1;11. Pictures were favorite objects of interest, but dishes of food and many other things were pointed out by the same means. The use of demonstratives with the gesture is a short-cut designation which saves linguistic identifications. It is a valuable help when specific words are lacking, and remains valuable as an effort-saving device, amply used by adults as well.

Pointing, with other words, was sometimes resorted to in a less standard way to clarify the reference of a statement. *Heiss* 1;7, when the reference was not at once understood, was interpreted by pointing to the radiator, for which she had no word. When she wanted to indicate where we were supposed to sit, she would point to the places, saying *Mama? Papa?* 1;8. The same utterance accompanied by pointing with the arm meant that we should follow her out of the room; in this situation, the

---

[82] Wundt p. 309.

[83] This view has points of contact with Wundt's theory that speech is expressive gesture in articulated form, but does not go to the same length.

gesture was the immediate forerunner of the linguistic expressions (*komm*) *mit* 1;8–10 and *come on* 1;10. She said *rock-rock* 1;8, pointing energetically to the rocking-chair in which she wished the ritual to be performed.

Not imitated, but original was the designation of objects by direct touch instead of pointing. When Hildegard wanted me to sit on a certain chair 1;6, she pounded on the seat and looked at me, silently; she laughed happily when I understood. When she wanted to be taken for a walk, she put her hands on her buggy and said *ride-ride* 1;8. To communicate the fact that she had teething-pains 1;8, she put her finger in the mouth with the demonstrative *da* of a three-word utterance, instead of simply pointing. These gestures were induced by the desire to be more specific. Pointing, after all, did not always preclude the possibility of misunderstanding. Rudimentarily, the urge for greater clarity was operating in gestures as well as in articulated utterances. Saving of effort is a desirable end; but being fully understood is even more desirable. If this were not so, spoken language might never be learned.

On a slightly different level was her report that her mother had spanked her 1;11; the demonstrative *da* was reinforced by clapping her buttocks with her hand. The desire to be specific was there, more than adults would feel necessary; it was, of course, an imitation of the adult's motion in spanking.

640. The use of the right index finger rather than the whole hand is specifically mentioned in the diary for the first time at B 1;0, not for pointing, but for calling attention to music. She had always been interested in music. Now she raised her finger and said ʔɪ with serious and absorbed facial expression, for piano playing, street musicians, singing, whistling, etc. The "word" and the gesture were demonstrative, but in a less concrete use, not pointing to the source of the music, but only calling attention to it. It is probable that the gesture was learned from adults. The verbal accompaniment varied (ʃ ʃ 1;0) or was absent. The gesture remained constant, except for the fact that it was often improved to beating time with the finger. A number of curious extensions of reference have been mentioned before (note to **623** and vol. 1, p. 134). Later on, the use of the gesture diminished, but it was deeply rooted; relapses occurred as late as 1;8 and 1;11; in the case of 1;8 she was half asleep. She understood the word "Musik" by 1;1, even in the disguised form "musikalisch", where the stress is shifted. She recognized four melodies by E 1;1 and liked to sing; but her singing did not reproduce any known melody, and she did not learn to say a word for music. The pre-linguistic gesture remained the only expression.[84]

A few other words were presented by the adults with a raised index

---

[84] Jervis has a special study of interest in music during the second year, with bibliography. The results are scanty.

finger for emphasis, and Hildegard imitated this gesture. The interjection *sh* 1;6, which meant "be quiet and go to sleep", was learned together with the gesture, which distinguished it from the homonyms *sch* and *shoe*. Because I raised a warning finger with *Augenblick!*, which meant "wait a moment and be cautious", she would sometimes do so too when she said the word 1;8. By this time the use of the gesture for music had become rare.

641. The hands and the right arm were also used for the following gestures. She learned clapping her hands 0;9 as the stereotype accompaniment of a nursery ditty. At 1;0 this gesture was transferred, by precept of adults, to the standard German nursery function of request. This was henceforth a very useful gesture, and it was used constantly by the child. The linguistic equivalent *bitte* was learned E 1;5; it immediately superseded the more primitive expression. One spontaneous relapse E 1;6 testifies to the persistence of gestures. At 1;5 Hildegard used the gesture of pounding her chest to indicate "it tastes good", also a standard practice; but this was only a synonym of spoken *m*, which had served the same purpose for nearly five months. The gesture was clearer than the "word", because **m:** also meant hunger, wish to eat, and food in general.

At 1;5 *all* in the sense of "all gone" was said with palms turned outward and thumbs spread, a gesture learned from the maid. Synonymous German *alle* 1;7 inherited the gesture at first.

At 1;6 she stated that her cousins were far away (in Milwaukee), underlining the idea of *away* with a gesture of the hand and with eyes looking into distant space. The statement became a fixed recital. Once it was released by hearing the word "Milwaukee" in a conversation. At 1;8 *Milwaukee* became the etymon for a word of the same vague meaning. Its synonymous character was evident by the similarity of the intonation and of the gesture, now a sweeping motion of the whole arm. This gesture was original.

The curious word **bu::** for thunder 1;11, possibly, but not probably, an original onomatopœia, was accompanied by a waving of the hand, which was certainly an original way of symbolizing a frequentative impression.

642. Nodding and shaking of the head were used for affirmative and negative ideas, as happens to be standard in English and German. As gestures accompanying words, their use was not restricted to the several affirmative and negative adverbs. Nodding appeared also, in original extension, with *thank you* 1;3–4, perhaps because situations which call for this "receipt" as a social obligation are positive in character. *Alle* occurred with head-shaking at 1;11; by this time Hildegard had analyzed the negative content of the word, which means "gone, exhausted".

Occasionally, gestures took the place of words at a rather late stage.

When asked what a person in a picture was doing, Hildegard indicated eating by smacking her lips 1;8. The verb *eat* (1;10) was not yet active, but the substitute *m* existed and was used for this purpose during the same month in the same situation. The use of the gesture was merely a playful variation of the response.

Facial expression, if it is permissible to call it a gesture, did not substitute for words, but accompanied them sometimes as a semantic reinforcement. This has been mentioned in connection with attention to music and with the expressions of the idea "far away". The commiserating exclamations *arme* 1;7 and *poor* 1;10 and the regretful interjection *oh* 1;3–4 were coördinated by intonation and facial expression.

Intonation leads over from gestures to linguistic expression, but is here included in the latter (**489 f.**), because it makes use of the speaking apparatus.

643. The meaning of gestures must first be understood before they can be imitated with meaning. No case of meaningless imitation of gestures is recorded. Yet, the learning of the meaning of gestures, even the simple pointing gesture, is an intellectual achievement. Dogs learn it, but not without first paying attention to the hand itself instead of the direction symbolically indicated by its position.

It is obvious that the meaning of words must first be understood before they can be imitated with meaning. Meaningless repetition can occur earlier, but there was little of it in Hildegard's case because of her cautious speaking habits. A complication arises out of the fact that words are not usually uttered in isolation, but in sentences. The child may understand the meaning of an utterance as a whole without being as yet able to analyze it in its component parts.[85] A phonetically and semantically prominent part of the sentence is selected for imitation by the child,[86] but made the carrier of the semantic content of the whole sentence. This is the cause of the distortion of perspective in the records of numerous observers who take early words at their face value as nouns, verbs, etc., whereas they really contain the meaning of sentences. This consideration applies with full force to the stage of one-word sentences. As the length of the child's sentences grows, word-analysis progresses, but not with a sudden jump. In two- and three-word sentences, the individual words get sharper outlines gradually, but cannot yet be compared, item by item, with their semantic prototypes.

Whether we face the meaning of sentences or that of words, there can be no doubt that understanding comes before meaningful imitation.

---

[85] Cf. Stern (p. 166), who credits Meumann with the first insight into these conditions. Delacroix (1930, p. 343 f., quoting Bally, *Traité de stylistique française* p. 78) calls attention to the fact that even adults do not nearly understand everything said or written in their mother tongue, without being conscious of it.

[86] Cf. vol. 1, p. 28 and note 67.

This has always been recognized, from the times of Aristotle on.[87] There is disagreement as to whether an extended period of pure comprehension, without speaking, precedes the stage of imitative speaking.[88] Stern (pp. 163–169) shows that the duration of this period is often overestimated and that it does not always exist. It differs individually from 0 to 7 months. The difficulty of establishing the length of the period can be illustrated on Hildegard's case. She understood, by the test of reaction, her own name at E 0;6. She said the first imitated word, *Bild*, at E 0;9. Thus it might be said that the period of pure comprehension extended over three months. The imitation of *Bild*, however, was uncertain and ephemeral and was at first not identified. It might easily have escaped notice, and then the first imitated word would have been *pretty* B 0;10, stretching the period to 3½ months. On the other hand, communicative articulated speaking began as early as M 0;8 with the interjection ʔa!. It was not imitative, but its existence makes it impossible to speak of a continuing stage of pure comprehension. Also, the understanding was at first strictly confined to her own name. It was not until M 0;8 that Hildegard began to understand "Daddy", "baby", and a few other words. Thus, speaking and understanding really began at the same time, M 0;8.[89] If we insist on imitative speaking, which I hold unjustified, the interval would be little more than a month, apart from the understanding of the reference of her name.

Gestures tie in with the problem of understanding. Stern (pp. 166–169) demonstrates that the gesture which accompanies the spoken word is a bridge for comprehension.

644. Apart from the problem of a stage of pure comprehension, there is no disagreement concerning the obvious fact that understanding precedes imitative speaking. Stern (p. 165) emphasizes that understanding progresses much more rapidly than speaking and displays much finer discrimination. This observation is fully borne out by Hildegard's record. The history of many words in vol. 1 begins with an extended period during which the word was understood, but not yet said. Few observers have gone into detail concerning the preponderance of words

---

[87] Pavlovitch p. 4; Aristotle states only that there are children who understand before being able to articulate. Cf., among many others, Schultze p. 26, Preyer pp. 93, 215 f., Romanes p. 123, note, Compayré p. 288, note 1; Fenton p. 139.

[88] Meumann (p. 165) calls the stage of mere understanding of presented words the stage of normal hearing-muteness. Cf. Schäfer's experimental study, especially p. 271; Jespersen p. 113; Decroly pp. 74 ff., 87; Bloch (1921) p. 705 f. Several authors make the point that children never make a mistake in understanding words which are homonyms in their own speech.

[89] Cf. vol. 1, p. 21.

merely understood over those imitated.[90] Such an endeavor, if carried on over more than the beginning stage of speaking, would increase the difficulty of a difficult task enormously, and nothing would be gained by it except a confirmation of what is obvious anyway.

Sully (p. 147) gives a rough sketch of the word-learning process, which makes it clear that understanding must come before speaking: "The child hears a particular sound used by another, and gradually associates it with the object, the occurrence, the situation, along with which it again and again presents itself. When this stage is reached he can understand the word-sound as used by another though he cannot as yet use it. Later, by a considerable interval, he learns to connect the particular sound with the appropriate vocal action required for its production. As soon as this connexion is formed his sign-making impulse imitatively appropriates it by repeating it in circumstances similar to those in which he has heard others employ it." Although the wording is not perfect, this description covers the situation well; the word "similar" at the end is well-chosen, because it allows for all semantic deviations from the standard.

645. In this connection it is worth while to review some specific examples from the word histories, which show the time interval between the first understanding and the first utterance.

Baby was understood, although in a greatly restricted meaning, at 0;8, that is to say, the child reacted to the hearing of the word in a manner approved by the standard speakers. It was said from memory at 1;2, without immediately preceding presentation. The interval was $5\frac{1}{2}$ months. An extension of meaning had taken place during the passive stage, beyond the standard limits. The phonetic history of a word in child-language begins with the first utterance. The semantic history begins with the first understanding of it.

Arm in compassionate exclamations like "der arme Wauwau!" was understood 1;2, spoken 1;7 (5 months' interval). Though there is no exact record, the interval is likely to have been even longer for the English synonym *poor* 1;10, which could remain in abeyance as long as its meaning was adequately expressed by the German equivalent. The bilingual situation tended to lengthen the interval in all cases of successive bilingual synonyms.

Papa was understood B 0;11, said with meaning E 1;0 ($1\frac{1}{2}$ months). *Mama* was understood E 0;11, said with meaning B 1;3 (over 3 months). The latter interval is reduced by the fact that perhaps at E 1;1 and certainly at E 1;2 the phonetic word *Papa* included "Mama" in its semantic coverage; *Papa* meant both "Papa" and "Mama".

---

[90] Deville lists words understood, but not said; but his lists are very incomplete. He states that at 1;3 it was impossible to record all words understood. Hoyer (p. 375) give statistics for the early months and find the proportion of words understood to words spoken to decrease from 9:1 at 0;10 to 7:2 at 1;1.

The corresponding figures are for *Handschuh* 1;5 and 1;10 (5 months); *mouth* 1;4 and 1;10 (6 months); "coat" (*Schnucks*) 1;3 and 1;10 (7 months); *train* 1;8 and 1;11 (3 months); *Wehweh* 0;11 and 1;8 (9 months); *Fritzchen* 1;2 and 1;8 (6 months); *patsch* 0;10 and 1;11 (13 months); *Hildegard* 0;6 and 1;11 (17 months). The latter example is the longest interval which I have noticed, excluding, of course, the great number of words which were understood but not said at all before 2;0. I disregard instances like *Kuss* 1;0 and 1;11 (11 months), because the English synonym *kiss* was slightly earlier; for the latter, 1;4 and 1;11, the interval was 7 months. If we focus the attention less strictly on the phonetic word, the history of the two synonyms combined yields an interval of 11 months.

The intervals recorded are minimum spans. Understanding is dated from the time that it was clearly shown by the child's reactions. Of course, in many cases the child may have understood the words earlier without giving evidence of it. Comprehension was undoubtedly often vague or dim at first. We must assume the same development from haziness to greater and greater clarity for passive meaning as we did for active meaning, with the difference that the development of passive understanding is faster than that of active expression.

646. In most of these instances, the active emergence of the word followed a renewed presentation shortly before. The child imitates a word, after many intervening presentations, when he is ready for its active use. In some cases, however, the word emerged when it had not been presented immediately before. It was remembered from earlier presentations.[91] This is bound to happen most frequently in the last months of the second year when the child's memory span has become longer (**649**). At 1;10 the diary notes specifically that many words came up from memory without having been used on the same occasion by the standard speakers. At 1;11 another notation says that Hildegard's new words were so numerous that we did not always understand them; this means that no clue for them was found in the present situation or in the immediately preceding presentation, that they rose from memory.

Occasionally, this phenomenon occurred much earlier. The word *baby* was first used 1;2 without preceding presentation, after 5½ months of passive practice. *Fritzchen*, the name of a doll, very familiar for 6 months, emerged from memory at 1;8. Most of the examples, however, were late. At 1;10 she said *aus* for "Licht aus" in a phonetic form which showed that it went back to the remembered German presentation, instead of the familiar form without a final consonant, which could just as well be based on the English synonym *out*. At 1;11 she named the

---

[91] Stern p. 135: "Summationswirkungen der natürlichen Umgangssprache. Worte, die oft gehört und verstanden worden waren, sind schliesslich so sehr in motorische Bereitschaft gesetzt, dass sie, auch ohne von neuem vorgesagt zu werden, bei geeigneter Gelegenheit erstmalig hervorspringen."

Löscher after she had not played with it for over 6 weeks nor heard the word. Toward the end of the year she uttered the wish, (*Let us go*) *way down* (*to the*) *beach* at home, therefore without the customary visual stimulus, and without immediate presentation of the word "beach".

The most striking instances of emergence from memory are those in which the inspirers of the imitation can be identified, but are no longer present.[92] At 1;2 Hildegard said *bim-bam* in exactly the same intonation which her aunt in Hamburg had used and for the same purpose. This was on the boat on the return trip to America, several days after the departure. Hildegard had imitated a variant form of the interjection at 1;1, but in more rudimentary form. The new form was not based on the memory of her own earlier imitation, but on the memory of the presented form.

At 1;11 she said *powder-puff* in a mutilated monosyllabic form. She had learned this word from a maid who had left three weeks before.[93]

647. The emergence of words from memory is a facet of the fact that word comprehension precedes word imitation.[94] Words are acquired passively sooner than actively. The active emergence is favored by renewed presentation. It is not surprising that the first active use of a word is usually preceded by a presentation of it. The presentation at the time when the child is ready to imitate the word activates the accumulated memory residues of previous presentations, which had engraved the phonetic configuration of the word with increasing distinctness on the child's mind, and at the same time had circumscribed its semantic area of reference. When the memory span becomes longer, the needs of the speaking situation can release the articulation without an immediately preceding presentation.

The lag in time between comprehension and utterance of words has found much attention in the literature of child-language.[95] It is often called "storing-up" (French: "emmagasinement").[96] Lewis (p. 96) objects to the term and substitutes "metalalia":[97] "Unfortunately a good deal of difficulty has been imported into the discussion of the subject by the use of the term 'emmagasinement', which since its introduction

---

[92] Cf. Grammont's observations concerning the after-effects of the pronunciation of an Italian nurse, one month after she had left (pp. 74, 76). A very striking case is reported by Cummings. A child began speaking three months after leaving Burma and after hearing only English in the meantime—at first all in Burmese, six months later everything in both English and Burmese. (In another year Burmese was forgotten completely.)

[93] The time indication, two weeks, vol. 1, p. 50, is an error. The diary says three weeks.

[94] Cf. Lewis p. 97 f.

[95] Cf. Jespersen p. 143.

[96] Cf. Grammont p. 81 ("emmagasinement et une sorte d'incubation"), Bloch (1921) p. 694 f.

[97] The term is taken from Stern p. 135.

by Le Dantec in 1899[98] has been repeatedly adopted, for instance by Delacroix[99] and those whom he cites, and by Lorimer.[100] But it seems no more justifiable to speak of 'storing-up' in this than in any other case of reinstatement of a past experience. What is it that is stored, and where?" To be sure, nothing material is stored in a physical sense; but then, we use words in figurative meanings all the time, and the established term is useful if it is understood figuratively, as it undoubtedly is by everybody.

Delacroix (1934, p. 104) explains this storing as due to a lack of initiative, to a certain timidness. This is only one way of looking at the phenomenon. One might just as well call it a wise restraint, a desire to be sure of results. In this light I have often represented Hildegard's aversion to hasty imitation of words. Besides, no matter whether a child is rash or cautious in embarking on active reproduction of speech, comprehension precedes speaking in the vast majority of instances. Every child understands many words long before he is ready to use them himself. In fact, this situation remains through life. We all understand many more words than we incorporate in our active vocabulary, and we continue to add items to it which had been stored in our memory for a shorter or longer period, as soon as we feel that they serve a speaking need.

648. Many children who are less reserved in their imitative proclivity,[101] reproduce some words which they hear before they understand their meaning. In fact, a stage of echolalia is sometimes postulated for all children, a stage of mechanical imitation preceding meaningful reproduction.[102] We have seen[103] that Hildegard lacked such a stage. The term "echo" has been used often in the record, but because of the absence of meaningless imitation its definition could be restricted, for purposes of this record, to meaningful imitation immediately after presentation.[104]

Echolalia, in the many cases in which it exists, occurs as a stage preceding meaningful speaking.[105] A special form of echolalia is the production of long sound-sequences in which no words are recognizable, but the intonation of adult speech is so faithfully reproduced that they sound like real speaking; one needs to listen closely to become con-

---

[98] F. Le Dantec, "Le mécanisme de l'imitation", Rev. philos. 10 (1899), p. 354.

[99] 1930, p. 290.

[100] F. Lorimer, *The growth of reason*, 1928, pp. 43, 49.

[101] I am not sure that I have ever used the word "proclivity" before; but I have known it for a long time. It has been stored in my memory.

[102] Most sweeping statement: Gutzmann p. 22. Cf. vol. 1, p. 22, note 38.

[103] Vol. 1, p. 22.

[104] Vol. 1, p. 6.

[105] Cf. further, Bloch (1921) p. 696 ("psittacisme" with his three children, late speakers, 1;7–2;3), Jespersen p. 135 ("Echoism"), Stern p. 162 f. (with further references; my observations agree with Preyer's, which Stern criticizes).

vinced that no meaning and no imitation of words is involved, but merely imitation of the speech melody, on the basis of long observation, not as an immediate echo.[106] Neither of my children ever used this type of echolalia, but I have observed it strikingly in another child (490).

Echolalia is often observed again later, when imitative speaking has already begun.[107] This phase was likewise not observed in Hildegard's language learning.[108]

649. The preceding discussions have to do with the development of memory. Echolalia concerns the memory of the phonetic form of utterances just heard and reveals degrees of capacity by its extensiveness; children echo the last syllable, the last word, several words, or the whole utterance. Even in meaningful few-word utterances of the early stages, limitations of memory for typical adult sentences are probably involved. The words spoken are often those which would stand at the end of complete standard sentences. This may well be a contributing reason why for instance, the subject is not expressed at first, because it does not usually stand near the end of sentences, and why formulas like "I want to" or "May I", "Will you" are suppressed, because they come at the beginning of sentences.

In this connection, it may be of interest to report a few general, non-linguistic observations concerning the span of memory, culled from the diary.[109] At first all actions and utterances were connected with visible, present cues. Interest in an object or a situation often involved recognition and therefore memory; but we disregard here all instances in which the memory needed a present stimulus to be released.

One of the first observations recorded is the incident at B 1;2 on the ocean liner, when Hildegard passed the door of the smoking lounge and beat time with her finger, because she had previously heard a trio performing there. There was still a visible cue (there is always some kind of a cue for everything), but it was not the object itself, but an event connected with it which was brought to mind. Running excitedly from the cabin to the place where the fire hose was rolled up, with the expectant

---

[106] Bateman (1914, p. 319) reports that his daughter joined the conversation of adults with "beautifully modulated periods quite devoid of meaning"; for other references cf. note to 490.

[107] Stern, loc. cit.; Lewis p. 101, with references (good characterization of the phonetic advantages and semantic disadvantages of echolalia); Bateman (1914) p. 317 f. (interesting case: two Chinese words submerge with the interruption of mechanical imitation at 1;3, emerge with its resumption at 1;6).

[108] Karla, on the other hand, had an unmistakable phase of echolalia at 1;9; cf. vol. 1, p. 22, note 40.

[109] Hetzer and Wislitzky have gone experimentally into minute detail with very young children, finding the memory of small events to increase its span from ½ minute at 0;10 to 17 minutes at 1;9–11. Expectation of regularly recurring events, based on memory, exists as early as 0;3. My own observations concern longer, more obvious spans of memory.

utterance *tick-tock* at the same time, did not even involve a visible cue; she could not see the red metal spool of the hose when she started out. She saw it several times every day; thus no long memory span was needed; but the operation of memory without a visual stimulus was noteworthy.

At 1;3 she said *Mama* and *Papa* in their absence, expressing her wish to see them. After a visit to Milwaukee, she began to say *Papa* as soon as she had alighted from the train, before the final ride home to our apartment, where I was awaiting her and her mother; she had not seen me for six days. Perhaps she realized that she was approaching home; if not, the awakening of a memory over a six-day interval was still a fact. Her mother had undoubtedly talked about me in the meantime, but not immediately before, and the stimulus of my presence was lacking all the time.

On the last two days of 1;3 she picked up matches, cigarette stubs and other trash from the sidewalk and carried them to the gutter. This morally laudable but hygienically objectionable pursuit had been a favorite occupation on the deck of the ocean boat seven weeks before. The close similarity makes it seem likely that memory over a long interval was involved rather than merely a renewed impulse of orderliness with accidentally similar results.[110] Otherwise the diary notes, a few days later, that memory was generally still connected with visible objects, but with associations leading from them or from linguistic stimuli to invisible objects. Thus, seeing me, she remembered the pencil which I had in the inside pocket of my coat and searched for it. Hearing "by-by" or "ausgehen", she echoed *by-by* and ran into her room to find her coat, hat, or buggy to implement the desire to go for a walk.

At B 1;5 the naming of absent persons in expectation of seeing them became frequent after a shorter or longer time of not seeing them. At 1;6 talk about her cousins in Milwaukee became habitual long after she had last seen them; a walk or ride, or hearing the name "Milwaukee", was sufficient to awaken the association. At 1;8, on a walk, she tried to lift a cake of snow which was much too big for her. Passing it again on the way back, her mother challenged her to lift it. She made a motion to follow the direction, but then desisted and said *big?*, shaking her head.

At 1;9 the word *Schnee* entered into temporarily fixed combinations with *bums* and *by-by*. A week after the snow had disappeared, she still said *bums, Schnee* with the game of letting herself fall backwards on the rug, as she had done in the snow. Again a week later, the question, "Do you want to go by-by?" released the answer *Schnee?*, because walks had recently been associated with snow. In both these cases, however,

---

[110] Egger (p. 19) also observed no memory for non-habitual phenomena before 1;3 in his children and grandchildren.

mechanical linguistic association between two words may have been more important than actual memory of the snow; the utterance of *bums* and *by-by* released the phonetic sequence which habitually followed it by linguistic rather than factual memory. The interrogative intonation in the second case may indicate that she became conscious of the clash between linguistic habit and the facts.

Also at 1;9, she pointed to the twin day-bed where her cousins had slept and stated *Marion? Dodo? Da!* That had been a week before. At 1;10 I told her that the cat had sore eyes. The cat was not present, but Hildegard understood. I checked after ten minutes. In question and answer she was able to reproduce the statement exactly, demonstrating a memory span of ten minutes for a purely linguistic communication, without any visual support at any time, whereas before that, objects, wishes, and actions induced words, or words led to objects and actions.

These incidental observations on memory can be linked with the previous discussion of tenses. The past tense can obviously not begin to develop until the child remembers events sufficiently removed from the present to induce a feeling for the inadequacy of the grammatical present tense. We have seen that Hildegard did not reach a formal distinction between the present and past tenses during the first two years (586). The lengthening of the memory span does not at once call forth formal distinctions in tenses.

650. There are instances and stages in children's speech development in which the linguistic memory of the child's own words is stronger than the memory of the words heard from standard speakers. This leads to temporary persistence of infantile forms and sudden replacement by perfected forms, when the presentation again takes greater effect; and it leads to plateaus in the linguistic development, the child operating with the acquired linguistic stock for a while instead of adding to it by imitation of new material. We have dealt with the fixation of imperfect forms[111] in the examination of the development of sounds.[112] The variable rate of progress and the existence of plateaus has been taken up in the analysis of the vocabulary.[113]

It is the former aspect which induces some observers to emphasize that improvement of form is due to a renewed imitation of the presented word and not to a gradual improvement of the child's former phonetic version.[114] This happens, to be sure. One of the most striking cases in Hildegard's record is the German word *Nackedei*, which had a very infantile form 1;7–2;0 without any development, and suddenly became

---

[111] Cf. vol. 2, index under Fixation, especially **496**.

[112] A good description of the phenomenon is given by Deville vol. 24, p. 30.

[113] Vol. 1, pp. 18, 161 f. The chapter on the First Year dwells on this point repeatedly.

[114] Grammont p. 81 (substitution, not gradual correction); Bloch (1913) p. 39 (child remembers presentation, not own imperfect form); Cohen.

phonetically perfect at 2;0, no doubt by a breach of the long-established habit and substitution of the presented form for the fixed mutilation of it. This jump from an imperfect to a perfect form, however, is merely a consequence of a prolonged phonetic fixation. The child became aware suddenly of the gap between the prototype and the habitual imitated form, and realized suddenly that she was now able to do better. There is no doubt in my mind that most improvements proceed gradually.[115] The volumes on vocabulary and sounds demonstrate this. Cases of progress with a jerk are the exception, not the rule. Of course, in either case it is the standard word which exerts its influence on the child's imitation; but it does so abruptly only after fixations which have stayed behind the child's phonetic capacity.

As to plateaus and stages of rapid development,[116] Stern (p. 178) equates them with the rhythmic wave motions, the alternating stages of slow and rapid development, which can be found in all aspects of mental growth. He takes phases of rapid advance in comprehension, coördinated with phases of slow progress in speaking, and contrasts between physical progress and linguistic progress as other facets of the same phenomenon. His exposition is quite satisfactory. I would only add that these phases of growth are not always mutually exclusive. Sometimes the child's energy is so productive that there is rapid growth in all those areas simultaneously.[117]

651. Many authors attempt to divide the process of language learning into a number of stages with broad characteristics.

Stern (p. 239) distinguishes a stage of substance, a stage of action, and a stage of relations and criteria. The last stage, that of abstractions, lies mostly beyond the period under observation in this record. The distinction between the first two stages suffers, as Bloch (1923, p. 671 f.) has pointed out,[118] from the transfer of standard grammatical classifications to child-language. "Nouns" mark actions as well as objects, especially during the one-word stage.

Charlotte Bühler (p. 149 f.) tabulates five successive stages of imitative speaking in detail under the categories of naming,[119] narration, interpretation, formal thinking, and synthesis, the last stage being

---

[115] Grammont (p. 82), in spite of his earlier strong statement to the contrary, admits that there is also correction of the child's form.

[116] Velten (p. 290 f.) observed a stage of swift development in morphology and syntax 2;2–5. By E 2;8 both were in agreement with standard English except for the weak past tense; this although his child's early linguistic development was very slow.

[117] Cf. vol. 1, p. 18.

[118] Cf. also Cassirer's criticism, reproduced by Grégoire, p. 81.

[119] Guillaume (p. 18) emphasizes that the learning of "names" is steady. There is no sudden revelation that every object has a name. The case of Helen Keller, of which much is made in the literature, is exceptional. Stern (pp. 190–193) seems to disagree.

reached, in the case of her own child, at 2;0. This logical classification overlaps in part our discussions of memory.

Other divisions into stages concern the procedure of imitation rather than the function or contents of speech. Cohen (p. 127) speaks of three stages as traditional: babbling, few words, and extensive speech. He implies that there should be more stages, but abstains from establishing any because there are not yet available enough records of individual children which describe their speech development linguistically. Trettien (p. 117) focuses his attention on three stages of imitative speaking: self-imitation (in the first months), conscious reproduction (second half of first year to third year), and reproductive speaking; his third stage falls beyond the time of this investigation. Allport restates the traditional stages in mechanistic terms: random articulation (= babbling and cooing); evoking the articulate elements by the speech of others, so-called "imitation" (= mechanical imitation, echolalia); and conditioning of the articulate elements, evoked by others, by objects and situations (= meaningful imitation). We have seen that the second stage was omitted by Hildegard.

Instead of engaging in the discussion of theories and explanations, we recapitulate here briefly the stages through which Hildegard's language learning passed, in linguistic terms: crying,[120] with purely physiological differentiation 0;0–1; cooing, second half 0;1; babbling[121] and inarticulate cries 0;2–9 (1;3) (340); understanding of her name E 0;6; transition to speaking: cries acquire meaning and become interjections,[122] a few babbling combinations acquire meaning and become words B 0;8; comprehension begins M 0;8; first imitative word E 0;9, with meaning. These stages are not neatly set off from each other, but overlap.

In imitative speaking, emotion prevailed at first, but statements of fact occurred early. No clear separation of the two conditions is possible. Statements were induced by interest, as in the speech of adults; interest

---

[120] Gutzmann (p. 3 f.) has a good characterization of crying as a useful physiological preparation for speaking. Note also his explanation (p. 5) why sucking, often considered an ancestor of speaking, is a handicap rather than a help for speaking.

[121] I am inclined to consider babbling as motor exercise, as does Delacroix (1934, p. 59), who states that deaf children babble like those who hear. K. Bühler (1926, p. 601) says: "*Lallen* est un héritage commun de l'humanité, et d'une uniformité complète chez les enfants de toutes les races." White observes that my Hildegard and O. F. Raum's two African babies "babbled about the same syllables and first words." Grégoire finds that national differences with regard to sounds are heard after a start with all possible sounds. This amounts to the same thing. Babbling, as I see it, is by definition not imitative. Language differences are reflected only in imitative speech, which should not be called babbling, no matter how imperfect the imitation may be.

[122] Cf. Macdougall p. 575: "His modified cries are true words—or, rather, interjectional sentences in their significance—which he employs because he finds them understood."

is not far removed from emotion. Intellectualization of speaking progressed.

Intellectualization coincides with progressive grammatical organization. Unorganized one-word sentences developed into more and more organized two-word and more-word sentences. Again these stages overlapped. Beginning with two-word sentences, a crude syntactic analysis set in, which became more and more refined. The morphological indications of syntactic relationships lagged far behind; few inflections developed; form words were below the threshold of attention. Phonetic learning proceeded apace, from crude one-phase imitations to rough contrasts, gradual refinements of contrasts, and refinements of imitative accuracy.

These developments were not concluded by the end of the second year. The termination of the study at the mechanical boundary of the turn to the third year corresponds to no boundary of the linguistic development. That is why further developments during the first two months of the third year were often indicated in parentheses. For the same reason the continuation of the learning process will be shown in diary form from the beginning of the third year. The first stages, however, are the most interesting ones. All processes of language learning were under way by the end of the second year. The gradual progress toward more exact reproduction of the presented standard, although still interesting to observe in its details, proceeded steadily in conformity with the intellectual and social maturation of the child,[123] with no major surprise developments.[124]

---

[123] Cf. Delacroix (1934), pp. 15, 16, 18.

[124] There are some marginal problems of linguistic development which must here be skipped. The influence of older siblings could not enter into Hildegard's language learning. It played a part in Karla's learning, but not until rather late. Hildegard did not play much with Karla until 1;6, when she began to be useful as a playmate. She did not talk nearly so much to the baby as the mother and even the father did. Bloch (1921, p. 693), whose three children were born four and five years apart, observes that under these conditions there is no linguistic influence of one child on the other (Hildegard and Karla are six years apart). Otherwise observations conflict; cf. Gale p. 46; Smith (1926) pp. 9, 63, (1935) p. 206. Smith is inclined to consider this difference as well as sex difference and even social differences as slight or uncertain (1926, pp. 60–63). Linguistic consciousness was occasionally observed in Hildegard (cf. Tappolet p. 408 for the fourth year); but it belongs to a later stage; examples can be found in the Diary (see index to it). During the first two years, attention to form detached from meaning was found in some cases referred to in vol. 2 (see index under Misunderstandings); these cases hardly deserve to be classified as evidence of linguistic consciousness; they belong to the months from 1;7. Another problem which is here omitted is that of the origin of language, of ontogenetic and phylogenetic parallelism, of relationships between the language learning of children and of mankind. This issue, although often mentioned in the literature of child-language, is purely speculative. An individual record cannot shed any light on it. Suffice it to state my conviction that man's learning to speak for the first time and children's learning to imitate a fully

652. The foregoing discussions were concerned with the language-learning process as such. There remains to be investigated the bilingual situation, which is a complication of the process involved in the case under observation.

I resist the temptation to generalize about the advantages or disadvantages of bilingualism, about which a sharp conflict of opinions exists. I shall instead offer some exact observations concerning the interplay of two languages in the learning of the child, engaging in theoretical considerations only so far as they seem warranted on the basis of experiences in this single case.

653. Supplementing the succinct analyses of vol. 1, pp. 159–161 (especially p. 161), 163, 176, 177–179 (especially p. 179), I record some more general details, first concerning the impact of the two languages on the child and her reaction.

Until 1;0 reactions to linguistic stimuli favored neither of the languages. They were generally understood in both languages and directions were executed with equal readiness. The fact that English and German are very similar, particularly on the elementary level corresponding to the stage, furthered this situation. We may assume that the phonetic perception of the child was still dim and coarsely differentiated. She may not even have taken cognizance of the differences between English and German stimuli, or only dimly so. This state continued for fully a month and a half after her arrival in Germany, where the German presentation became much more powerful.

At the end of 1;0 it was observed that, for the first time, a direction was understood and obeyed in German, but not in English. When she was asked, "Kannst du allein stehen?" she would delightedly demonstrate her new prowess of standing up without holding on. Her mother tried the same question in English, but the child did not react.

By B 1;2 Hildegard had forgotten the few English words which she had learned to say, with the exception of the persistent word *pretty*, whereas she had learned to say several German words. At the end of the sojourn in Germany 1;2, she no longer understood English.

Thirteen days after the return to America (1;2), she just began to understand simple English directions again, but still understood everything in German, more complicated directions only in German. The change of environment retarded the acquisition of new words temporarily (vol. 1, p. 152). During 1;3 new words in English and German were in balance and few in number. By B 1;4 the English was rapidly catching up with the advantage which the German had gained. Later

---

developed language are two basically different processes; and that, on the other hand, there is no closer empirical approach to the problem of language origin than the study of how children rebuild for themselves the organization of the world as it is codified in language. Cf. Stern pp. 307–327, Conradi pp. 333–337, Richter pp. 76 f., 85, 92, Guillaume p. 228 f.

in the month, she understood familiar commands in English and in German; but in many cases, especially for longer explanations, her mother, who does not speak German with ease, still felt impelled to resort to German.

The diary notes at this time that Hildegard did not associate the languages with definite persons. She said the new English word *up* to me as freely as to other persons. This condition is typical of Hildegard's early bilingualism. She directed German words to English speakers as well. This was observed as late as 1;11, when a misunderstanding was caused by her use of a German word (see *nass*) before English-speaking children, although she disposed of bilingual synonyms by this time. Her sentences were mixed of German and English words. She constructed a unified linguistic medium of her own out of the bilingual presentation (vol. 1, p. 179). The separation of the two languages belonged in her case to a later stage.[125]

Under the surface, however, the feeling for language differences was being prepared. I had my eyes open for the emergence of such phenomena; but tentative observations of this kind recorded in the diary sometimes proved to be unfounded later. At 1;8 she used *nass*, rarely, as an alternate for the synonym *wet*, and *heiss* as an alternate for *hot*, apparently with appreciation of the fact that she commanded two linguistic forms for the same idea, but not with discrimination of languages or associated persons. While eating an egg at 1;9, she called it alternatingly *Ei* and *egg*, apparently the German form meant for me, the English for her mother; but such impressions were still untrustworthy. During the same days she used *nein* playfully as a variation of the ordinary *no* before either of us. The two-word statement with *nass*, mentioned above, was addressed to me, although *wet* was more familiar. This may have been accidental, but it is likely that a subconscious association with the person who would use this word made it rise into use at the moment.

At the very end of the second year, Hildegard sometimes said (*Gute*) *Nacht, Papa* to me although her ordinary greeting was *night*. This was shortly after the infantile *night-night*, without the final consonants, had given way to the more mature unreduplicated English form with an aspirated final stop. The German version was undoubtedly induced by the greeting which she had heard hundreds of times from me on the same occasion. Before that she must have said the English word more than a hundred times to me as well as to her mother. A distinction by persons was beginning to emerge, but was far from being an established principle. The example was a first flicker of the later unfolding of two separate language systems.

---

[125] Geissler (p. 23) assigns consciousness of bilingualism to the beginning of the third year. Karla, at E 1;11, was once heard to say *please* and then, more to herself, just to show that she understood it to be identical in meaning, *bitte*. This shows consciousness of synonymy, but not necessarily of bilingualism.

In the meantime the struggle between the two language models must have gone on constantly under the surface. It was involved every time that the child decided to adopt a word from one language for active reproduction, when the synonym from the other language was passively familiar too. It was also involved when she decided to discard a word from one language, which she had been using, and replace it by a synonym from the other language. Examples of the struggle of bilingual synonyms and of language shifts in vocabulary shall be examined next.

654. Such shifts[126] were most conspicuous in the latter months of the second year, when Hildegard adopted English resolutely as her leading model. On a reduced scale they took place before, whenever the linguistic environment was changed, and sometimes without external inducement.

The first change in linguistic environment came with the arrival in Germany 0;11. This event entailed the loss of English words and the acquisition of German words; but since there had been only two definitely English words before, and one of them, *pretty*, was not given up, only one word was actually replaced, namely *there* 0;10 by *da* 1;0. She heard the latter often from her German grandfather. The influence of English was not completely eliminated. Among the unstable forms which the name of her aunt, *Gertrud*, took was one which seemed phonetically to be based on the American pronunciation which her mother used, although a form with the German stressed vowel became more frequent.

After the return to America 1;2, the English was slow to come back, as we have seen; but after a few months it became definitely the favored model. Since, however, the German presentation did not cease, the struggle of the languages went on. Hildegard learned *ja* at 1;3, tried *yes* at 1;4, but decided in favor of *ja* at 1;5, probably for phonetic reasons; the exact imitation of the German form was more satisfying than the reproduction of the English word without the final fricative.

The same reason may account for the eventual adoption of English *no* rather than German *nein*. Hildegard did say *nein* with the final consonant, but she articulated it with a self-conscious distinctness which revealed that it was contrary to her normal phonetic pattern. The struggle of the two languages for supremacy is evident in the history of these words. Hildegard seemed to understand "no, no" as a warning at 0;8 and 0;10, earlier than "nein, nein" in the same function; but when she understood the latter E 0;11,[127] her reaction was much more definite; this was in Germany. Back in America, she reacted mechanically by head-shaking to "nein" at 1;3, to "no" at 1;4. Both *no, no* and *nein, nein* were said at 1;6 in the restricted function of reporting denial of

---

[126] Cf. vol. 1, p. 176.
[127] The time indication, E 0;10, in vol. 1, p. 112 is an error. The time is given correctly as E 0;11 on p. 109.

permission, a reflection of the warning function in the presentation. In the second half of the same month, *no* had fuller meaning, *nein* receded. From 1;9 *no* alone was used.

Hot and *heiss* were in long-lasting competition. *Hot* came first 1;4. At 1;5 it was replaced by *heiss*, although the position of English was becoming stronger at that time. The diary marks this event as the first instance of a replacement of a word from one language by the synonym from the other; actually *there* > *da* was much earlier, 1;0. The replacement was temporary, however. *Hot* returned to its leading position, which it held definitely from 1;6, *heiss* occurring only in scattered instances 1;7, 1;8, and 1;10. The struggle was decided in favor of *hot*, although *heiss* was not judged to be inactive by the end of the year. *Hot* was favored in spite of the fact that it did not have the final consonant until 1;11, whereas *heiss* had it regularly from 1;7, experimentally even at 1;5. In the later months the English model was so much more powerful that even a phonetically more satisfactory German form could not stand up against the competition of an English model.

My 1;6, originally based on *mine*, but soon serving as pronoun and adjective alike, was English in origin and remained predominantly English. Occasionally, from 1;7 to 1;11, the more variable German forms, *mein, meine, meins* appeared, but always ephemerally. The isolated pronunciation with an exaggerated final **n** at 1;11 might go back to *mine* as well as to *mein*. The word normally lacked a final consonant. The German model was operating on the word, but without lasting effect. English was victorious throughout the history of the word.

All was learned from the maid's presentation "all gone" 1;5 with an expressive gesture. At 1;7 it was definitely replaced by the German synonym *alle*, the pronunciation of which is quite different, and was quite different in the child's representation. The gesture, however, was transferred to it, which underscored the identity of meaning. The etymological kinship was presumably not recognized by the child. The English word reappeared 1;10 in the perfected combination *all gone*, which was, however, only one of many similar combinations of the adverb *all* with an adjective. Nor was it at all common, whereas *alle* was one of Hildegard's most frequent words. In this case the German won, soon and lastingly, during a period when the strength of English was constantly increasing.[128] (At 2;1, however, after I had been absent for six weeks, *alle* had been replaced by *all gone*.)

Wet was said 1;7, *nass* B 1;8. The two words were in competition for the remainder of the year. *Wet* was more frequent, but *nass* was not rare.

---

[128] There must be something appealing in the German word. It lasts for generations, as a loan-translation, in the English of Americans of German descent. Expressions like "The coffee is all", meaning "gone", can be heard in Midwestern English on a German substratum one or two generations removed from immigration, as an isolated phenomenon within perfect English.

In fact, Hildegard felt it to be so completely synonymous that she did not hesitate to vary the common combination *all wet* into *all nass*, in which *all* is unmistakably English. (At 2;1 this German word had also been displaced by the English synonym.)

A clear case of language shift is German *Ball* 1;0-9 to English *ball* 1;9-11. The similarity of the synonyms is greater in the spelling than in the sound. The difference in the pronunciation of -l was unmistakably reflected in the diphthongs of Hildegard's forms. There was one month of struggle between the two prototypes, 1;9.

The bilingual struggle did not always result in such a clear-cut decision. *Egg* and *Ei* came into use at 1;8 one day apart. Both continued through the year in active use, although *Ei* might conceivably have suffered from the interference of the older homonyms *I* 1;5 and *eye* 1;7. Even after *ball* had been converted from German into English form, *Ei* continued to be used in a hybrid compound, *Ei-ball*, along with *egg-ball*, to designate a rubber ball in the shape of an Easter egg. A coordination with the language of the person addressed was suspected at 1;9, but was neither certain nor lasting.

The functionally useful and therefore very frequent word *bitte* held the field alone for over three months, 1;5-8, after a long pre-linguistic stage 0;9-1;5. The English synonym *please* was induced 1;9 by persistent training on the part of the maid, who knew no German. During 1;9 it was used in combination with *bitte*, that is to say, it did not replace the latter, but was added to it redundantly. During 1;10, to be sure, *please* was much more frequent than *bitte*. This reflects the often observed phenomenon that new acquisitions were overused for a while. *Bitte* was not displaced to the end of the year. *Please* remained more conventional; *bitte* was the spontaneous expression of a wish. This is a case in which the more recently dominant language did not succeed in displacing the old synonym because it was too well established. The easier phonetic form of *bitte* and its more satisfactory representation in the child's form may have contributed to the decision.[129]

When the German word and its English synonym were entirely different, as in the preceding instance, it was easy to follow the interplay. On account of the close linguistic kinship of English and German, there were many more instances in which the two etyma had similar form. Even then it was sometimes possible to trace a child-form definitely to one language or the other, as in the shift from *Eiskrem* 1;9 to *ice cream* 1;11. The crude phonetic form of the child's words often precluded definite assignment to one language, even though there was a clear distinction in the pronunciation of the standard words, as in the case of

---

[129] In Karla's case, in which the English medium prevailed from the beginning, *bitte* was also first, M 1;7, but was completely displaced by *please* as early as E 1;7, in spite of its imperfect phonetic reproduction.

aus and *out*. Smaller phonetic differences, as between *Auto* and *auto*, could not be followed with assurance, because the child's variations in the vowel of the stressed syllable can be explained by reasons other than exact imitation of the standard pronunciations. The difficulty of this unraveling process has been illustrated in detail in the example of *Buch, book* (vol. 1, p. 59), in which the standard differences were too fine for the child's phonetic discrimination. Thus, in a great number of instances, the synonyms from both languages had to be given as joint etyma. A leaning toward the English etymon at the end of the year could be assumed in many cases, but more on the basis of the general observation that English prevailed at that time, than on grounds of exact phonetic proof.

More examples could be given, both for language shifts and for maintenance of bilingual synonyms (cf. vol. 1, pp. 176–179); but the principles operating in the interplay of the two languages are sufficiently demonstrated by the foregoing samples.

655. The fact, repeatedly emphasized, that Hildegard did not yet try to keep the two language instruments apart, but built a hybrid system out of the elements of both, is brought out in spotlight illumination by certain instances, in which she replaced a word presented in one language by a word from the other in her own, immediately following reaction. This was, of course, always a word which happened to be current in her own speech. Passively she realized that she was faced with two languages, which contained interchangeable words of identical reference. This must be considered a preparatory stage for the active bilingualism of a later time.[130]

At B 1;4 I told her "Aufstehen!" She complied and said *up*, which the maid had just taught her in a different situation. To call this a translation would be rash. She understood the German word, at least its stressed prefix, performed the action of standing up, and the motion conjured up the English word which had just become associated with an upward motion. This is not conscious translation, but it is transposition from one language medium into another via an act which was linked by association with words in both. It differs from translation in the ordinary sense merely by the unconscious character of the process and by the need for the bridge of action. The path did not yet lead from the word of one language to the corresponding word of the other directly, without an intermediary.

There is one instance in which Hildegard performed a purely linguistic translation, and it was early, B 1;6. Her mother told her not to do something. When she did not obey, the mother asked "What did Mama tell you?" Hildegard reproduced the injunction, *No, no*. Driving home the

---

[130] Cassirer (1933; as cited by Grégoire p. 81) says that the word is an objective part of the object. A bilingual child learns early to detach the phonetic word from the thing designated.

point, the mother continued: "Don't you know what 'no, no' means?" Hildegard's answer was: *Nein, nein.* She took the verb "mean" in a linguistic sense and explained the meaning by a translation into German, not to be facetious, of course, but because of a misunderstanding. This remained the only instance of actual translation. It foreshadows the growth of a double linguistic system.

The remaining cases are more like the first one. They usually had a bridge of objects or actions. At 1;8, upon the challenge, *"Licht aus!"*, she switched the light off and said *Light out.* The adverb took German form eventually, but the noun was always English. This shows, incidentally, that the words were analyzed separately, did not form one immutable complex, as they might well do, being tied in stereotype combination to one act.

At 1;9, being told to say "no more", she reacted immediately and regularly with *no mehr.* This was a purely linguistic transformation without visual aid, but translation was not intended. Hildegard knew that "more" and "mehr" meant the same thing; *mehr* was an established and frequent word of hers (1;5), whereas *more* had only been tried and dropped at 1;6. She simply replaced the English word, which she understood, by the German word, which she used for the same purposes. "No" was left unchanged because it was familiar; she did not use "nicht". She maintained her freedom of choice with regard to the words which she imitated, and had as yet no qualms about mixing languages. Passive bilingualism was involved, but the purism of active bilingualism was not yet an aim of her speech, which served practical ends only.

At 1;10, my wife once said to me, "Look at the cars!", commenting on the numerous cars parked in our street during a football game in the near-by stadium. Hildegard, who could not see the cars from the position in which she was, echoed *Auto*, in an exact reproduction of the German form of the word. This was only accidentally a translation from English into German. Essentially it meant a reaction by an active word, rather neutral with regard to its linguistic provenience, to an English word which was merely understood. If Hildegard had chosen a more English form of the word *auto*, as she did earlier and later, bilingualism would have played no part in the process.

At 1;11, trying to settle her for sleep at night, I told her: "Alle kleinen Kinder sind jetzt im Bett". Her echo was: *All babies Bett.* "Alle" was replaced by English *all* and, more conspicuously, "kleinen Kinder" by *babies*, which was her regular word for big as well as small children. Since "Baby" is used in German, too, bilingualism shows more clearly in "alle" > *all*. The point, again, was not translation, but replacement of a passively familiar form by the actively current one.

Her first interrogative, *where*, entered into her vocabulary hesitatingly during 1;11. The second time it was used was in a hiding game which I played with her. Thus it was in this instance a translation from

German "wo", but not with the intention of translating. She understood both words, but had made her choice in favor of the English word.
(During 2;1, *where* became established, and then the phonetically similar German "wer", which means "who", was misunderstood as "where",
668.)

At the end of the year, the combination *right da* was common. It was
based on English "right there", the rejected "there" being replaced by
the deeply rooted German *da*. There is no similar idiom in German.
By this time she spoke English, with surface intrusion of established
German vocabulary items.

(The most striking instance of substitution of more familiar words
came 2;1, when "Three little kittens lost their mittens" was reproduced
as *Three meows lost Handschuhe*, in total disregard of the rhyme. The
disregard for form in favor of content was probably furthered by the
bilingualism, **660**.)[131]

656. We have explained the examples of vocabulary shifts from one
language to the other as due to the substitution of familiar terms for
unfamiliar ones. A double aspect of familiarity is involved in this. Some
words were more familiar because Hildegard had used them for a long
time. This type of familiarity favored German words, because the influence of German on her language was stronger in the earlier months of
the second year. Other words were more familiar because she heard them
more often. In the later months, when her English-speaking environment became wider because she got around more and played with neighbor children, English became the language to which she responded more
readily and the English elements of her vocabulary multiplied. There
must have been many occasions when the German words which she used
were not understood by others. This defeated the communicative purpose of speaking and was a powerful inducement for lexical shifts from
German to English.

As long as she got along with a vocabulary drawn from both languages,
she had no hesitation to combine items from both in single statements
of more than one word. Examples could not occur before the one-word
stage was overcome. The first instances were *down bitte* and *bitte up*
1;7. *Bitte* was so stable as an ingredient of wish expression that it continued long to be used with English words: *dolly* 1;8, *please* 1;9, *drink*
1;10. English *up* (1;4) was equally well established. It was combined

---

[131] Replacement by a more familiar term took place also in the many instances
in which she understood, but did not learn to say a synonym from the other language. For instance, she understood "Auf Wiedersehen", my regular farewell greeting, as early as 1;5, but never said it (until 2;1). She substituted *by-by*, which
had been active since 1;3. Karla, on the other hand, used the German term as
early as 1;1, blended it with *by-by* later, and eventually abandoned it in favor of
the easier English term. No such striking blend of bilingual synonyms occurred
in Hildegard's language (**457**). She kept the two languages apart as far as the individual vocabulary items were concerned.

with German *mehr* 1;7 in the sense of "higher up". *Mehr* (1;5) in turn was freely combined with English words: *mehr light* 1;8, meaning "another lamp". This usage continued throughout the second year (in fact, *mehr* was so well rooted that it survived the period of my prolonged absence 2;1, when most German words were lost). *Wehweh eye* is another case of 1;8. Its bilingual character is more questionable, because the mother had adopted the German nursery term for pain into her English speech. *Big Schnee*, however, for "too big a cake of snow", was clearly a bilingual combination modeled on the conventional combination of adjective and noun.

At 1;9 we find *no mehr* as a direct imitation of "no more" with substitution of the familiar German synonym (655); and, in a better organized statement of four words, *This (is a) big book—da!* I omit here dubious instances like *mehr milk* because the noun might also come from German *Milch*.

At 1;10 we have *This (is) nass; all nass* as a variant of frequent *all wet;* and *by-by dunkel*.

At 1;11, with greater fluency of speech and improving organization of sentences, the examples multiply. Although Hildegard's language was now definitely dominated by English, enough established German words survived, which were inserted in English utterances. Bilingual phrases: *No, not da; right da; Ei-ball.* Bilingual sentences: *Ja, Mama da bite; Hottey da; Cry-baby da; Choo-choo da; Da my ball; Meow not da; (May I) da slide down; (Put) all balls da; (Carry) this da down* (unless *da* stands for "carry" rather than "da"); *Ask Mama this aus; This dolly up Bett; Miau up Baum; I spiel this; I spiel ball; Don't spiel, Miau; Mehr bathe; Mehr sh* (the interjection "sh", which developed into a verb meaning "sleep", is English); *Häng up* (in two different four-word sentences; based on English "hang up", but with substitution of the phonetic equivalent of the German verb).

(The poem of the three little kittens, mentioned before, end of 655, had, in addition to substitutions from German, the phrase *all pooh* for "our mittens we have soiled", 2;1. Instead of using German *schmutzig*, which she was just beginning to learn, Hildegard chose the English interjection which served as her equivalent for "dirty" from 1;11. The familiar term was substituted. The complication of bilingualism is incidental. Bilingualism, however, helps to break down the intimate association between form and content. A bilingual child will pay more attention to things referred to, situations and actions described, and ideas expressed, than to the phonetic forms pronounced.)

657. Hildegard mixed English and German words freely in her phrases and sentences; but she did not often blend different bilingual synonyms into one hybrid word-form.[132] In the section on blending (457), the

---

[132] Karla blended *by-by* and *auf Wiedersehen* into one form, *(by-)by-dersehn;* cf. vol. 1, p. 47 and note to 655, at the end.

possible instances were examined; but nearly all the examples were found
to be doubtful. The only instance in which bilingual blending was
definitely assumed was the first form of *paper, Papier* 1;8 (474), which
yielded to a form based on English alone at 1;10.

The many cases in which the English and the German etymon are
so similar that they cannot be traced separately in Hildegard's forms
(654), do not invalidate the claim that she kept the two languages
asunder in the individual words. When both prototypes abutted, by
the rules of regular phonetic treatment, in the same form, there is no
reason to speak of an interference of one language with the other.

In scrutinizing the sound-system which Hildegard evolved, I have
looked persistently for effects of the bilingual presentation. I have not
found much. This is largely due to the fact that the phonetic features
in which English and German differ were not yet learned by the child,
for instance the rounded front vowels in German, the dental fricatives
in English. Nor can this deficiency be charged to the bilingual situation.
The sounds in question are late with monolingual children as well.

Passing in review the phonetic items for which the possibility of bilingual interference with the learning process was thought of, we find the
results to be rather negative. Two German words beginning with **ts**
were attempted at 1;11 (136). The representation of the affricate was
imperfect and wavering. Parenthetically it was stated that Hildegard
did not learn perfect **ts-** until 4;1, and the prevailing English habits of
pronunciation were blamed. This is probably true for the later years,
but nothing can be proved for the first two years. Final **ts** and, on the
whole, medial **ts**, which occur in English as well as in German, were
imitated just as imperfectly as initial **ts**, which is regular only in German
(316).

Hildegard's habit of using the glottal stop before initial vowels gave
the impression of being based on standard German habits of pronunciation. Again, one cannot be sure of that. English words with initial vowel
often have it when pronounced in isolation, and Hildegard's utterances
were not yet sufficiently fluent to make individual words lose the characteristics which they had had during the long time when they had been
said more or less in isolation (241).

English long vowels, except in final position, were reproduced as pure
vowels, as in German. The omission of the faint American diphthongal
off-glide is a natural simplification, performed also by monolingual
children (note to 293). Bilingual influence was considered improbable.

The most striking impact of the bilingual presentation is the fact that
Hildegard heard two kinds of l, the flat-tongued German l and the
English l with a raised back tongue. In final position this resulted in
vowel substitutes of different types, front vowels for German l, back
vowels for English l, although the substitute tended eventually to be
the neutral ə (304). In prematurely perfect pronunciations of -l- in

the German word *alle*, Hildegard used English 1 at 1;7, German 1 at 1;10 (391 note, 425). In initial position, English and German 1 did not have the same substitutes at first, but were both represented by j later on (196). It can be said that the exposure to two languages resulted in a broadened phonetic experience. Hildegard knew two varieties of 1 and imitated both of them. She treated them as variants of the same sound, however, and did not learn to distinguish them functionally. The effect of the bilingual presentation did not last (425).

German ç, although a frequent sound and physiologically as easy to produce as the favored ʋoiced equivalent j, was avoided. This was thought to be due to the fact that it is not a regular sound in English; but the corresponding velar fricative x is also missing in English and yet it was not avoided and sometimes even imitated correctly (305).

Terminal unvoicing is an outstanding feature distinguishing German from English. In Hildegard's speech it was a regular principle, which held sway until the second half of the third year. Yet it cannot be imputed to the German model with assurance. It is a sort of assimilation which operates frequently in standard languages and in the speech of non-German monolingual children (312).

The end result of the re-examination is negative (21, 426). Hildegard had already a wider experience, passively, with varieties of sounds than monolingual children. Actively, however, her sound-system scarcely exceeded that of monolinguals. She did use ʒ, which is not normal in German, and x, which does not occur in standard English. The former, common only in English dʒ, never corresponded to standard ʃ, however; and the latter was much more frequently due to an inaccuracy of imitation than to reproduction of the standard sound. Both sounds were introduced into words coming from both languages. Each might have occurred if Hildegard had been exposed to only one language. They prove nothing for a phonetic effect of bilingualism.

(In later years, when English was Hildegard's natural language and German was pushed back into a subsidiary position, her German pronunciation was affected by her English habits of articulation; the same thing happened in reverse after the second sojourn in Germany; but no such effect could be ascertained with assurance during the first two years, when the two languages were more nearly in balance.)

658. We can hardly expect to find an influence of bilingualism on the morphology as long as grammatical endings were almost completely undeveloped, which was the condition of Hildegard's language by the end of the second year (590). Since she began to learn the English plural formation at the end of the year, it would not be surprising to find her adding one of the English plural endings to German nouns. Actually, however, no such case of analogy was found (567). This does not prove that she kept the morphology of the two languages apart, since most English nouns, too, were still used in plural function without a formal sign.

The patterns "foot, feet" and "Fuss, Füsse" were in competition. *Feet* was first, 1;10. *Fuss* was the only singular, M 1;11. A week later the plural *Füsse* was used, and on the next day again the English plural *feet*. *Fuss* and *Füsse* were rendered in phonetically divergent forms; the child did not seem to be aware of any link in pattern. We have here in all likelihood three separate vocabulary items imitated phonetically, with no appreciation of pattern.

The incipient use of an ending to mark possessive function (**568**) did not present an occasion for a clash of languages. The endings of both languages would have resulted in the same substitute sound, so that it is not even possible to decide which language was the source. The corresponding English and German analytic forms were not used by the child; prepositions and articles remained inactive.

A striking fact in the development of Hildegard's verb is the absence of an ending in her German infinitives. Since observers of monolingual German children state that the infinitive is early, this condition was attributed to English influence (**575**). At the time when the German infinitive ending could be represented phonetically, Hildegard's language was predominantly English, and in English the infinitive has the same pure-stem form as the imperative. This fact may have given the imperative, or the pure stem, a stronger position in her speech than would be the case without bilingualism. Still, even this effect is not certain. It is quite thinkable that this child, as a German monolingual, would have chosen an individual route, favoring the pure stem, which is heard often enough in German imperatives and is also early in monolingual German children's speech (cf. **576**). It might, on that basis alone, have been the common form of the verb, which was not yet split into formally distinct subdivisions to indicate different functions.

In the conjugation of the present tense, hybrid forms were tentatively assumed in several instances in the original diary. In the systematic review (**577**), however, it became evident that the assumptions were erroneous. The common form of the verb was used, unmodified by endings, in English and German.

Thus, no definite effect of bilingualism on the morphology was found. To be sure, this is largely attributable to the fact that Hildegard's grammatical forms were quite undeveloped. (In later years, because of the common admixture of English words to German sentences, some hybrid forms appeared, English words being given German endings and prefixes.[133] The reverse cases are much rarer.[134] On the whole, she avoided morphological hybrids (**932**), although complete English words in German utterances remained frequent.)

---

[133] Examples of German infinitives from English verbs: schleiden 832, crushen, anlichten 846, pouren 942, practicen, sparkeln 961; participles: geyawnt 830, gepeelt 854, gesmilet 947, gebelcht 950; noun plurals: cheeken 940, monthe 949.

[134] English possessives of German nouns: Heinzes 854, jeder Mensches 937. These cases are significant because they occurred in German sentences, the former even in Germany. They may be German analogical formations, however.

659. In the syntax, we observe constantly the free mixing of English and German vocabulary within one utterance. Just for that reason, it is hardly possible to find an influence of the constructions of one language on those of the other. In the first place, nearly all of Hildegard's constructions were still so primitive and incomplete that no language difference can be established. Then, English and German constructions, on the simple level of a child's everyday speech, are so similar that not many differences can be expected to crop up. Finally, if she had used a clearly English construction, like "I want him to come," with nothing but German words, this would have been merely an accident of vocabulary choice. This construction, which was just beginning to develop at the end of the year (563), is English; but its use with German words could not be called an application of an English pattern to German speech, because she did not yet use the two languages as separate instruments. Besides, no such extreme case occurred.

A few cases of puzzling word-order were tentatively explained by a wavering between the models of the two languages, which differ in word-order more than in any other syntactic feature (561). The incompleteness of Hildegard's utterances precluded certainty about the explanation, however. Actually, she had absorbed neither English nor German syntactic patterns with sufficient assurance to banish variations of word-order used for psychological reasons.

Thus, in the field of syntax, too, no effect of bilingualism can be definitely established in the first two years. (Later, when Hildegard used the two languages separately, the English influence on the structure of sentences and on the composition of idiomatic phrases became very noticeable; for a time after the second sojourn in Germany, also the influence of German on English.)

660. In looking back over the effect of bilingualism on Hildegard's early language, we find that it was striking in her vocabulary, because she chose words from both languages as carriers of her communications, and combined them into utterances with no regard for their linguistic provenience. She was the sole arbiter of her choice, which favored now one language, now the other, with shifts of emphasis due to changes of linguistic environment, but never entirely determined by it. Synonyms from both languages for the same purpose were already in use, but there was no attempt yet to split the one medium of communication into two parallel ones.

The layman is inclined to focus his attention on the vocabulary. The linguist knows that the vocabulary is the least characteristic feature of a language, comparable to the ornamentation of a building rather than to its structure. When we examine the less obvious features of Hildegard's early language, the sounds, the forms, the syntax, the word-formation, we find very few effects of bilingualism. She adopted into her speech the features which the two languages have in common, and on the elementary level, English and German are very similar.[135]

Nor can the poverty of her morphology and syntax be charged against the bilingualism. In mixed languages like Pidgin-English, a decay of complex linguistic mechanisms is often observed. The hypothesis suggests itself that in Hildegard's case, conversely, the bilingual exposure prevented the development of the finer mechanisms of linguistic expression. This cannot be disproved, but neither can it be proved. At the early age of two, many children's speech is better developed than Hildegard's was, but many others speak less well or even do not speak at all, within the range of normal development. Early in the third year, her English sentences developed rapidly and normally. It would be hazardous to attribute the delay to the bilingualism. She simply was not ready for organized sentences by the end of the second year, but took that step in an entirely normal manner soon thereafter. Nothing in the later development indicates that her learning of English was impeded by the interference of German, although there is no doubt that her German suffered permanently from the overpowering influence of English, even during the seven months in Germany. This means no more than that her bilingualism was imperfect. She obtained only a limited command of German, but—and this is important—not at the expense of the mastery of English. Much later, in high school, she proved to be a mediocre student. She had difficulty with Latin and mathematics, subjects in which strict logical thinking is needed; but English remained one of her best subjects.

Lack of originality in thinking is a feature which many students would be willing to charge against bilingualism. Caution is necessary, however. Many monolingual children have just as much difficulty with Latin and mathematics. Her low performance in these subjects is not too much out of line with her I.Q. She should be a high-average student. The fact that she obtains only a low average is easily explained by her indolence and lack of interests. To impute these characteristics to a handicap caused by bilingualism would be equally hazardous. Nobody can say that she would not have developed them as a monolingual. In fact, they may only be a passing feature of adolescence.

In this connection, attention should be called to an observation which occurs several times in the record of the first two years, and more frequently in later years. Hildegard never clung to words, as monolingual children are often reported to do. She did not insist on the exact wording

---

[135] Later on, there was much influence of one language on the other in vocabulary, idiomatic phrases, and syntax; very little in sounds, morphology, and word-formation. Eventually, the development of the dominant language, English, was not impaired; the secondary language, German, remained handicapped by the overpowering position of English.

of fairy tales. She often reproduced even memorized materials with substitution of other words (cf. *meow, Handschuh, church* in the Vocabulary). I attribute this attitude of detachment from words confidently to the bilingualism. Constantly hearing the same things referred to by different words from two languages, she had her attention drawn to essentials, to content instead of form. This fact would seem to favor thinking over vague and empty verbalism. The absence of parrot-like imitation and the avoidance of the use of words not understood, often explained in this record by the personal characteristics of caution and conservatism, is in line with this effect of bilingualism and may well have been engendered by it. A bilingual, who constantly hears two words for one thing, is compelled to pay more attention to the meaning expressed than to the word used to express it, whereas the monolingual is often satisfied with a hazy definition of a word and will use it without understanding it fully.[136]

Thus, apart from the accomplishment of understanding and using two languages, which nearly everyone would rate as a gain, I see in early bilingualism the advantage that it trains the child to think instead of merely speaking half mechanically (594). Of course, I see the other side. A monolingual develops, through the compelling influence of his single language, a simpler and therefore more forceful view of the world. I do not overlook the difficulties inherent in growth nourished from a split root instead of a single strong tap root. It will lead to conflicts, which can wreck a weak personality, but will improve the mettle of a strong one, who can overcome the difficulties. The difference is the same as between a highly educated and an uneducated person. Ignorance and superstition make the decisions of life simple. Education does not make life easier, but better and richer. Few would condemn education for this reason. Bilingualism should be seen in the same light.

With these prospects we have strayed far from the first two years, from the factual record into the philosophy of language and into the philosophy of education and of life. I do not propose to follow these lines of thought further in this place.[137] Some readers may wish to know what I have come to think about infant bilingualism on the basis of my experience. That is why I have indulged in this brief excursion.

I return in the following volume to the factual record, namely the diaries of Hildegard's and Karla's further linguistic development from the end of the second year on. Bilingualism plays a prominent part particularly in Hildegard's record, which includes her seven months in Germany at the age of five.

---

[136] Cf. Geissler p. 79.

[137] I may write about bilingualism in general, and about bilingualism of small children in particular, separately later on.

References

in addition to those listed in vols. 1 and 2

Bateman, W. G.: "The naming of colors by children: The Binet test". Pedagogical Seminary 22 (1915), pp. 469–486. (Cited as Bateman, "Colors". Abstract in National Yearbook p. 497. Summary of research and examination of 600 school children in Montana. Bibliography of 33 items.)

Bean, C. H.: "An unusual opportunity to investigate the psychology of language". Journal of Genetic Psychology 40 (1932), pp. 181–202. (Child, born blind, gained sight through operations 1;4. Condensation of extensive material, too succinct. No phonetic transcriptions. Generalizations. Linguistically not satisfactory.)

Beckmann, H.: "Die Entwicklung der Zahlleistung bei 2–6jährigen Kindern". Zeitschrift für angewandte Psychologie 22 (1923), pp. 1–72.

Bloch, Oscar: "Langage d'action dans les premiers stades du langage de l'enfant". Journal de Psychologie 20 (1923), pp. 670–674. (Lecture, pp. 670–672, and discussion, pp. 672–674, by Marcel Cohen among others. Criticism of Stern's stages of language learning. Same view as at end of Bloch 1921.)

Bohn, William E.: "A child's questions". Pedagogical Seminary 23 (1916), pp. 120–122. (Shows wide range and depth of questions of one intelligent child 1;5–5;0.)

————: "First steps in verbal expression." Pedagogical Seminary 21 (1914), pp. 578–595. (Abstract in Yearbook p. 499 f. Same girl 0;8–2;2. Special attention given to development of sentence, no interest in sounds. Emphasizes pleasure in communication over practical ends of speaking. Unusually conscious learner. Sensible observer.)

Boyd, William: "The development of sentence structure in childhood." British Journal of Psychology, General Section, 17 (1926–27), pp. 181–191. (Abstract in Yearbook p. 501. Notes down 1250 unselected sentences of his daughter each year 2;0–8;0 around birthday, studies development of sentences systematically, and compares them with random conversational sentences culled from 18 novelists.)

Bühler, Karl: "Les lois générales d'évolution dans le langage de l'enfant". Journal de Psychologie 23 (1926), pp. 597–607. (Translated from German by P. Guillaume. Good statement of great outlines of development as a promising basis for the study of the origin of language. Criticism of Wundt.)

Cassirer, Ernst: An essay on man; an introduction to a philosophy of human culture. New Haven, Yale University Press, 1944. XI, 237 pp. (Not on child language. Chapter VIII, "Language", gives a good rapid survey of the history of linguistic science.)

Chamberlain, Alexander F.: The child. London, 1901. (Comprehensive examination of literature by an anthropological linguist. Interest in parallelism of child-language and aboriginal languages.)

Chambers, W. G.: "How words get meanings." Pedagogical Seminary 11 (1904), pp. 30–50. (Expansion of vocabulary and meanings in school years studied by means of questionnaires sent to teachers; papers with five definitions from 2922 "children", age 5–27, mostly 6–18.)

Vᵉ congrès international des linguistes 1939. I Réponses au questionnaire. Bruges, (1939). (Papers preparatory to a meeting which was not held. Fruitful brief general discussion of the effect of bilingualism on the inner speech-form by many scholars in several languages, pp. 25–36. Children's bilingualism mentioned only once, p. 29, by B. Terracini.)

Cooley, C. H.: "A study of the early use of self-words by a child." Psychological Review 15 (1908), pp. 339–357. (Abstract in Yearbook p. 504. Observations 0;0–2;9, chiefly after 1;8. "I" and semantically related words. Not seen.)

Court, S. R. A.: "Numbers, time, and space in the first five years of a child's life." Pedagogical Seminary 27 (1920), pp. 71–89. (Abstract in Yearbook p. 504. One child, age 1;8 to age 5. Observation and leading questions. Not seen.)

Cummings, Florence S.: "When do babies learn to talk?" Parents' Magazine 15 (1940), p. 45. (Title misleading. Interesting case of English-Burmese bilingualism, which developed three months after departure from Burma.)

Curme, George O.: A grammar of the German language. Revised edition, New York, Macmillan, 1922. XII, 623 pp. (Not on child language.)

———: Parts of speech and accidence. Vol. 2 of A grammar of the English language. Boston, Heath, (1935). XV, 370 pp. (Not on child language.)

———: Syntax. Vol. 3 of A grammar of the English language. Boston, Heath, (1931). XV, 616 pp. (Not on child language.)

Davis, Edith A.: "The form and function of children's questions." Child Development 3 (1932), pp. 57–74. (3650 unselected spontaneous questions asked by 73 children in home situations. Questionnaires, answered very unevenly by mothers. No definite conclusions. Titles in bibliography very inaccurate.)

Egger, Émile: Observations et réflexions sur le développement de l'intelligence et du langage chez les enfants. Paris, 1879, fifth edition 1887. 103 pp. Also German translation from the fifth edition by Hildegard Gassner, Leipzig, 1903, 73 pp. (Important early study, by a classical philologist, of his children and grandchildren, originally a lecture, 1871. Sensible generalities with a few interesting examples. Parallels to Greek and Latin sound-changes. Phonetic observations pp. 69–72, conventional transcription.)

Erdmann, K. O.: Die Bedeutung des Wortes. Leipzig, 1900, ³1922, ⁴1926. 226 pp. (I used the third edition. Scholarly treatment of descriptive semantics, incidentally on child-language.)

Fisher, Mary S.: Language patterns of preschool children. New York, Columbia University Teachers' College, 1934. 88 pp. Also as thesis, Columbia University. (72 superior children observed for nine hours, stenographic record; age 1;10–5;0, most children 2;0–3;11. Interest centered on sentences rather than vocabulary. Favors Piaget, criticizes McCarthy. Of moderate value for sentence structure.)

Fröschels, Emil: Psychologie der Sprache. Leipzig-Vienna, 1925. 186 pp. (Speech therapist. Chief interest: aphasia. Forerunner of Jakobson in certain respects.)

Gabelentz, G. v. d.: Die Sprachwissenschaft. Leipzig, 1891; second edition, 1901. XXI, 520 pp. (Masterful work on general linguistics. Scattered references to child-language. Calls for more records, p. 67.)

Gheorgov, I. A.: "Ein Beitrag zur grammatischen Entwicklung der Kindersprache." Archiv für die gesamte Psychologie 11 (1908), pp. 242–432. Also separately, Leipzig, Engelmann, 1908, 191 pp. (Cited without indication of year. Most comprehensive study of development of morphology, Bulgarian. Two sons treated separately, to 3;7 and 2;8 respectively, in exact parallelism of chapters; one chapter each on syntax. No conspectus, but backward glances from second son to first. Thorough study written by a university professor in Sofia.)

————: "Die ersten Anfänge des sprachlichen Ausdrucks für das Selbstbewusstsein bei Kindern." Archiv für die gesamte Psychologie 5 (1905), pp. 329–404. Also separately, Sammlung von Abhandlungen zur psychologischen Pädagogik, vol. 2, nr. 1, Leipzig, 1905. (Inspired by Preyer. Same material as preceding title. Babbling stage omitted. Treatment not phonetic. Extensive extracts from diaries, with interest centered on expression of ego. Tabulation of results, p. 392 ff., compared with early literature.)

Goodenough, Florence L.: "The use of pronouns by young children: a note on the development of self-awareness." Journal of Genetic Psychology 52 (1938), pp. 333–346. (203 children in nursery school and kindergarten studied with McCarthy method.)

Guillaume, P.: "Les débuts de la phrase dans le langage de l'enfant." Journal de Psychologie 24 (1927), pp. 1–25. (Abstract in Yearbook p. 513. Children, two to five years old, in nursery school; his boy and another child, not identified. Good general observations, mostly concerning nouns and verbs. Backward glances to second year included.)

————: "Le développement des éléments formels dans le langage de l'enfant." Journal de Psychologie 24 (1927), pp. 203–229. (Psychologically and linguistically sound and sane discussion of principles, with sparse examples; not a systematic treatment of morphology. Goes beyond age 2;0. Important.)

Hermann, Eduard: Review of Karl Bühler, Sprachtheorie. Göttingische gelehrte Anzeigen 198 (1936), pp. 542–553.

Hetzer, Hildegard and Reindorf, B.: "Sprachentwicklung und soziales Milieu." Zeitschrift für angewandte Psychologie 29 (1928), pp. 449–462. (Difference in early language learning between children in cultured and uncultured families.)

———— and Wislitzky, S.: "Experimente über Erwartung und Erinnerung beim Kleinkind." Zeitschrift für Psychologie 118 (1931), pp. 128–141. (Memory span of small children, 0;3–1;11.)

Jervis, Jessie L.: "Akustische Rezeption im zweiten Lebensjahr." Zeitschrift für Psychologie 123 (1931), pp. 259–290. (Especially appreciation of music. Bibliography.)

Jespersen, Otto: "L'individu et la communauté linguistique." Journal de Psychologie 24 (1927), pp. 573–590. (Only incidentally on child language. References without indication of year mean the book listed in vol. 1.)

Kainz, Friedrich: "Der Ursprung der Sprache." Deutsche Vierteljahrsschrift für Literaturwissenschaft und Geistesgeschichte 15 (1937), pp. 1–33. (Status of research on the origin of language. Article not satisfactory. Uses child language as one approach to the solution of the problem, pp. 8–10.)

Leopold, W.: "Der Mitteilungsvorgang und die 'innere Sprachform'." Anglia 56 (1932), pp. 1–22. (Not on child-language.)

Lewis, M. M : "The beginning of reference to past and future in a child's speech." British Journal of Educational Psychology 7 (1937), pp. 39–56. Summaries in French and German, p. 56. (Excellent investigation of the development of reference to time in a boy, ages 1–3, disregarding formal expression of tenses. "Lewis" without indication of year refers to book, Infant Speech, as in vol. 2.)

Lindner, Gustav: Aus dem Naturgarten der Kindersprache; ein Beitrag zur kindlichen Sprach- und Geistesentwicklung in den ersten vier Lebensjahren. Leipzig, 1898. 122 pp. (An educator's report on his second son. Material collected 1883-1887. Important early study.)

Meumann, E.: "Die Entstehung der ersten Wortbedeutungen beim Kinde." Philosophische Studien 20 (1902), pp. 152-214. Also separately, Leipzig, Engelmann, 1902, second edition 1908, 69 pp. (Summarized and continued in book, Die Sprache des Kindes, Zürich, 1903. Theory, examples from literature, few observations of his own. Of historical importance for emphasis on voluntaristic and emotional urges, which are stressed but not exaggerated.)

————: Review of K. L. Schäfer, "Die psychologische Deutung der ersten Sprachäusserungen des Kindes." Archiv für die gesamte Psychologie 11 (1908), p. 158 f. (Refutation of Schäfer's attack.)

Moore, Kathleen C.: "The mental development of a child." Psychological Review, Monograph Supplement, vol. 1 (1895-96), nr. 3. 150 pp. (Abstract in Yearbook p. 522. Part IV, Language, pp. 115-145: sounds, words, sentences. Her boy's language during first two years. Good observer, good method, but material condensed too much; no adequate transcription of pronunciation. Sees important problems, but does not handle them successfully.)

Müller, Paul: "Die Begriffe der Sechsjährigen." Archiv für die gesamte Psychologie 72 (1929), pp. 115-178. (Concepts and words of six-year-old children. Survey of earlier research pp. 115-126, only pedagogical and psychological writers.)

Nausester, Walter: Denken, Sprechen und Lehren. Berlin, Weidmann, 1901-06. 2 vols. in 1, 193 and 246 pp. (Interesting studies of style by a school man, who recommends child-language as a model of style, as an instrument of life, instead of the lifeless language of grammar. Grammar means morphology. About child-language merely in a theoretical way.)

————: "Die grammatische Form der Kindersprache." Zeitschrift für pädagogische Psychologie 8 (1906), pp. 214-233. (Cited as vol. 8, p. . . .. Riding the same hobby: the noble language and child-language avoid giving importance to inflectional endings. General and theoretical, no observations. Often sensible, but not important for child-language.)

————: Das Kind und die Form der Sprache. Berlin, 1904. 51 pp. (37 pp. text; pp. 38-51 proverbs, to illustrate superfluity of inflections. Lively, readable book, interesting. Based on Preyer, whom he admires. More valuable for comparison of natural speech and paper language than for theories about child-language.)

Neugebauer, Hanna: "Aus der Sprachentwicklung meines Sohnes." Zeitschrift für angewandte Psychologie 9 (1915), pp. 298-306. (Psychological orientation, but many interesting observations about language learning, second and third year. The boy had an unusual degree of linguistic consciousness.)

————: "Sprachliche Eigenbildungen meines Sohnes." Zeitschrift für Kinderforschung 19 (1914), pp. 174-181, 242-246, 362-370. (Very interesting study of an unusually original child: invention and original handling of language material, to 2;8.)

————: Über die Entwicklung der Frage in der frühen Kindheit." Zeitschrift für angewandte Psychologie 8 (1913-14), pp. 145-153. (Classification of her son's questions, second and third years. Follows Stern, with long parallel quotations. Cited by author's name without indication of year.)

Nice, Margaret M.: "The development of a child's vocabulary in relation to environment." Pedagogical Seminary 22 (1915), pp. 35–64. (Abstract in Yearbook p. 523. Not seen. Cited without indication of year.)

———: "Length of sentences as a criterion of a child's progress in speech." Journal of Educational Psychology 16 (1925), pp. 370–379. (Abstract in Yearbook p. 524 f. Good small sampling of cases.)

Ogden, Charles K.: Opposition, a linguistic and psychological analysis. London, 1932. 103 pp. (Not on child language. Logical analysis of opposites in language, for the sake of Basic English; written in anything but Basic English.)

Perez, Bernard: "Le développement des idées abstraites chez l'enfant." Revue philosophique 40 (1895), pp. 449–467. (Good investigation of general concepts to age seven.)

Piaget, Jean: The child's conception of the world. New York, 1929. Translated from French, La représentation du monde chez l'enfant, Paris, 1926. (Little about language. Imitation and originality in child language. Based on Stern.)

———: Judgment and reasoning in the child. New York, 1928. 260 pp. Translated from French, Le jugement et le raisonnement chez l'enfant, Neuchatel-Paris, 1924. (Logical analysis. Thinking and linguistic expression correlated.)

Reumuth, K.: Die logische Beschaffenheit der kindlichen Sprachanfänge. Leipzig, 1919. (Not seen. Accounts in Elsa Köhler p. 194 f. and Richter pp. 105–107: Method of phenomenology; reaction against emphasis on will and emotion, but not one-sided overstressing of intellect.)

Reynolds, Martha May: Negativism of pre-school children; an observational and experimental study. New York, Columbia University Teachers' College, 1928. VIII, 126 pp. Also published as thesis. (229 children, 2;0–5;6. Negativism in behavior; linguistic negativism only p. 122 f.)

Schäfer, P.: "Beobachtungen und Versuche an einem Kinde in der Entwicklungsperiode des reinen Sprachverständnisses." Zeitschrift für pädagogische Psychologie 23 (1922), pp. 259–289. (Interesting experimental study of learning by instruction, from 0;9.)

Schlag, J.: "Grundsätzliches zu einem Häufigkeitswörterbuche der Kindersprache." Zeitschrift für pädagogische Psychologie 18 (1917), pp. 216–226. (Counts frequency of words of a second-year grade-school class and of a girl before entering school, using Kaeding's frequency count as a model.)

Smith, Madorah E.: "Grammatical errors in the speech of preschool children." Child Development 4 (1933), pp. 183–190. (Statistical investigation of 220 children, 1;6 to age 6; few details. Purist approach; common colloquial usages counted as errors. Range of age groups too wide.)

———: "A study of some factors influencing the development of the sentence in preschool children." Journal of Genetic Psychology 46 (1935), pp. 182–212. (220 children in Iowa and Hawaii, 1;6–6;0; length of sentences, syntax, morphology.)

Snyder, Alice D.: "Notes on the talk of a two-and-a-half year old boy." Pedagogical Seminary 21 (1914), pp. 412–424. (Abstract in Yearbook p. 529. Irregular notes taken during one summer, 2;5–8, on selected topics, particularly types of sentences, questions. Useful.)

Sperber, Hans: Einführung in die Bedeutungslehre. Bonn-Leipzig, 1923. (Not on child-language.)

Stalnaker, Elizabeth: "Language of the preschool child". Child Development 4 (1933), pp. 229–236. (Nine children 2;4 to age 4 in West Virginia; total conversation of each child during one and a half hour on five days recorded. Adult colloquialisms included in "incorrect forms". Of moderate value.)

Tappolet, Ernst: "Die Sprache des Kindes." Deutsche Rundschau 131 (1907), pp. 399–411. (Lively narration of his own observations, which do not extend to the study of sounds. Swiss German; French and Italian examples included. Not many references to the literature of the field.)

Tihany, L. C.: Review of Miklós Zsirai, Finnugor Rokonságunk. Speculum 13 (1938), pp. 259–263. (Not on child-language.)

Treitel, Leopold: "Haben kleine Kinder Begriffe?" Archiv für die gesamte Psychologie 3 (1904), pp. 341–346. (Not very clear. Of marginal interest for discussion of small children's concepts.)

Trettien, A. W.: "Psychology of the language interest of children." Pedagogical Seminary 11 (1904), pp. 113–177. (Theory of the development of child language, based mostly on the literature and on observations of parents and teachers without much identification; very few observations of his own. Good correlation of early scholarship in rapid survey. Extends to pre-adolescent period. Bibliography of 91 items includes many titles not easily found elsewhere; many inaccuracies.)

Usnadze, D.: "Die Begriffsbildung im vorschulpflichtigen Alter." Zeitschrift für angewandte Psychologie 34 (1929), pp. 138–212. (Not seen. Abstract in Zeitschrift für Psychologie 122, 1931, p. 152: Classification of objects by children three to seven years old.)

Wallon, Henri: "L'interrogation chez l'enfant." Journal de Psychologie 21 (1924), pp. 170–182. (Good psychological, not grammatical, discussion of questions, with broad treatment of two pathological cases. Uses Preyer, criticizes Stern.)

Weisgerber, Leo: Muttersprache und Geistesbildung. Göttingen, 1929. (Not on child language.)

———: "Die Stellung der Sprache im Aufbau der Gesamtkultur," I. Wörter und Sachen 15 (1933), pp. 134–224. (Only incidentally on bilingualism of children, p. 212 f.)

Weiss, A. P.: A theoretical basis of human behavior. Columbus, Ohio, 1925; second edition, 1929. (Theory of language as seen by a behaviorist. Incidentally on child language.)

White, Alice Marsden: "When scientists listen to babies." Parents' Magazine 20 (1945), No. 5, pp. 28, 116–118. (Babbling of Hildegard Leopold and two African babies compared.)

Winkler, E.: Grundlegung der Stilistik. Bielefeld-Leipzig, 1929. (Not seen. Quoted on concepts by E. Köhler p. 202 f.)

Index

Names of authors are printed in Roman type, *topics* in *italics*. The few items in parentheses refer to Karla alone. References to sections include the notes to the sections.